THE
END
OF THE
AMERICAN
FUTURE

PETER SCHRAG

SIMON AND SCHUSTER · NEW YORK

SBN 671-21581-7
LIBRARY OF CONGRESS CATALOG CARD NUMBER: 73-7923
DESIGNED BY IRVING PERKINS
MANUFACTURED IN THE UNITED STATES OF AMERICA
BY THE BOOK PRESS, BRATTLEBORO, VT.

1   2   3   4   5   6   7   8   9   10

CONTENTS

FOREWORD

I

In the spring of 1968 an age came to an end. No one could then fully comprehend what was happening, nor could anyone begin to imagine what, if anything, would replace it. Events moved too rapidly and too unpredictably—the Tet offensive in Vietnam, Lyndon Johnson's decision not to run for reelection, the assassinations of Robert Kennedy and Martin Luther King, Jr., and, later, that summer, the Democratic convention and the demonstrations in Chicago. Those of us who were trying to cover the country as journalists listened to supposedly intelligent and articulate people talking about the dark core of violence in America, about the ugly domestic consequences of an ugly war, and about the serious possibility that the country would destroy itself in riot, revolution or civil war. Simultaneously "alienation" had become a household word—the alienation of blacks, students, Chicanos, Indians, blue-collar workers, and, a year later, the alienation of the middle class itself. The country—though we hardly understood that either—had begun to define itself as a collection of minorities, rhetorically a Balkanized republic of disaffected groups.

In the avalanche of rhetoric it was never clear just what people were alienated from: the sick society, the racist society, the uptight middle class, the system. The decade had begun in celebration and was about to end in a holocaust. Vietnam had something to do with it, but was Vietnam a cause or a symptom, was it an aberration or a reflection? Was the war responsible for the failures of the Great Society, or was Vietnam itself a convenient way not to confront the problems and inequities at home? In theory, the ordinary processes of politics were supposed to mediate between competing interest groups and to mitigate conflict, but that mediation had always assumed some fundamental social and cultural consensus and required a common language. Quite obviously a portion of that consensus had broken down. The Chicago convention seemed to demonstrate that certain kinds of social and political discourse were no longer possible, that ordinary political rhetoric was more inadequate than ever, and that politics in the traditional sense could no longer make the connections with ordinary life—however superficial—that it had once made. There seemed, moreover, to be a new (or, at least, newly visible) demonic streak in the nation's soul, a vein of madness, that might be explained but never understood. The best and most hopeful among us were being killed with an apparent inevitability that could easily be regarded as an expression of some buried impulse in the national will. Not that those assassinations were necessarily the work of political conspiracies (as some people insisted), but that there was something in us that seemed no longer able to tolerate the demands of grandeur and spirit.

Yet none of that, even if accurate, explained very much. There was no way to be certain just what had changed or why the language of conventional American politics no longer worked. Was it simply that politics had become overburdened, that expectations were too high, that people were demanding too much? By the end of the sixties almost everything was becoming a political issue, and each issue was escalated into a rhetorical choice between salvation and annihilation, utopia and apocalypse. For two hundred years the country had defined itself in terms of possibilities, and it was that very sense of possibility and optimism that had brought the order of consistent assumptions and a common language. We had institutionalized the dreams of the Renaissance and the hopes of the Reformation: we could control spirits and perform magic, could renew the earth and transform men, and everything we once said and read about ourselves had been a variation on that theme—its verification, its higher criticism, its correction, its disputes of doctrine—until writing about America became a great deal like writing theology. Government itself had become the place of ultimate appeal in the American cosmos—when all else failed, there was still Washington; but what if government should fail, too?

There were no hard indices that things had gotten as bad in the late sixties as the rhetoric suggested; the statistics were, at worst, inconclusive, the language was prone to overkill, and there was at least a possibility that the very intractability of American politics—a common complaint among students, blacks and others—was a consequence not of exclusion but, as Daniel Bell suggested, of increasing participation in the political process. The more players, the theory went, the less satisfied each of them would be. Yet that hypothesis itself suggested that democratic possibilities were limited, that the system could work only if it were not forced to accommodate too many groups or too many demands, that mediation itself could work only up to a point. It also raised the question of why the country had become so politicized, why everything from sex to literature had become a political issue, and why the political process had been so burdened. Was everyone going to the arena of last resort because all else had seemed to fail? The language of American politics had always assumed an inevitable rise in the conditions of American life; the inevitability had been taken for granted, and the disputes focused only on means, speed and emphasis. But what if a growing number of people no longer believed in that inevitability—if their very demands were based on doubt? Then the language and the process might themselves become irrelevant, might apply only to a place that no longer existed or one in which people no longer believed. Were people talking about themselves as minorities because they regarded themselves as strangers in a place that was supposed to be their own?

II

I have been trying to write about life in America for nearly a decade, sometimes covering the events that make headlines; but more often I have found myself in ordinary places—schools, factories, union halls, churches, bus stations, race tracks, community meetings, in towns named Mason City, Quincy, Lowell, Greenfield, Stockton, Winnetka or Jackson—looking, as the song said, for America. It is a place too large and complex to comprehend, a place too much loved and too much hated, a place that people re-spelled, for the purposes of abuse, "Amerika," a name too sacred and too profane. Every time one looked for something, one would also find something else—hope, despair, resentment, affirmation—peeling off like the layers of an onion. Sometimes all that one could recall was the blur, and so one made lists: the midnight fires of the steel mills in Pittsburgh and Gary and Bethlehem, and the reflected light in the faces of the changing shifts; the aggression of neon on people-vacant Los Angeles avenues after dark; the faces passing through the tiled arteries of identical airports; the cacophony of a hundred AM radio stations from everywhere competing for dial space and signal strength in the Nebraska night; the tumbleweed blowing indifferently alongside the car in the Texas desert; the orange suits in a Tennessee stadium on an autumn afternoon, and the black faces in a Mississippi church; the voices from the lectern, the pulpit, the soapbox, the tube, voices of admonition, counsel, warning, exhortation.

Still, there had been things that made sense and brought order. And the thing that had once brought the most order, the thing one took for granted, was the sense of possibilities, a quality that had shaped our language along with everything else. That sense is still there, but after 1968—either because the perceptions of the journalist had changed or, more likely, if eyes and ears were at all reliable, because the country was changing—it had become muted, qualified, conditional. It was as if the country had begun looking for itself, as if its perceptions of time had changed, and as if the interwoven strands once inadequately labeled "the mainstream," "the future," and the "American dream" had become increasingly unreliable or unattractive. The dramatic events of 1968, of course, had not been causes, but symptoms— though the symptoms themselves profoundly affected the national mood. Vietnam and the failures of the Great Society and the New Frontier "proved" something, but the thing they proved, however described, seemed to transcend those failures and to suggest that if there were, indeed, new limitations (or limitations newly perceived) they were not merely the limitations of programs (or demonstrations of things "government should not attempt to do") but limitations on more fundamental possibilities. Before 1968 the places and people associated with national "problems" were covered as aberrations—the ghetto, Appalachia, the back country of Mississippi—variations from some national norm; after 1968 one began to see—or imagined one saw—most places and people as somehow uneasy and vaguely uncertain.

I set out to write this book as a way of looking at America at a moment of social, political and moral crisis. That was in the summer of 1970—a time, as I then tried to describe it, of adjustment, a "turning around," when many people seemed to speak seriously about threats of disunity, repression and depersonalization. "How," I asked in an outline, "do people place their lives, problems and identity in perspective? What kind of national identity is there, what sort of Americanism is possible, what sort of reconciliation, if any, is there with the chance that the future is limited, that life is finite, that tragedy and pain are ubiquitous, and that all frontiers are closing?" I conceived of it as a journalistic book focusing on particular groups, regions and ideas which would concern itself primarily with the question "Do Americans still believe in the rising curves of possibility and, if not, how are they adjusting to their new sense of doubt?" In the two years that followed I spoke with people in every region of the country—more factories, schools and union halls, visits to places that stretched from Haverhill, Massachusetts, to Los Angeles, and from Rapid City, South Dakota, to Miami Beach and Laurel, Mississippi—but I tried to relate those conversations to the matters of national discourse about what was happening to the country, and to what I sensed was a growing intellectual despair about the chances of resolving major social problems. Inevitably I asked questions—of myself, and often of others—about what was happening to traditionally distinctive American places, practices and ideas. What had happened to the idea of the frontier, not as a physical place but as a metaphor for change and mobility, what had happened to the concept of the West, to the idea of work, to the ideology and faith of the middle class? What was happening in the South, which, in the late sixties, was emerging as a region that some people regarded as the source of new possibilities, what was happening to the young who had themselves, for a brief moment, bemused so many people with a vision of the greening of America, and what was happening to the national faith in brains which, in the twenty years after World War II, seemed to represent solutions to all the world's problems? I covered portions of the 1972 presidential campaign, as well as a number of state and local campaigns (in 1970 and 1972) as a way of looking not only at the country but as a way of testing the relevance of political language. For a time in 1970 and 1971 I had written some speech drafts for George McGovern (who seemed to me by far the most promising alternative on almost every major national issue), and I began to realize then how difficult it was—not just for me, but for anyone—to articulate a coherent vision for the country and to make connections with what seemed to me nearly inexpressible feelings which had, at least temporarily, outrun the possibilities of political language. Many journalists who covered the 1972 election would later observe that the country was tired of change, wanted a rest from new programs and activity, yet it seemed to me that that very desire was also a reflection of the national doubt in the country's possibilities. The years since 1968 have represented, in a great many ways, a coming to terms with limitations and a simultaneous acceptance of the inequities that American rhetoric had once promised to eliminate. The 1972 election was a way to get into those matters, and so I have used it as a means of starting the book, a launching vehicle into other elements of American life.

As I think about the book now I wonder again, as I often did during the period of research and writing, how much my own feelings conditioned my view of the country and the hundreds of interviews I conducted. Yet in the last few months—the last months of 1972 and the first months of 1973—a number of things have occurred that seem, if anything, to reconfirm my impressions: the relative passivity of the country in the face of the unlimited and senseless bombing of Indochina, the simultaneous announcements of stock-market prosperity and reduction of social services, the abandonment of attempts by the national government to enforce civil-rights laws and to produce equality in employment and housing, the national willingness to tolerate restrictions on the press and intimidation of journalists, and, in general, the willingness to accept things as they are, to tolerate, to come to terms, and to preserve the remains of personal privilege. Finally there is the festering matter of Watergate itself, perhaps the most serious political scandal in American history. Richard Nixon, if he survives as president, is likely to do so only at the price of a crippled capacity to govern, and there is a growing possibility, as I write, that he will not survive at all. Yet the national response—shock, fear, anger—does not yet begin to raise the more fundamental questions associated with the scandal: it is blamed on the President's isolation or on the cynicism of Haldeman, Ehrlichman and Mitchell, or on sheer stupidity, and not on the widening gap between national political ideals and social aspirations on the one hand and political and social realities on the other. When the language of consensus fails, cohesion and political success are forged by more devious means. When establishments collapse, opportunists and upstarts often replace them. Two months before I wrote these lines, the national commission planning the official bicentennial for 1976 confessed that, after months of deliberation, it was still unable to formulate plans for the celebration. Such a failure would have been inconceivable in the more primitive months preceding July 4, 1876: a century ago time seemed to be on our side. Now we are no longer sure.

III

This book owes a great deal to a great many people. Some of them are quoted, but a number, quoted and anonymous, helped far more than the text can possibly suggest. In a book such as this, it is often impossible to know just where ideas, suggestions and assistance first originated. But I know that the following—among many others—are those who contributed: William Simon, John Gagnon, Colin Greer, Midge Decter, Norman Cousins, Willie Morris, James Cass, Nicholas Kisburg, Michael Korda, Ellen Levine, Ivan Illich, Ted Van Dyk, Studs Terkel, Leonard Stevens, Barry and Marcia Farrell, Joan Didion, Jay and Alberta Murphy, Stan Murphy, Edward Cole, Jason Berry, Joseph Huttie, Clifford and Virginia Durr, David Mathews, Robert Spiegel, Bill Field, Carolyn Tobian, Steven Arkin, Tom Jolas, H. Brandt Ayres, Jack MacNider, Richard Reeves, Stanley Sheinbaum, Norman Podhoretz, Paul Jacobs, Robert Heilbroner, Roland Gelatt, Susan Cohen, Gerry and Dick Meister, Tom Cottle, Didi Lorillard, Jack Garvey, George Cunningham, Neil Evans, Edgar Friedenberg, Irving M. Levine, Judith M. Herman, Gino Baroni, David Pinsky, Steven M. Roberts, Henry Goldman, and, most particularly, Sheila Canning, who has helped more than she will ever understand. I also owe thanks to the National Project on Ethnic America of the American Jewish Committee, from which I have borrowed and stolen for a number of years, to

Joint Council 16 of the Teamsters Union, to the Fraternal Order of Steel Haulers, to my students at the University of Massachusetts in 1970–71, and to many organizations which tolerate the impositions of journalists who can be only of limited help to them, if, indeed, they are any help at all. I'm also deeply grateful to the John Simon Guggenheim Foundation, which provided the fellowship that supported the research that led to this book. Most of all, as usual, there was the incalculable input of Diane Divoky, who sees and perceives things that escape ordinary mortals. I'm certain that many of these people do not agree with my views, a fact which makes me appreciate their assistance and generosity that much more.

San Francisco
May 15, 1973

THE END
OF THE
AMERICAN
FUTURE

ONE:

BYE-BYE,
MISS AMERICAN PIE

I

*"I want to call our country home from the destruction in Asia;
I want to call this country home to the Constitution; I want to
call the country home from the politics of image making and
deception to the politics of hope and reconciliation . . ."*

The prophetic voice is familiar, seems to rise from the soil itself, and the Biblical rhythms flow so easily that, for the moment, this time and this place seem to encompass all American
existence. Baltic, South Dakota, May 1971: the thirty-nine Norman Rockwell graduates, girls in white, boys in blue, the gowns
concealing only an occasional miniskirt or a pair of clogs, the
boys' mortarboards edged only rarely with hair hesitantly growing toward the collar, all respectful, yet very much in possession, people in a familiar place, a place understood and under
control, the families in the bleachers and on the folding chairs on
the gymnasium floor, the men in their sports shirts and their
steel-rimmed glasses, the babies in strollers, the younger brothers and grandmothers and cousins and friends, the print dresses
and the denims, the programs fanning for the relief of a breeze,
the invocation and the benediction, "The Battle Hymn of the
Republic," and, along the gymnasium walls, the pennants of the
Opposition—Oldham, Salem, West Central, Ramona, Rutland,
Egan. In the fall they will cheer again, repeating the familiar
cycle, autumn Saturdays of football, winter Wednesdays and

23

Fridays in this room, listening to the same instruments and music, watching the same uniforms, measuring the same possibilities—the possibility of a new quarterback or a new tractor or another crop—and waiting for spring again. A cluster of people stand in the breeze just outside the open doors, but beyond them no one stirs on the dusty streets or in the momentarily deserted houses or in the fields where the streets abruptly end and which stretch across the rolling Dakota prairie to the Missouri on the west, to Minnesota on the east, to Nebraska and Iowa, lapping at other little towns with other teams and other kids, sustaining corn and cattle and a sense that if only people elsewhere were as sane as those at home, the country could once more be understood. *"I want to call our country home from its wandering abroad, I want to get on with the redemption of our nation—this great and good land . . . Let us test the current practices of this nation against the ideals we cherish most; is the pursuit of happiness going well with us as a nation?"—speaking now of God-given resources, of war and peace, of the young before him, quoting that "admonition of olden times": "I have set before you life or death, blessing or cursing; therefore choose life that thy seed may prevail."*

He has been an announced candidate now for almost six months, but he still remains a lonely figure, traveling by automobile across his home state, trying to tell them that he is serious in his wish to be President. We do not yet know that he has a plan—a careful and necessary strategy—and when he tries to tell us we ignore him as a pursuer of fantasy; it is only later that we will briefly regard him as a consummate politician. For now it is his very aloneness that seems most appealing and that gives the prophetic voice its authentic ring; and thus he charms us with our own illusions. In the past year his sideburns have grown a little longer, the colors of his ties and shirts bolder, and some of his people say he is a little too mod for the folks in Baltic or Ramona or even Sioux Falls, yet the deference in manner blunts the affront, cools it, and seems to change its course. He is comfortable here, is more in place than in Washington or New York or Chicago; there is less noise here, less need for the strident, less pressure for that preemptive quality that keeps the channels in tune and the message clear. They know what he has been saying Out There, read his statements in the *Argus Leader*, and hear them on KELO: George McGovern on Vietnam, McGovern on hunger and poverty, McGovern on the military, McGovern on dissent, McGovern on amnesty, McGovern saying domestic problems are more dangerous to national security than the possibility of military attack, but when he brings it here, when he shakes their hands, when he finds the tone and cadences of the plains, the message is no longer exotic or even subversive, and the man is one of your own. After the ceremony ends they will cluster around him, extending that diffident courtesy which, all democratic egalitarianism aside, humility always extends to fame. He will ask about people he knows, will discuss farm prices and irrigation projects, promising to raise agricultural parity and to pursue federal assistance on items that only he and they can fully understand. Yet it is only here that it all comes together, where the language works, where they still seem to speak simple English. Later we will hear him in other, more *remote* places, in New Hampshire and Wisconsin and California, will watch him speak to factory workers and blacks and housewives, and will note varying degrees of enthusiasm, varying levels of intensity, some of them warm, some merely distant and courteous. Many of those subsequent attempts to communicate will be slightly off key, nuances passing in space, words misunderstood in translation. Here they know what he is; elsewhere they try to imagine something that he never was.

There is, in these early days, something tentative about the man, the place and the time. The common style in Baltic suggests the best of the past and the best of what one may hope for the future, but it seems forever in search of connections to the ugliness of a larger moment, and so the present itself becomes more like a mathematical median than a manifestation of contemporary reality: Here the rural life of the plains can somehow be squared with the prospects for a stable world, the parsimony of the farmer with proposed restrictions on the military budget. They cheer when he tells them that it's time the prosperous Europeans stopped expecting the United States to maintain a NATO force of 300,000 men and started paying for their own defense, and they respond when he cites polls indicating that sixty percent of Americans don't believe the pronouncements of their government, yet just as surely they would respond if he told them that moral values are in jeopardy, or that the family is breaking down, or that too many rich kids are going crazy with sex and drugs. It is the style, the accent, the familiarity that saves him: Withdrawal from Vietnam (even before it became fashionable) was clearly acceptable as long as a man responded to his constituents, tried to help the farmers and spoke the right language, and even amnesty might be regarded as a sign of honesty and charity rather than a symptom of liberal permissiveness. Standing outside the open doors of the Baltic High School gymnasium, it is easy to imagine that this world goes on forever, and what appears on the tube or in the paper is merely the fantasy of a maniac.

In the succeeding eighteen months, as the politician sheds the prophet's skin and grows the more familiar hide of the contender, we will begin to understand both the assets and the limitations of his style and background, will come to know what the country beyond has made him. We will watch as he makes his famous "discovery"—retrospectively dated February 18, 1972, and placed in a shoe factory in New Hampshire—that he can appeal to blue-collar workers and ethnics, people who, as he once said privately in South Dakota, "aren't considered Middle Americans around here"; the subsequent discovery—placed at a church rally in Watts during the California primary—that black people will respond; and the still more startling discovery (especially for those who admired him *because* they expected him to lose) that he could manipulate delegates and conventions as well as the old professionals. And yet one has to begin here, has to begin in this place, not because this is where he began but because this is where order was supposed to reside, because the history of the previous four years had seemingly affected this place least. In this kind of region politicians could survive—liberals from farm-belt states—until they were needed; here the brawls that destroyed a Lindsay or that produced a Buckley or that emasculated a Humphrey could be averted under the umbrella of farm supports, "candor" and simple talk. This is where sentiment placed the real America, even while desire took it elsewhere.

It is our shrine to simplicity, the place where Things are supposed to work, where telephones are answered, where officials are accessible and people responsive. It is the kind of place that the people at Common Cause—that great public-interest lobby—dream about when they talk about the need for accountability in public institutions, and when they lament the lack of responsiveness among officials. You can get to see the mayor, the doctors (some of them) make house calls, and the plumber comes in a hurry. Not that they are all that virtuous or that things are all that wonderful. Wages are low, jobs are scarce, and new industry is reluctant to come in, discouraged by the isolation of the region—by distance itself—and by a crowd of cozy loyal oligarchs who like their cheap labor. Local problems, moreover, are rendered invisible: there are virtually no blacks, the Indians are kept on their reservations—when they come to town they are regarded as a police problem—and the poor, like the people of Watts, pay exorbitant rents to live in rundown houses that look reasonably pleasant from the street. You are reminded of a barely articulate alienation, the sort of alienation that proceeds from an instinctive comprehension of immediate things—the repair of an engine, the care of the soil, the management of cattle—but that cannot fathom the capricious behavior of distant systems and forces, cannot understand either the rebellion of the young or the practices of the government against which that rebellion is ostensibly directed. For a century the ambitious and the hopeful have been packing up and moving elsewhere—off to college, off to the cities, off to California—and the population of the state, now under 700,000, continues to decline. "People really seem to lack direction," says a reporter newly arrived from California (no jobs there either). "There's no feeling about tomorrow, no sense of the future, and the result is apathy."

What remains is the moral sense, the ingrained voice of the prophet, and it is that which connects the antiquity of the plains with the presumed modernity of the students. Talk about populism, talk about the Dakota farmers who supported La Follette, talk about the Scandinavian Socialists who opted for state-owned cement plants and flour mills—talk about all the things that were supposed to make George McGovern a voice of the new party of the people and you ignore the central fact of his appeal, the prime liability in his understanding. His own support in South Dakota, he often said, comes from "farmers, preachers and teachers." Scrape him a little and he turns into William Jennings Bryan; scrape him still further and he begins to resemble Jonathan Edwards. "This chamber," he had said on the floor of the Senate, "reeks with blood. Every Senator here is partly responsible for that human wreckage at Walter Reed and Bethesda Naval and all across our land—young boys without legs, or arms, or genitals, or faces, or hopes. There aren't very many of these blasted and broken boys who think this war is a glorious adventure. Don't talk to them about bugging out, or national honor, or courage. It doesn't take any courage at all for a Congressman, or a Senator, or a President to wrap himself in the flag and say we're staying in Vietnam. Because it isn't our blood that is being shed." *This chamber reeks with blood.* He would lecture all of us, this son of a Methodist preacher, this man of conscience—would see the war as the prime excrescence of a morally endangered society (just as others would seize on drugs or pornography or obscenity) and would try to save us from our sins. *"This may be the last chance,"* he said in that swing through South Dakota, *"the last chance to reverse the drift toward militarism and repression. . . ."* The last chance. *"The American people are prepared to respond to leadership that called upon them to turn away from military adventurism to the reconstruction of American society. That is a leadership of reconciliation which could unite the coalition of silence and the coalition of conscience for the common good. I want to redeem what is finest in America."*

II

In four years we had had it all: The Chicago Democratic convention of 1968, the inauguration of Richard Nixon, the "New American Revolution," the face of John Mitchell, Honor American Day, Woodstock, Altamont, Hendrix, Joplin, the closing of the Fillmore and the breaking up of the Beatles, the Chicago conspiracy trial, Harrisburg, Ellsberg, the Panther trials, Angela Davis, Charlie Manson, Sirhan Sirhan, Cambodia, Laos, Haiphong, the bombs, the dikes, and finally another Democratic convention which was supposed to set things right but which, in the final analysis, only traded one elite for another. "We have endured a long night of the American spirit," Richard Nixon had said in his first inaugural. "But as our eyes catch the dimness of the first rays of dawn, let us not curse the remaining dark. Let us gather the light." "Bring Us Together" had been the first slogan of the new Administration, although it was soon dropped. Four years later McGovern would speak of healing and reconciliation. *"There's a new day coming,"* he would say in the shopping malls, his voice beginning to crack, though no one could quite imagine what the new day would look like.

It had been the undoing of the sixties; by the time the decade ended it was difficult even to remember what the beginning felt like. Memory always reshapes the meaning of the ordinary in favor of the present. The optimism of Lyndon Johnson and Jack Kennedy sounded almost quaint, *The Greening of America*, published in 1970, became a best-selling joke on the liberal middle class—no corporate executives were running off barefoot to lie in the grass—and the beautiful things that had started with the Beatles and the hippies and the flower children ended with scenes of the Hell's Angels busting up rock festivals and of fourteen-year-olds from Scarsdale freaking out on speed in the East Village. The war had been "wound down," had been brought to a higher level of technical efficiency, so that while the boys were being brought home we managed to drop the equivalent of one Hiroshima bomb every week, a million tons of explosives every year; we had learned about My Lai and Lieutenant Calley, about Attica and George Jackson, about the Vietnam Veterans Against the War, about Dita Beard (whom Daniel Ellsberg once called the Lieutenant Calley of the ITT case), about prayer breakfasts at the White House, about Jesus Freaks and wiretaps and about the way five Presidents had systematically deceived their constituents about what was happening in Vietnam. And yet all that seemed more like a set of symptoms, even abstractions, than the substantive facts of American existence. Most people didn't want to know about the Atticas or the My Lais, or, if forced to confront them, could only assert that the killing must have been justified. They wanted lies, insisted on deception, demanded reassurances that the Panthers had shot first, or that the prisoners were slitting the throats of the hostages, or that the Vietnamese children carried grenades. Abstractions on the evening news. The reality was taxes, unemployment, and the price of beef at the supermarket. We had created a new set of headlines and erased the old without very much change in the facts of everyday existence: Remember Appalachia, remember all those news clips of shacks in some Kentucky coal camp where hollow-cheeked men spoke about coal dust and food stamps and rotten schools; remember the pictures of the black women with their seven kids telling about the welfare, the social workers, the landlords; remember all that talk about "the urban problem" and all the ways that the corporations and the cities and the federal government were going to get together to solve it; remember Vista and the Peace Corps; remember the Great Society and the New Frontier?

In these difficult years [Nixon had said in that first inaugural], America has suffered from a fever of words; from inflated rhetoric that promises more than it can deliver; from angry rhetoric that fans discontents into hatreds; from bombastic rhetoric that postures instead of persuading.

We cannot learn from one another until we stop shouting at one another—until we speak quietly enough so that our words can be heard as well as our voices.

For its part, government will listen. We will strive to listen in new ways—to the voices of quiet anguish, the voices that speak without words, the voices of the heart, to the injured voices, the anxious voices, the voices that have despaired of being heard.

Those who have been left out, we will try to bring in.

Those left behind, we will help catch up.

A great deal had happened since Nixon took office, but the accumulated effect of those happenings had more to do with the state of the American mind than it did with the features of the landscape. We had canceled previous commitments without taking on new ones: 1972 felt more like 1955 than the mid-sixties. "Most people," said a reporter during the Wisconsin primary, "know they're in this snowball and that it won't stop. They know the problem isn't temporary; it'll go on even after Nixon." No new day was coming. The apocalyptic issues of the previous decade faded into a limbo of forgotten sociology—studies of presidential commissions, plans to integrate schools and communities, programs to eliminate poverty—and were replaced by a tentative coming to terms with the inequities, brutality and uncertainty of American life. Quite clearly the "inflated rhetoric" of the sixties had promised more than it could deliver, but it did so only because it assumed that fundamentally things in America were more hopeful than in fact they turned out to be. History and tradition had seemed to indicate —long, long ago, before memory became dim—that through relatively cheap social action we could remedy severe domestic problems, resolve world crises, and rescue nations in the cause of righteousness; we had believed that large reforms came in small packages labeled education, health or housing which could be bought painlessly as funds became available. Acquiring them would not (we thought) affect the privileges of others. In four years of the Great Society we began to discover (as we should always have known) that the advantages of those who had power and resources were inextricably tied to the disadvantages of those who did not. We learned that it was impossible to maintain suburban homogeneity and integrated communities at the same time, that part of the wealth of Pittsburgh and New York depends on the mining of cheap Appalachian coal and the exploitation of mountaineers, and that it was impossible to use schools and colleges as instruments to select some people for economic advancement without using the same institutions to reject others. By the time of the 1968 conventions we already understood that the New Deal had finally come to an end, and that Lyndon Johnson's well-intentioned liberalism was almost as anachronistic as the Neanderthal Goldwaterism we had rejected in 1964. It was not the nomination of George McGovern that broke up the old coalition, or the reform of the Democratic Party under the McGovern rules; the coalition had been breaking up for a generation because the ideology and aspirations that once sustained it could apply only to a nation on the make, not to one that had outrun its vision of the future.

Traditional economic disorders, inflation and unemployment [wrote Richard Goodwin on the eve of the 1972 Democratic convention] have produced studies and debates so voluminous they constitute an independent problem of waste disposal. Less visible but far more influential is the fact that the real income of an American majority has virtually stagnated for half a decade. Combined with a decay of other conditions of life, this means that the standard of living has declined. The change may be slight, economically unimportant, but statistics do not reveal the devastation of this reality. For . . . most of two hundred years, a continual improvement in the conditions of life, in the circumstances of every diligent family, has been an article of American faith, an expectation woven into the acts and decisions of every individual . . . Economic stagnation is real, but it is also a visible symbol for more spirit-shrinking afflictions. Material well-being is only an instrument for the pursuit of more fulfilling, freer lives. Yet wealth has brought not liberation, but increasing confinement. The pleasures of place, of neighborhood and street, are eroded by physical decay and psychic eviction; work, the principal object of human vitality, declines from satisfaction to obligation to pain; the organic units which provide one with the acceptance and respect of fellow-family and community and place crumble under powerful, ill-comprehended forces of dissolution. The individual realizes that he no longer shapes the conditions of his existence, that he has become an instrument, an object, of some uncontrollable social process. Impotence can stimulate defiance; but more often it breeds insecurity, fear, hostility, and even violence. Not long ago, the prototype of impotent humanity killed a President.

American liberalism had been founded on the premise of an indefinitely expanding future, and liberal policy grew from the belief that if men were free from artificial restraints (or if they received temporary assistance to overcome obstacles), then progress would inevitably follow. Every problem in America was an aberration—depressions, unemployment, disease, perhaps even death—and every program was temporary. The curves would rise forever, lower left to upper right—population, production, abundance, opportunity, the good life, even that quality once known to the nineteenth century as "the moral condition," the rise in one curve merely confirming or anticipating the rise in others. More babies meant more business, more cars meant a better life, wealth affirmed virtue. David Potter, who (among many others) had called Americans the people of plenty, a nation where economic abundance shaped the very essence of the national character and where history itself had seemed to be an ally of aspiration, once pointed out that it was by the stratagem "of refusing to accept the factors given, of drawing on nature's surplus and technology's tricks, that America has often dealt with her problems of social reform." American hostility to the concept of class struggle, he suggested, was founded on the national reluctance "to entertain the thought that American wealth had ceased to grow, and that we can no longer raise the standard of living without lowering it somewhere else." And what was true in the economic sphere could be regarded as a paradigm for everything else: for religion and morality, for the greater good life, for political institutions, and for American influence in the world. Inevitably tomorrow would be better than today, inevitably time was on your side. There was no need for substantial restructuring, certainly no need for anything like a socialist revolution, since everyone would soon have everything—be everything, control everything —he needed. The frontier, any frontier, was the American answer to Marx.

The refrain lasted for more than three hundred years and may, from sheer force of habit, last fifty years more. In the dark one whistles familiar tunes. And yet it was precisely that confidence which had been waning for a generation and which, after the temporary hiatus of the early sixties, seems to have become so irreparably disconnected from the present. It was even hard, after the first Nixon years, to recall what it felt like, hard to recall the anger of the liberals at the Chicago convention when they fully realized—though perhaps without comprehending— just what had finally come to an end. It was not simply that the old heroes had turned fat and become villains, that "labor leaders" had been transformed into bosses or that people like Hubert Humphrey were regarded as fatuous fools; nor was it even the fact that it was the Democrats themselves who had made the war; it was, more than anything else, the beginning of the realization that liberalism could no longer articulate a comprehensive vision, that the programs, even if they had not run afoul of the Vietnam War (a condition impossible to imagine), could not have worked since they did not address what Goodwin, one of the angriest of the Chicago liberals, would later call "a social and economic process unsuited to modern conditions." The liberal system no longer worked because too many people had stopped believing in the curves.

The evidence, though substantial, defied the ordinary data of journalism. In 1971 Albert H. Cantril and Charles W. Roll, Jr., summarizing a national poll of American expectations, concluded that "Americans sense that their country has lost rather than gained ground over the past five years . . . Looking ahead, people expect the United States in 1976—our bicentennial year—to be merely where it was a full decade earlier, having barely recovered the reverses of the last half-decade." There were similar returns from other surveys. In one poll, conducted among students in 1971 for the JDR (John D. Rockefeller) Fund, thirty percent of the respondents declared that they would prefer to live in some country other than the United States; although the campuses were quiet, the survey concluded, students "are more uneasy and worried than in 1970. Only a handful believe our national policies will lead to peace or economic well-being." For a decade the rate of increase in American productivity had been declining, and the indications of the early seventies, despite the ritual optimism of official spokesmen, and despite the "recovery" of 1972, suggested that the decline would not be an aberration. "As productivity in particular occupations increases," said Kenneth Boulding, "the proportion of the economy in improving industries declines and the proportion in technically stagnant industries, such as education, government (and) medicine, increases. It seems highly probable therefore that there will be a substantial decline in the rate of increase in gross productivity in the next few decades." Limitations on natural resources, ecological considerations, competition from other nations and a variety of related elements were likely to compound that decline, even to make it desirable. Boulding talked about a "crisis of closure"—the realization that growth and development can no longer be linear, do not take place on an infinite plane: "The crisis is that of an image of the future. One might almost describe it as eschatological ecology."

By themselves, polls and statistics and quotations were not enough; it was rather what people didn't say or didn't do, or what they resisted, that told the story. You felt it in the small towns and saw it in the cities and heard it in the pronouncements of the politicians; it did not have a coherent voice, lacked a language, and yet that lack itself seemed to be part of the problem. We had no way, not yet, of really asking the question "What's bugging you?" and getting a useful set of answers, no way of expressing what people now believe or expect. The future was always implicit in American speech; without it we were tongue-tied. Everywhere people were pointing to something else—to the absentee owners of the local plant, to the pollution from the city upstream, to the junkies, to the bureaucrats in the state house, to "Washington" or "Detroit" or "the media" or "the Pentagon." The possibility of local action and independent enterprise seemed increasingly remote, the boosters had disappeared, and the prospect of a new housing development or a new factory was greeted with mixed feelings. Slowly people were beginning to learn to live in an indefinite present.

At bottom [Robert Heilbroner had written in 1960] our troubled state of mind reflects an inability to see the future in an historic context. If current events strike us as all surprise and shock it is because we cannot see those events in a meaningful framework. . . . More than anything else, our disorientation before the future reveals a loss of historic identity, an incapacity to grasp our historic situation. Unlike our forefathers who lived very much *in* history and *for* history, we ourselves appear to be adrift in an historic void.

For a few years John F. Kennedy's style and rhetoric seemed to repeal that observation: Here, it seemed, was a man astride historical forces, a man who did live in history and who expected to restore history to the national will. But all that quickly came to an end and was replaced by an inchoate feeling that history had become an uncertain ally, perhaps even an enemy, that time might be against you, and that Americans had lost their providential favors. Perhaps the whole decade of the sixties had been a fluke, a last explosion of euphoria; perhaps Nixon had in fact been Eisenhower's successor.

You got it in all sorts of versions, could hear it from the unemployed fishermen in Gloucester and San Francisco, or from lawyers in small Midwestern cities, or from kids along the highway, or from politicians at national conventions, or in the corner bar, or in the welfare office, or in the songs of the rock musicians, or in any of a hundred other places; not the voice of anger or despair, but merely the separate voices of people trying to come to terms—the revolution of declining expectations. "You try hard," says the old Republican politician in Ashtabula, "but you have to make compromises." "A great place to raise kids," says the booster in Mason City, Iowa, "if only the packing plant doesn't close down." "We got the new plant," says the lawyer in Newton, Kansas, "but they brought their own people, and our people are still unemployed." The clichés of accommodation replace the rhetoric of growth, and the fear of crowding and decay overwhelm the facts of expansion: *Another goddam Los Angeles . . . The corporate farms cutting you up . . . winding down the war, I guess . . . the welfare load . . . taxes . . . can't walk the streets at night . . . beer cans on the beach . . . nobody wants to work*—acceptable symptoms of an unexplained disease. The great refrain of the age was "alienation," the fashion was nostalgia, and the marching song, by Don McLean, an elegy of allusions that not even the writer could trans-the fashion was nostalgia, and the marching song, "American Pie," by Don McLean, an elegy of allusions that not even the writer could translate:

> Bye-Bye, Miss American Pie
> Drove my Chevy to the levee but the levee was dry.
> Them good ole boys were drinkin' whiskey and rye
> Singin' this'll be the day that I die,
> This'll be the day that I die.

And in the streets the children screamed,
The lovers cried and the poets dreamed.
But not a word was spoken
The church bells all were broken.
And the three men I admire most,
The Father, Son and the Holy Ghost,
They caught the last train for the coast
The day the music died.

What we desperately needed was a language, because the disenchantment was inexpressible. We could talk about inflation or unemployment, about race relations or "the urban problem," about the war and the economy. But all those things suggested specific and presumably temporary difficulties, departures from a healthy norm, and not the more pervasive uneasiness that has been variously described as the American Malaise or the American Resignation. What did losing ground mean? What were the reverses, and how did one recover them? What was it that the country had lost?

The facile answer was that it had lost its virginity, but that was hardly enough. In *The End of American Innocence*, written in the 1950s, Henry May spoke about a "permanent flaw in American nineteenth century thought: its inveterate optimism," an optimism which held that the main guarantee of American morality, ultimately the good life, "was neither in the mind of God nor in tradition, but in the unfolding American future." We had been chronicling the end of American innocence for at least a century; it has been our favorite topic, Melville's topic, the theme of Henry James, the lament of Henry Adams, and the subject of countless tracts, novels, studies and speeches: World War I represented the end, or the coming of the railroad, or World War II, or the assassination of John F. Kennedy or Robert Kennedy or Martin Luther King, Jr., or Hiroshima, or the Sharon Tate murders or the Chicago Democratic convention. Our innocence was always coming to an end, had been coming to an end ever since the Puritan fathers at Massachusetts Bay cut down the Maypole at Merrymount. Yet what *they* knew—the writers, the novelists, the critics—most people apparently didn't know at all, or didn't talk about if they did. Those of us who tried to read American literature in school, and who discussed those ideas in college, were subsequently surprised to find that Twain's humor had been remembered and his despair forgotten, had learned to regard the Melvilles and the Thoreaus as uncomfortable abstractions and had taught ourselves that, despite all that literature, America—the real America Out There—had cheerfully disregarded their gloom and was inventing new futures for itself as rapidly as it could develop the gadgets and appliances and life styles on which those futures would be based. What you discovered now was that futures were no longer being invented, that psychic curves were flattening out, that people suspected the boom was over. This kind of image, wrote Boulding,

implies a high value on modesty rather than grandeur. There is no room for "great societies" in the spaceship. It implies conservationism to the point of conservatism rather than expansionism. It implies a high value on taking things easy, on conflict management. There is no room in the spaceship for men on white horses, and very little room for horsing around. We cannot afford to have war, revolution, or dialectical processes. Everything must be directed towards the preservation of precarious order rather than experimentation with new forms. We have to stress equality rather than incentives, simply in order to minimize uncertainty and conflict. . . .

Economists have never been very cheerful about the stationary state, and a permanent, planetwide stationary state, from which there seemed to be no possible means of escape, might be a very depressing prospect indeed. What is even more depressing is that a stationary state might not even be stable simply because of the intensification of conflicts within it. In the progressive state, conflicts can be resolved fairly easily by progress itself. The poor can get richer without the rich getting poorer. In the stationary state, if the poor are to get richer, then the rich must get poorer, and what is even more frightening, if the rich are to get richer, they can only do so by increasing their exploitation of the poor. . . . In a mood that was not intended to be congratulatory I once defined Maoist economics as the substitution of euphoria for commodities. In the stationary state, one has the haunting feeling that this trick might be highly valuable.

Perhaps it hadn't yet come to all that—hadn't reached the verge of the gloomy predictions published by the Club of Rome in *The Limits to Growth* or by the other apocalyptic visionaries of resource depletion and overpopulation; maybe there would be new technological tricks to maintain growth and mitigate the exhaustion of natural resources; you still heard people talking about solar energy and about the imminent prospect of developing inexpensive processes to desalinize sea water; there was even evidence that population, in America at least, was about to regulate itself, that the birth rate had fallen to a figure approaching the maintenance level. Yet just as surely there had developed, in the space of a few years, a sort of entropic consciousness in America, a feeling that there were no places left to go, and that the price of growth (in whatever form) was getting higher every day. Each item in the consumer catalogue was coming closer to the limits of its marginal utility: the very things which had once been major American symbols of progress had been transformed into negatives—the smoking factory chimney, the automobile, the boom town, the new tract of houses. Who would have ever thought that a Republican President of the United States would boast of the restrictions he had placed on the economy?

The ritual optimism, of course, was still there. The charts from the President's Council of Economic Advisers, from the Labor Department and from the Federal Reserve System contained the familiar projections: a continuing rise in gross national product, new investments in plant and equipment, more jobs, higher incomes. "The Gross National Product of our economy," said a Labor Department booklet published in 1970, "may increase to $1.4 trillion in 1980, about 50 percent more than in 1970 and three times the level in 1950—given high employment levels and expected productivity gains," and by 1972 the projections had become even more optimistic (even while the economy lagged): $1.5 trillion by 1980, a median family income of $15,000, a shorter work week, better housing, better transportation, better everything. In the context of those predictions the continuing problems of unemployment and inflation appeared, ironically, to support the optimists: We were not debating the premises of the economy or the necessity for fundamentally new arrangements, but only the tactics by which we could eliminate those nasty little dips and squiggles from the curve of indefinite progress.

There would be changes: We were moving from a production economy to a service economy; we would be harder pressed by competition from the low-wage nations; we would need new sources of raw materials; we would have to consider the impact of growth on the environment, and we might even have to revise our long-standing belief in the connection between a growing prosperity and a growing population.

The more time we save in making goods [said *Fortune* in 1970], the more time we spend providing services. During the last twenty years, output of goods has more than doubled, but productivity of the goods industries rose so much that the number of people producing the goods increased only from 28 million to 29 million. But behold the services. The number of people providing them increased by no less than 70 percent, from 28 million to nearly 48 million. . . . The trend seems bound to continue. By 1980 service jobs will again account for the overwhelming bulk of the increase in total employment. By 1990 the services may well account for more than 70 percent of all jobs.

Everything was an opportunity: industry would be set to solving social problems, building new cities, operating schools, selling police and fire protection, developing mass-transit facilities, and, most important, creating the technology of pollution control. The environment would take its place alongside the housing shortage and the ghetto problem as the great source of new profits. "There is almost no social problem," said E. B. Weiss, a vice-president of Doyle Dane Bernbach, Inc., in *Advertising Age*, "for which industry could not develop a wanted service—at a profit." And yet everyone knew that "efficiency" and increased productivity in the service sectors were hard to come by, that no one had yet figured out what it meant to make a cop or a schoolteacher more efficient, let alone how to do it; that the heralded participation of private industry in rebuilding the inner cities had turned into a bust; that the first new ventures in mass transit (with the possible exception of a new system in the San Francisco Bay area) were not even on the drawing boards; that Amtrak was a sham; and that the experiments with performance-contracting in public education (turning entire schools over to private industry) had produced no perceptible improvement in measured skills and no saving to the taxpayers. Even more significant, there was no indication that the great rise in industrial productivity of the fifties about which *Fortune* spoke so glowingly would continue, meaning that there was no certainty that there would be any money available to pay for the alleviation of those social problems or to sustain the service economy which *Fortune* predicted; on the contrary, there was every indication that the quality of services was, on the one hand, deteriorating badly and, on the other, rising so rapidly in cost as to go beyond the means (or, at least, the willingness) of the average man to pay: medical services, school taxes, college tuition, the repair of cars and appliances.

Most important, however, was the growing belief that those social problems would never be solved, that the cities were probably beyond hope, and that most of the programs of the New Frontier and the Great Society (or the industrial efforts which would succeed them) were doomed to futility because their intended beneficiaries—and we all knew who they were—were too shiftless and stupid for help. In discovering the limitations on resources, we had also rediscovered the limits of biology and genetics, what might be called the exhausted lode of human potential, and so we watched (generally with official approval) while a whole group of once liberal intellectuals—Nathan Glazer, Edward Banfield, Richard Herrnstein, Arthur Jensen, Daniel P. Moynihan and Irving Kristol, among others—constructed the intellectual rationale for benign neglect. Once the curves began to flatten out, the entire liberal argument was in jeopardy, because it had never contemplated, and would not now consider, any fundamental restructuring or redistribution of national wealth and power. "Economic growth at a relatively stable and high rate of approximately three and a half percent per annum, allowing for annual variations," wrote Zbigniew Brzezinski, one of the prophets of the "Technetronic Era," "seems to be the *sine qua non* for the continued evolution of American society toward a situation in which liberty and equality will buttress but not vitiate one another. This is particularly true of poverty and race relations, in which even social goodwill will be powerless to accomplish much in the event of a significant economic slowdown." Here too the future was gradually being exhausted; as the country sorted itself out, as opportunities (in jobs and education) enabled the heretofore disadvantaged to move up—if, indeed, they did—the residue would increasingly be composed of genetically inferior material; what was left behind, in the ghettoes or in Appalachia, were the biological losers. Existing welfare programs, moreover, tended to exacerbate the problem; it "deprived the poor [in Glazer's words] of what was for them —as for the poor who preceded them—the best and indeed only way to the improvement of their condition, the way that involved commitment to work and the strengthening of family ties." In an article in *Social Policy* called "The American Resignation: The New Assault on Equality," S. M. Miller and Ronnie Steinberg Ratner summarized the argument: (1) There is nothing wrong with America that lowering our aspirations won't solve; (2) things are much better than people seem to think; (3) blame the victim; (4) things will get worse if you try to make them better.

We are told [they wrote] that the condition of the poor and the Blacks has improved and that measures to improve their status still fur-

43

ther will have a destructive effect both on them and on the larger society. As evidence the retreatists from social change cite the social turbulence, the dangers of population, and the middle- and working-class backlash, the inflationary spiral, and the unredeemed and unredeemable promises, all of which, they note, marred the late 1960s.

What the new sociological data seemed to prove was that nothing made much difference, that schools could not produce either equality or economic opportunity, that intelligence and family background (whether racially or culturally determined) were the most powerful influences on later achievement, that more money did not necessarily produce better schools, that all forms of social intervention were, when you came right down to it, hopeless. The "urban crisis," which had once been a positive code word for Blacks, was replaced by "busing," and that meant keeping everybody in his place. "Welfare" had become our prime social problem, not poverty.

III

We all knew, those of us who went to Miami to cover it, that nothing would happen at the Republican national convention which nominated Richard Nixon for his second term as President of the United States. The proceedings had been so carefully scripted in advance—had, as it turned out, been programed to the last hand gesture and the release of the last balloon—that there remained only the ironic pleasure of watching people who were supposed to be the political powers of Kansas and Michigan and Ohio being used as spear carriers in a pageant. The Young Voters for the President (YVP, or Vippies), a contingent of three thousand red, white and blue fraternity types (many of them were too young to vote) were shuttled from hotel to hotel and from the airport to the convention hall to provide a suitable backdrop for an Administration obviously embarrassed by (and jealous of) the youth quotient of the opposition. While the delegates drank their corporate booze on yachts tied up in Indian Creek or sat through perfunctory caucuses or lined up for Tricia Nixon's autograph in the lobby of the Fontainebleau Hotel, the Management, locked behind three tiers of security guards in the Doral ("Closed to the Public"), orchestrated the convention with a hermetic perfection suitable only to a candidate who found nothing peculiar in being photographed for a campaign film walking along the beach with his shoes on.

They cheered on cue, and the spontaneous demonstrations were managed with contemptuous precision, yet anyone who had ever attended a Southeastern Conference football game could also feel a familiar intensity, even hysteria, when the delegates on the floor and the Nixon Youth in the galleries erupted at the climax of nomination. They really felt something, had won a great victory, had beaten a determined enemy, had triumphed over something that must have been frightening and relentless. Yet who, or what, was it? Where was the opposition? They had all known it would happen like this: Congressman Pete McCloskey of California, who had tried to challenge the President on the war, had been exiled from the convention, and while he was graciously permitted the one delegate vote he had won in the New Mexico primary, he was stripped of the delegate who should have cast it (1,377 for Nixon, one for McCloskey); thus there was not one voice in the hall to question the President on any issue—the war, the economy, none of it—even though many professed to have misgivings. George McGovern, meanwhile, was so far behind and so disorganized that he constituted more of a laugh than a threat (causing the Republicans to promote Ramsey Clark, just returned from Hanoi, into the role of co-villain); the theoretically divisive issues concerning the make-up of the 1976 convention, issues largely invented by the press for autostimulation, had been eliminated before most of the delegates had even arrived, and the potentially troublesome figures of the party—Rockefeller, Reagan, Percy—had been either bought off or consigned to oblivion. John Gardner, a Republican and once the Secretary of Health, Education and Welfare, wandered through the lobby of the Fontainebleau ungreeted and unrecognized, the ghost of another age; he was representing Common Cause, the organization he established to make institutions of government more responsive, but now he had a hard time finding a handshake; John Lindsay, convert to the Democrats (who paid no attention to him, either) was never mentioned, and Charles Goodell, until 1970 a U.S. Senator from New York—still a Republican, though he had also challenged Nixon on the war—was not even in town. And yet it was not that the assembled delegates were celebrating the triumph of the Right or the almost certain Nixon victory in November: You knew—again from those football games—that such catatonic hysteria went deeper than a touchdown, or a game won, or even a Conference Championship, it came from a lifetime of shit, from an existence that could admit nothing except duty and principle, that understood somehow that duty and principle were under siege, were forever being disparaged by the smart folks Out There, and that had long learned that even their America, the old Protestant Heaven-on-Earth (Jesusland, Mailer once called it), was more dour than advertised. When they chanted "Four more years" you couldn't help feel that it was intended just the way it was heard, a threat as well as a promise: Vengeance on America. They hated us—the press, the kids, the funky dissenters—probably hated even the technicians who were running them around, certainly hated the incomprehensibility of a world they imagined they never made, and now, for a moment, they could scream it all back, could unbutton their inhibitions, could wear their idiotic hats and buttons, could sweat and stomp, could smear the shit in our faces. For a moment.

The important thing here was not what had happened in Miami, but what had happened before, and which now was. The sentimental vision saw these Republicans as the Real America (different, certainly, from the Democrats of what they called the McGovern Convention): white, kempt, successful. Certainly that was how they saw themselves: the responsible people. They were older, richer, far richer, than the Democrats, more Protestant—were, when you came down to it, the best assembly of wealthy WASPs to be found anywhere. It didn't matter, therefore, that the convention hall was sealed off from the outside world (security), or that, after three or four days in Miami, it became hard to imagine that another world still existed beyond this strip, or that their war was still going on, or that people were out of work, or that some were still going hungry. These Republicans could speak, feel, think and act for America itself because that is who they imagined they were; it had, after all, been their country, and now it seemed that the polls, with McGovern trailing sixty-four to thirty, indicated that, despite the noise outside, it would be their country again. And yet, when you probed, when you talked to them in the lobbies of the hotels or interrupted their scripted boredom on the convention floor, you learned a startling fact. They too were coming to terms. They all agreed that if Nixon had run on a platform promising the things he had actually done in the previous four years, the arms agreements with the Russians, the trip to China, wage and price controls, the termination of the draft, and the Moynihan proposals for family assistance (essentially the same idea as McGovern's "radical" guaranteed-income proposals, though cheaper)—if all these things had been proposed they would have regarded Nixon as a dangerous extremist, a madman. But now they had learned to accept those things, even to like them, and when the campaign film showed Nixon drinking toasts with Mao Tse-tung and Chou En-lai they cheered, just as they would cheer when he spoke Wallace-talk about busing. *"People realize things are complicated,"* said a woman delegate *from small-town Missouri; "you have to trust the leadership, because you know that you couldn't unravel things yourself."* And so it went with all of them—*Change Without Chaos* was the theme of the film and the refrain of the delegates: of old Leverett Saltonstall, onetime everything from Massachusetts, now attending his tenth convention, who didn't like the phrase "coming to terms" but did think the party was catching up to something (and who allowed that McGovern was a sort of Andrew Jackson but that Nixon was more adaptable than John Quincy Adams had been in 1828, and would change rather than lose); of Tena Anderson of South Dakota, the youngest delegate in the hall, who conceded there were no jobs for the kids coming out of college but felt that Nixon represented the best chance for change; of Ted Lavit of Kentucky, who agreed that the country was coming to terms with its limitations, and who also felt that Nixon shouldn't get the credit for ending what Lavit called the "turmoil" of 1968 (though obviously Nixon was taking it); of Congressman Manuel Lujan of New Mexico, who kept saying that "we've learned something in the last four years," meaning that you could damn well abandon your principles if it meant more federal aid for the taxpayers at home; of Representative Keith G. Sebelius of Kansas, a one-time Goldwater Republican, who kept saying that the big wheat deal with the Russians sure was a wonderful thing and had raised the price of wheat for Kansas farmers by some thirty-five cents a bushel; of Norman A. Hodges, head of the Green Power Foundation, the corporation that grew out of the Watts riots, and one of the few black Republican delegates in Miami, who pointed out one morning at breakfast that "civil rights is not where this administration is at, green power is where it's at," and who made it clear, perhaps without meaning to, that you hustled your goodies anywhere you could get them, but especially among those powerful enough to hand out the contracts; of the black Wallace supporter who had drifted into the black Republican caucus at the Fontainebleau to announce that *"there's no point integratin' with sociologists and schoolteachers—man, you do that and you'll always be poor; the only people I'm interested in integratin' with are the Du Ponts and the Rockefellers"*; or of Gerald Ford, the House Minority Leader, who called a press conference to attack

McGovern's already familiar proposal to cut the military budget by some $30 billion and who concluded by conceding that such a cut would destroy the economy. They cheered because they had a winner, but they also cheered because Nixon had done them the greatest of favors: he had liberated them from their principles.

The journalists kept speaking about the complacency, the sub-urban-country-club smugness, the cosmetic wealth ("My country," said Kurt Vonnegut, Jr., who was covering for *Harper's*, "and I hate it"), and yet it wasn't really anyone's country, not altogether, nor was it all that smug. Some of them knew that the hermetic environment—the guards, the barricades, the script—wasn't of their choosing, that it had been chosen for them, and a good many more behaved like passengers in a crippled airplane who had no choice but to trust the pilot (however mad or incompetent he might be) to bring them safely down. The police around the convention hall kept driving the more curious delegates away from the surrounding fences to avert any possible confrontation or exchange between them and the Vietnam Veterans Against the War who were demonstrating outside. Inside and around the convention hotels, the Quaker kids who were handing out leaflets about the bombing found few takers (they had been refused permission to set up a table), while the Vippies, most of whom admitted that they came from wealthy families, cheered madly when a trio of imported pro-Nixon blue-collar workers spoke about the wonders of hard work. If there was a vision of the future, very few of them, kids or adults, could manage to express it; the task was to keep the thing functioning, to protect what you had, to try to disregard the inner doubts and suspicions, and to grab off a little piece for yourself. The problem, finally, was not only smugness but anxiety.

The language didn't matter anymore—either the words or the pictures on the screen. For three days they were fed the familiar rhetoric about American honor, hand-me-down words from McGovern about "this great and good country," echoes of John

Kennedy, "Let us take risks for peace, but let us never risk the security of the United States of America," and reminders about how "a person should get what he works for and work for what he gets," and yet it all came back to one thing: an attempt to reassure those who had something—a little wealth, a little influence, a little security—that it would not be taken away. In Nixon's acceptance speech, wage and price controls were translated into "our new economic policies" and then into free enterprise; the Family Assistance Program became welfare reform, and that, in turn, became the work ethic, but McGovern's similar proposal, a guaranteed $4,000 for a family of four, "insulted the intelligence of American voters." Nothing was offered or promised except those things which would help hold the line and, at the same time, maintain, wherever possible, the ritual language of American politics. "Because of our American economic policies we have built a great building of economic wealth and might," Nixon said. "It is by far the tallest building in the world and we are still adding to it. Because some of the windows are broken, they say tear it down and start again. We say, replace the windows and keep building." The United States, he said, contrary to the facts, has the "highest rate of growth of any nation." People on welfare in the United States, he said, as the delegates prepared to depart for the corporate yachts, "would be rich in most of the nations of the world today." At the end of his speech, referring to his visit to a Leningrad cemetery during his trip to Russia, he demonstrated just how cynical the Republicans had become:

At the cemetery I saw a picture of a twelve-year-old girl. She was a beautiful child. Her name was Tanya. I read her diary. It tells the terrible story of the war. In the simple words of a child, she wrote of the deaths of the members of her family. Zhenia in December. Granny in January. Then Yeka. Then Uncle Vasya. Then Mama in May. And finally—these were the last words in her diary: "All are dead. Only Tanya is left." Let us think of Tanya and of the other Tanyas, and their brothers and sisters everywhere in Russia, in China, in America, as we proudly meet our responsibilities for leadership in the world worthy of a great people.

It was one of the heaviest weeks of bombing in the war; the following week, the Army announced that the investigation of the My Lai massacre was closed. Maybe these people in Miami knew it was the end of the line, that politics had become only ritual, nothing more, and that all decisions (or could they even be called decisions?) were corporate and predetermined. Four years before, in the same place, newscaster David Brinkley had said something on NBC about ideology "becoming anachronistic, irrelevant and obsolete. To say this convention is ideological is silly . . . hardly worth discussing." Yet clearly there was an ideology, the ideology of suburban politics and corporate management: The country, like this convention, would be run by corporate means, corporate people and corporate ideals; and the imagery of the civics textbook, which had once likened shareholders to citizens, would be turned on its head. The delegates had become stockholders, the Administration became management, and the country was a corporate enterprise to be maintained. *The tallest building in the world,* Nixon had said, *corporate headquarters.* That's what those people meant about things being complicated, about trusting the leadership, and that's why they didn't mind being herded behind those fences and being scripted for the viewers at home. What was important was the image, the image of efficiency, of unanimity and cosmetic hygiene. Secrecy and deception, here and throughout the world, were therefore not only tolerable but imperative: they helped maintain the image and relieved the shareholders of whatever nagging moral or political doubts they might still entertain. You didn't want to know about the bombing or the killing, and you were glad when they told you it wasn't happening. Fuck Tanya. More important, secrecy and deception maintained the illusion of national grandeur, helped preserve the purity of the ritual. Through a decade of war and a generation of coming to terms, the thing they had learned best was to yield their citizenship—their right to make noise, to complain, to act—in return for shares.

But they had also learned something else, even if they were still unwilling to express it: that ultimately the demands of the poor, the black, the old and the sick could only be met at their expense. That the enterprise, the thing in which they held shares, might ever grow again in any substantial way was, despite the rhetoric, beyond their expectations. Thus they were willing to make their alliance with old enemies—with the unions or the ethnics or with anyone else who could be persuaded that he was among those who might be charged with the unpaid claims of the system. If they could make their anxiety pervasive enough, then they might become the core of the new majority that their leaders dreamed of. In the meantime, they would try to maintain the value of those shares.

IV

Richard Nixon had, in fact, done something new, and he might therefore gain the place in history that he craved so much. He had become a caretaker. The problem for him (and for the majority of the Republican delegates) was to take the political and economic system, no matter how imperfect it might be, and keep it running. Forget the inequities. Poverty and inequality were political luxuries for another time. That was the meaning of law and order, of property-tax relief, of revenue sharing, of the proposed value-added tax, of the accommodations with Russia and China, of wage and price controls, of devaluation, of the whole attempt, in fact if not in rhetoric, to cool it. He was presiding over the liquidation of the empire. Although it all came under the cover of "traditional" American principles—decentralizing power, restricting the federal government, encouraging free enterprise, and celebrating the value of hard work—it

wasn't traditional Americanism at all. The "traditional" principles had assumed that growth was unlimited and that things, if
left alone, would pretty much take care of themselves. (In fact,
of course, they never did: for a century and a half the government had, when necessary, subsidized "initiative" with land
grants, loans, and special favors for railroads, canal companies
and other ventures.) Now the problem was to avert bankruptcy
—real and imagined, economic, moral and political—to bail out
state and local governments, school systems, universities, corporations, taxpayers, to get the streets cleaned and the garbage collected, to put limits on the demands of those who were impatient
to get a piece of the action, to strengthen, as he often said, "the
peace forces as against the criminal forces," to come to terms
with limited international power, to sell compromise, and to tone
down aspirations. The delegates in Miami kept trying to explain
how "we can no longer ignore the 800 million people of main-
land China" without being very explicit about what had happened to the high principles which for twenty years had regarded accommodation as treasonable; they kept trying to square
revenue sharing with Republican ideals—using the federal government's power to tax for bailing out local government—and
became incoherent; they wanted to make it clear that they were
still Republicans (or "traditional" Americans) and succeeded
only in suggesting that they belonged to no party except Nixon's.

He had been the perfect President because he had developed
an uncanny sense of national limitations—knew that the limits
existed and was prepared to accept them. But he also knew that
political language was inadequate to the task, so, when necessary, he obfuscated or lied or simply reversed the meaning of
words.

One way of looking at the political process in the first, preconvention
phase of 1968 [wrote Lewis Chester, Godfrey Hodgson and Bruce Page
in *An American Melodrama*] is as a series of filters, systematically eliminating all the strongest political personalities, until only the safest and

blandest were left. . . . In American Presidential politics, the race may be to the swift, but the battle certainly isn't to the strong. In their very different ways, Johnson, Rockefeller, McCarthy and Wallace all addressed themselves to what were generally regarded as the main issues far more specifically and unambiguously than Humphrey and Nixon, for all their floods of positive papers, policy papers, and the rest. It was the men who were eliminated, not the men who were nominated, who told the American people frankly where they stood on the war, on race, poverty and crime. It can be said without epigrammatic exaggeration that Humphrey managed to be nominated because he talked about every issue except the one that mattered to his party; and Nixon was elected because he talked about every issue except the ones that mattered to the country. . . .

Every politician, of course, understands the uses of ambiguity: the more divided the electorate, the more ambiguous the language has to be. And yet, despite the classic avoidance of issues, Nixon, both as candidate and as President, managed to connect with the American Resignation, turned even his vacuous lack of style into an asset. It had become increasingly clear in the last two years of the Johnson Administration that the country wanted welfare for itself, that many of the programs which had been designed for the poor and the deprived were being turned to the relief of the middle class. By the time Johnson left office the bulk of Title I money (designed for compensatory education for poor children) was being used indiscriminately by local school systems to balance budgets, buy new equipment, and reduce the tax load; congressional pressure was mounting to convert all categorical aid into general aid, which meant federal money without strings to be used at the discretion of local officials; resentment against welfare threatened to produce taxpayer revolts; and references to poverty or the "urban problem"—for a few years almost equivalent to motherhood—produced nothing more positive than indifference. Most of all, the country wanted out of Vietnam, was tired of the casualty lists, the futility, and, by inference, tired of all adventure. Nixon did confront the issues that mattered.

Many of the programs turned sour, some of them because they ran afoul of local interests, some for lack of funding or through mismanagement, but most because the so-called affluent society became increasingly less certain of its affluence, its power, its ability to grow, and its capacity to manage. Perhaps it was Nixon's very lack of convictions that enabled him to understand, to sense that what the country wanted most of all was to climb off its liberal limbs and to move toward what Boulding called "a more modest society: the end of growth and grandeur." Despite the greatest-nation rhetoric, almost everything Nixon proposed represented some kind of accommodation and almost everything he did suggested retrenchment. No new adventures were promised, and when a "New American Revolution" was finally unveiled in his 1971 State of the Union Message it consisted only of a complex and not very heady realignment of federal departments and agencies, a new organization chart. There was still "the lift of a driving dream," but the recurring theme was "emphasis on developing better ways of managing what we have" and "facing the realities of the world today." China was part of those realities, the weakness of the dollar, the price of Japanese cars and radios, domestic poverty, the over-burdened taxpayer, unemployment, inflation. "The American malaise," said Herbert J. Gans, a Columbia University sociologist, early in 1972, "is almost entirely domestic, and although the President seems to believe that it stems from too much wealth and easy living, it has actually developed in part out of the inability of people further to improve their standard of living. Specifically, it has resulted from . . . the closing of the gap between people's aspirations and expectations, and a recent widening of the gap between these expectations and their achievement." The main reaction, therefore (said Gans) is "a counsel for more modest expectations and a return to traditional values which themselves call for modest expectations. . . . Such reactions are deemed necessary to uphold the social order and keep America from falling apart."

55

Nixon tried all these things, and yet the policy ran a different course. The counsel for modest expectations was there, but the proposals were designed to help those who were already established, to take the burden off the property tax, to shift aid from categorical social programs (i.e., the poor) to general aid (i.e., the middle class), to save institutions rather than needy people (the school system rather than the ghetto child) and to maintain profits—even to increase them—before wages. Partly, of course, the policy was old-fashioned Republicanism; it included all the classic rationales about investment credits, plant expansion, and the necessity to stimulate growth, and it obviously (judging by profits and wages) helped the rich more than the poor. And yet the final expectation was not growth but maintenance—to permit the majority to continue to live at the level to which they were accustomed. There was already enough idle plant capacity to produce more than could be sold. Nixon's incentives could produce no great new cornucopia, nor did they create much optimism; what that investment could do was make production more efficient (meaning fewer jobs and faster assembly lines), create marginal products to replace or supplement things most people already considered adequate (especially if they didn't break down), and build new plants overseas where labor was cheaper and the workers were cooperative. Detroit might be dragged kicking and screaming into the creation of safer automobiles—bumpers, for example, which matched those produced in 1935—or of engines which reduced polluting emissions, but its heart was not in innovation. ("The possibility of further technological improvement in our business is not as great as in the past," said Edward N. Cole, the president of General Motors. What was needed was "intensive efforts to cut costs and to increase the efficiency of all of our operations.") The government operated on the theory that protection of the environment could be built into the price of the product—emission-control devices, resource depletion, even the cost of ultimate recycling (you pay not only for the goods but for the cost of getting rid of them when they become junk)—yet that was no way to make them more accessible to the have-nots. Add a few hundred dollars to the price of a car and you may improve the quality of the air, but you make transportation all the more inaccessible to the poor. Although Nixonomics could take credit for new jobs, at least temporarily, it failed to reduce either unemployment or inflation. The prime importance of the new policies, therefore, lay in their recognition that liberal capitalism was finished, that the market and the business community alone could no longer be trusted with the decisions. "The money manager in the green eyeshade," said "Adam Smith,"

will no longer be operating in a world where the market determines totally what is produced (and induced) nor in a society run by business decisions. Capital is scarcer and profits are thinner. He is still looking for three stocks that will double, but the range of his options has decreased. He has always looked not just at profits . . . but at the rate of change in estimated profits . . . and in the long run—the broad run, the macro scene, whatever—*his expectations are diminished.*

Since the country was clearly entering an age of more modest expectations, was now part of a finite and self-enclosed world, the old Marxist considerations reentered the picture: international competition for markets and resources, domestic competition between worker and capitalist, between rich and poor. Those considerations had, of course, always been there, but could once be deferred or mitigated through indefinite appeals to new frontiers—meaning growth. Increasingly those appeals were now being exhausted, and it was the growing awareness of that exhaustion which had created much of the sandwich-board millennialism of the late sixties. The end was at hand. At the same time, however, the apocalyptic and the Marxist became so confused as to preclude any consistent criticism of the system which, in the view of the so-called Left, exploited both the environment and the poor slobs who were trying to buck their way into the middle class. For Nixon, therefore, the business of postponing the millennium could be used to separate the pollution-minded middle class (which saw the issues as a suburban zoning problem) from the political radicals who bravely predicted that the revolution was imminent. Ecology was domesticated, despite the suspicion of a few kooks that the scheduling of Earth Day on Lenin's birthday was more than coincidence, the radicals were prosecuted and the press was intimidated. More important, he managed, with the help of the apocalyptic rhetoric of the radicals themselves, to make a majority of Americans think of themselves as potential losers in any confrontation—to regard themselves as taxpayers, property owners and consumers, people too affluent and comfortable to rebel, yet not affluent enough to feel like giving anything away. Better not to think about Vietnamese massacres or the collapse of the system or the fire next time. Maybe everything was running out, air, water, time, resources, but what was the alternative? Cool it, and try to keep it going like it was. Play ball.

He did not create the mood—rather, it created him—but he understood and took advantage of it. The old unity of WASP Americanism had finally broken down in the sixties, had lost its magnetic attraction, its self-confidence, its faith in its capacity to manage, and its ability to impose discipline without coercion. Many of the young, the black, the Chicanos, the Indians, and a growing number of white ethnics no longer wanted to join the mainstream on the old cultural terms—wanted to do their own thing, were inventing their own history and trying to create their own heroes—and the polls indicated that while most people still believed they might do all right economically (or that their children might), their faith in the national future had sharply declined. Every man for himself. Simultaneously, and for related reasons, the old liberal coalition had come unstuck, had gone particularistic, while its former constituents pursued luxury issues in their separate ways: women's liberation, abortion, Black Power, La Raza, legalized marijuana, gay liberation and all the rest. Those of us who were in Chicago at the 1968 Democratic convention naïvely believed that it was America that was falling apart, when, in fact, it was only American liberalism. Nearly everyone in the counterculture was the child of a Democrat. The fallout from that dissolution, however, was noisy and sometimes violent enough to scare the rest of the country half to death. The nation had to be brought together again, by any means possible, and so Nixon embarked on the multiple courses designed to restore "order"—unleashing the cops or the grand jury or Spiro Agnew on dissent, synthesizing a form of middle Americanism with prayer breakfasts and football, or with Julie and David, and trying to create sufficient economic and class fear to maintain at least the illusion of consensus. When the Nixon "recession" first began in 1969–70, Norman Podhoretz, the editor of *Commentary* and once a fully accredited liberal, suggested that from the point of view of the Administration a certain level of unemployment might be a good way of disciplining the rebellious young, and especially the college students. It was only because they knew that jobs were available for the asking that they could afford to be so contemptuous of the system. Frighten them enough with unemployment and you would bring them back into line. It was a way of rolling back time, he suggested, of recreating what Charles Reich had called Consciousness I or Consciousness II, the old American spirit. Yet when one talked later with students on the campus, at Berkeley or UCLA or Emery or the University of Massachusetts, the most common refrain was apathy. The idealism of the sixties and the euphoria of the counterculture had, at least temporarily, gone sour, but very little replaced them. People had simply separated their social despair from their personal lives; they were looking for jobs, but they no longer believed in much of anything except self-preservation. Nixon escalated the alienation, but he also calmed things down.

He was the ultimately "reasonable" man, and his particular form of reasonableness became a perfect setting for an Administration charged with the receivership of a half century of liberal faith. The point was not to try to put it together again, but to divest as rapidly as possible. Nixon's lack of personal style was in itself helpful because it obviated the necessity to identify with any distinctive group or language or region, was itself a way of speaking ambiguously. And yet style, or lack of it, was misleading because Nixon had such vast capacities for adaptation and self-denial, was, as Richard Poirier wrote, so "extraordinarily intelligent when it comes to the difference between literary and political values," was, in short, so much of an actor, that even the *absence* of style couldn't be trusted. What was more important was the conviction of so many old liberals themselves—liberal capitalists as well as political liberals like Podhoretz or Pat Moynihan or Irving Kristol—that it was lack of reason itself (the irrationality of the young, the excessive "illiberal" demands of the black and poor, the anti-intellectualism of the students) which had caused the problems in the first place. Any "reasonable" man, therefore, was preferable to a collection of idealists lurching between utopian and apocalyptic visions of the future. Nixon, though he had once been the arch-enemy, had, if nothing else, the advantage of being familiar: he would play Hindenburg to the American Weimar and thereby avert the possibility of worse. Most important, however, was the simple lack of alternatives. The 1972 Nixon slogan "Reelect the President" had, despite its potential for an Art Buchwald–Russell Baker type of humor, a compelling logic. If not Nixon, who? Where was the man who could manage a nation that had exhausted its convictions? In Europe one might repair to the remains of a conservative tradition, might call in the Tories or the Gaullists, but America had no such tradition, had no feudal background, lacked an established church and a disciplined sense of class and place. The extreme Right in America was closer to Tom Paine than to Edmund Burke.

After liberalism and short of fundamental change, there was only accommodation, conformity, law and order, and Nixon himself. "Reelect the President" suggested survival and stability without the benefit of either consensus or conviction. Nixon would take care of things until political conviction could reassert itself, or until repression and accommodation made conviction unnecessary. There were obvious dangers—dangers even beyond the familiar concerns about a Nixon Supreme Court, about John Mitchell's Justice Department, or about the continuing brutality in Vietnam:

It never seems to occur to the Nixonian kind of American [Poirier wrote] that the accidents and misfortunes that befall them should be blamed not on efforts to disrupt systems but on the very nature of the systems they have imposed on themselves, that what appear to be minority or dissident voices may in fact be calls to a truer ordering of things than those invented for the advancement of careers or of empires. It is therefore genuinely difficult for Nixon to understand the resistance of the Vietnamese to proposals or working arrangements that seem to him eminently reasonable, even generous. Their continued struggle for independence of our hegemony is to him a willful resistance to the natural order of things. They are "one small country," as Henry Kissinger put it. There is a Nixonian testiness in that phrase, an impatience with assertions of human "freedom and dignity" that threaten such systematic efforts at the mechanization of life as Nixon proposes to extend from himself to the nation and, by a Great Power accommodation, to the world.

With peculiar mixtures of generosity and intimidation, Nixon's method for controlling the unmanageable aspects of life has evident dangers. So great is his faith in the logic of conformity, in the studied correction of mistakes, so convinced does he make himself that he has done all any reasonable man can be expected to do under the circumstances—forgetting that he has in large part created them—that any persistence thereafter of deviation is taken as an intolerable affront to America and to reason. . . . The soap opera of easy accommodation can, for him and for many Americans, turn under stress rather quickly into the melodrama of betrayal. To encompass the reality of Richard Nixon in America and of America in Richard Nixon requires the wildest and yet the most subtle balance of comedy and melodrama, soap opera and satire, documentation and parody, reason and madness. We are still healthy enough to understand such a spectacle should anyone be imaginative enough to contrive it.

61

What that suggested, finally, was that the residue of American idealism and liberalism, the things which were not interred with their bones, could, as they had in Vietnam, turn to the most excessive kind of brutality, that what you tried to save from the frontier was machismo, that what you clung to from the fifties was nostalgia, that what you tried to preserve from the decencies of the small town was sentimentality on the one hand and an obsolete repressive moral code on the other, and that what you retained from the great age of industrial development was corporate power and indifference. Instead of trying to enable people to reconnect with belief and meaning, you institutionalized the separation, trivialized religion, and made "law" contemptible, and instead of appealing to the residues of hope you played to the mounting fear. War, of course, became peace, and submission freedom, but what was more significant (and unanticipated by Orwell) was that self-interest became social responsibility and that a minority of the poor became the oppressors of the majority. When even paranoia was turned on its head, when the threat came from the weak, it was clear how little the majority trusted its own future.

Still, he had managed to cool it, had taught the country to accept even its social blemishes, its injustice and its inequities. Remember how it was, back in 1968?

At home our horrified people watched our cities burn [said the Republican platform of 1972], crime burgeon, campuses dissolve into chaos. A mishmash of social experimentalism, producing such fiscal extravaganzas as the abortive war on poverty, combined with war pressures to drive up taxes and balloon the cost of living. Working men and women found their living standards fixed or falling, the victim of inflation. Nationwide, welfare skyrocketed out of control. The history of our country may record other crises more costly in material goods, but none so demoralizing to the American people. To millions of Americans it seemed we had lost our way. . . .

Now, four years later, a new leadership with new policies for new programs has restored reason and order. No longer buffeted by internal

62

violence and division, we are on a course in calmer seas with a sure, steady hand at the helm.

Richard Nixon, they said in Miami, had saved the system. He had not made things a whole lot better—they did not, at any rate, feel much better—but he had kept them from getting worse. People on the outside, the Naders and the McGoverns and the reporters from the liberal press, might speak of the awesome corporate power that they held, yet neither the delegates nor the country felt all that powerful. In their obsession with strength and security (of neighborhoods and apartment houses, airlines and nations) there was a growing understanding that no region of the earth remained exempt, that the world was a fragile place, and that no place could be pacified indefinitely. They, like the nation, were vulnerable.

V

For McGovern the problem was to find a voice. The euphoria had begun to wane even before the candidate had been officially nominated. A hundred-to-one shot, a man who had campaigned in New Hampshire out of two motel rooms and a sedan, had become the candidate of the majority party and, having become that candidate, would be cast in the role of a splinter-faction contender. After the convention, even the so-called youth vote was no longer certain, and the labor block, supposedly the backbone of the Democratic Party, was said to be defecting. A joke, even a man to feel sorry for, but no longer a serious contender. Where had he won those primaries, among what people, in what state, in what country? On the evening he won in California, a June night that now seems terribly long ago, five thousand of us were jammed into the Hollywood Palladium, waiting for him to claim his victory. A few weeks before, the Field Cali-

63

fornia poll had given him a lead of some fifteen percentage points over Hubert Humphrey, but as the returns came in it was clear that the margin would be smaller, that McGovern had already started to slip. "I can't believe we've won the whole thing," he would say when he did arrive, and the rock band played "Let the Sun Shine," but by then the troops of the campaign, kids from New York and Wisconsin and California, were already complaining about how the old pols were taking over, how their man had started to fudge on the issues, how it was turning into just another sellout. McGovern got his cheers when he arrived, but the more-than-perfunctory outbursts were reserved for the announcement that Shirley Chisholm had won four percent of the vote in New Mexico (or was it New Jersey?). They loved losers.

"It's our party now," said one of the young workers that night. "The kids *are* the Democratic Party. We have the lists and we know the techniques; we've done the canvassing and registered the voters. There is no other Democratic Party. Without us they would have been dead, and now they're trying to take it away from us."

"It's a big country," someone replied. "Maybe kids aren't enough." A month later in Miami Beach, Alexander Barkan, the political director of the AFL-CIO, would shake his fist in the face of a McGovern supporter: "You so-called responsible leaders of this party seem to think the kids and the kooks and the Bella Abzugs can win you some elections. Well, we're going to let them try to do it for you this year. We're not."

The bigger he got, the more disenchanted they became: He was backtracking on women's rights and abortion, was coming to terms with the bosses, was manipulating the Democratic convention and violating the purity of their separate uncompromisable positions. At the very moment that he became the candidate of the party he was no longer the candidate of those who called themselves the People. They would still support him after the convention, but the enthusiasm was gone and the campaign became a chore. During a primary stop at a shopping mall in Concord, California, where the signs had invited people to "Come See George McGovern with Shirley MacLaine"—a sort of double bill—three thousand screaming kids greeted his appearance, leading MacLaine to observe that McGovern "has given charisma a new meaning." And so he had, but rather than being the charisma of the low key that she imagined—the simple man from the small town in the battle for decency—it was merely the charisma of a loser. Once he won the nomination, even that charisma would be tarnished: How could they be what they were if they really felt that their man was in charge? Their very identity seemed to be based on their status in defeat—an elite in their secret desire to be whipped. It was the one way to prove that you were special. "We're great believers in momentum—now," Frank Mankiewicz, McGovern's political adviser, had said after the Wisconsin primary, but on the night they won in California the momentum was already running down.

McGovern was never completely certain whose candidate he was. When he began to run in the winter of 1970–71 he believed that the real task was getting nominated; beating Nixon, he thought, would be easy: Nixon was vulnerable on the war, on the economy, on his own Tricky Dick image. Put the old Democratic Party together with the New Politics people—the kids who had been locked out of the Chicago convention in 1968, the McCarthy and Kennedy reformers, the idealists, the Movement—and you would have a nearly unbeatable combination. Neither Humphrey nor Muskie could do that; Humphrey's reputation as a liberal was forever doubtful after 1968, and Muskie, as Mankiewicz used to say during the primaries, had no base: he wasn't the peace candidate or the candidate of the blacks or the women or even, when you came down to it, the defense industry, and his support would evaporate. What McGovern did not understand was the difficulty of holding the coalition together: he did have a base, but there was no reason to believe that he could build on it, that the old Democrats would hold still any more than the new Democrats held still for Hubert Humphrey four years before. The ideological demands of his own constituency, moreover, turned out to be as exacting as the self-interest demands of any collection of labor bosses, big-city machines or Democratic Party fat cats. He would have to maintain his purity on causes which most of the country regarded as marginal (or which it opposed): marijuana, abortion, women's rights—the luxury issues. Many of his New Politics people tended to be moralists rather than politicians, were not willing to wheel and deal, did not understand that winning was everything, and thus threatened to turn the 1972 convention into a French Parliament of irreconcilable factions. In the process of getting himself nominated, McGovern was replacing Nixon as the enemy, and the luxury issues replaced Vietnam, militarism, civil liberties and economic injustice as the essential topics of McGovernite concern.

McGovern himself was too decent and, in a sense, too rural to understand. From the moment that he decided to run—a decision that he had all but made a year after Nixon's election—some of his supporters had urged him to turn his attention to blue-collar frustrations, to study the sources of Wallace's appeal, and to run as a sort of urban populist against the banks, the corporations and the utilities. Ultimately, and especially after Wallace's victory in Florida, he began to do that; what this Administration offers, he had said in Nashua, New Hampshire, is "socialism for the rich and capitalism for the workingman"; the shoe workers cheered, and that night, sitting around the hotel, his staff people all suddenly started thinking the same thing. "We could win that vote, could run against Wallace and maybe beat him." And yet McGovern's own instincts remained alien to the urban style; he did not understand their voices and they never understood his. Although he was labeled a populist—for a while, thanks to Wallace, almost every candidate was—it never came naturally. Even in his taped television commercials, where he was recorded listening and speaking to factory workers, people talking about dirt and hazards and exploitation at the plant, he sounded more like your worried grandmother than a tough bastard who would lead eighty million angry Americans in an assault on corporate power. His labor supporters continually urged him to go out and give 'em hell, and there were moments when he could be stirred to genuine anger, and when that anger found its crowd response, but he always seemed uncomfortable among the ethnics, white, brown or black, always a man groping for connections.

He had, in fact, never been a populist, was, if anything, a Midwestern progressive, a man in the small-town tradition of William Allen White or Robert La Follette. His political hero had been Adlai Stevenson, and his home was the pulpit, the lectern and the small gathering, not the garment district on a hot day or the subway at rush hour or the factory gate when the shifts changed. It was hard ever to imagine him with his tie pulled down, his shirtsleeves rolled up, delivering a sweaty harangue to an angry crowd. He was a man more likely to pronounce his curse upon the complexities of urban life or international power than to try to understand the amorality of political compromise; unlike Nixon, he really believed in political morality rather than simply employing it as a weapon for partisan advantage. During the primaries, the pundits said that McGovern's manner mitigated his message, that people just couldn't think of that man as a dangerous radical, and that was why he was winning. But there was also something about him that suggested unbounded innocence; the wheat farmer of South Dakota and the shoe worker in New Hampshire were not necessarily the same people as the steelworkers of Pittsburgh or the rubber workers of Akron. How did the small-town preacher's son sound in those regions where life had never been very good, and where civility, reason and decency had always been matters of distant aspiration rather than facts of immediate experience? Could McGovern

THE END OF THE AMERICAN FUTURE

ever persuade those Gary steelworkers or the blacks in Harlem that he had an instinctive comprehension of how rotten life can be? Could a man who had not made his compromise with ugliness and brutality ever be trusted to understand? The Eagleton affair seemed to be a reminder of that softness—he was a patsy; first he got taken into something he didn't want, and then he compounded the mistake by abandoning his friend. Even the Watergate bugging scandal seemed to prove that the Republicans were tougher and meaner than the Democrats. Politicians were *supposed* to be dirty, and the bigger they were, the dirtier they were expected to be.

The most serious difficulty for McGovern, however, was that he entered the campaign with the liabilities of a liberal elitism that had become disconnected from its working-class base and couldn't find its way back. Norman Podhoretz, who had shed his own liberal baggage, was generally correct when, in the early fall of 1972, he characterized McGovern as a new arrival in the realm of workingman's politics:

Lately the talk has all been of tax reform and the redistribution of wealth, but this was not an issue indigenous to the New Politics or to the "McGovern phenomenon"; it was taken over from George Wallace, and the carelessness with which the McGovern proposals have been thought out is perhaps a sign of the fundamental indifference to such matters which the New Politics movement until so recently felt. For what this movement really cares about is not the distribution of economic power but the distribution of political power. It wishes to "participate in the decisions that affect our lives" and it wishes to govern, but it has no clear idea of what, in addition to participating and governing, it wishes to do. Consequently it has *itself* become the issue. Why has the AFL-CIO, which until the nomination of McGovern obsessively kept declaring that its main political priority was the defeat of Nixon, refused to endorse McGovern? Asked this question, George Meany, I. W. Abel and the other anti-McGovern labor leaders fish for unconvincing explanations in McGovern's voting record, when what is actually bothering them is the hostility of the New Politics toward organized labor ("It isn't worth the powder it would take to blow it up," I once heard a leading McGovern strategist say of the labor movement) and the contempt of the New Politics people for the ordinary workingman and the "racism" and vulgar materialism which allegedly define his character.

Through the primaries, McGovern's staff often argued that the reason their candidate had so little big-labor support lay in the fact that the union leaders knew they couldn't control him, a self-flattering and partially correct proposition that failed to mitigate McGovern's subsequent difficulties with a substantial proportion of the rank and file. What was probably more revealing was the simple lack of comprehension, not only in the McGovern camp, but in the society at large, of the varied and uncertain ways that working Americans defined themselves, and of the extremely complex (if not impossible) task it was to make connections not only among the separate labor constituencies but within the differing self-images of "workingman," "middle class," "consumer," "homeowner" and all the rest. A good many disaffected factory workers made it quite clear that they didn't feel happy about either Nixon or McGovern, just as Meany didn't, or, for that matter, about Humphrey or Muskie or any of the others. I recall talking to one man in Sheboygan who thought it might be a good thing to elect Wallace—if the voters could get him out of office in a hurry if he didn't work out. "You mean in the third inning?" I asked. "No," he replied, "I mean in the first." A few days later, on the eve of the Wisconsin primary, Elliot Cutler, who was working on the Muskie staff, observed, "No one is really touching the voters—we're all moving blindly toward the issues." McGovern, as the new boy in town, the unfamiliar face (and, as it turned out, the man with the most effective organization), was able to win that battle of indifference. And yet the very act of winning, in Wisconsin and Oregon, in New Jersey and California and ultimately, of course, in Miami Beach, destroyed the new-boy freshness, converting him from a promising rookie to an established fumbler. During the primaries his staff always assumed that exposure would help McGovern and weaken Muskie, and that, in fact, is what happened. But once the primaries were over and McGovern was all but nominated, he began to suffer the same fate. His attacks were too vague and often too pontifical, the solutions too specific, and so he frightened as many people as he persuaded.

For McGovern the task was obvious: to unify the young, the poor, the lower middle class, and as much of the middle class as he could rally against the "interests"—meaning the polluters, the beneficiaries of special favors, the fat cats, and whatever exploiters, real or imagined, could be conjured up. The issues were all apparent: the growing concentration of corporate power, the lax enforcement of mine and factory safety laws, the cozy settlement of antitrust cases in return for corporate campaign contributions, the widespread malfeasance, if not fraud, that deprived workers of their pension rights, the rigorous enforcement of wage controls on the one hand and the loose enforcement of price controls on the other, and the growing concentration of private wealth in the hands of a privileged minority. *In 1950, the two hundred largest American corporations held half the total assets devoted to manufacturing; in 1970 more than half such assets were held by the one hundred largest corporations. In 1971, according to Ralph Nader, the government's own studies indicated that if monopoly industries were broken up prices would fall by at least twenty-five percent. In 1970, the lowest fifth of the population in income—those earning under $3,000— received 3.2 percent of the national income, while the highest fifth, those earning over $12,000 a year, received nearly half. In 1971 the Administration raised price supports of milk, and therefore the price to the consumer, in return for a $300,000 campaign contribution from dairy interests; in 1969, according to the* Corporate Examiner *(a publication of the National Council of Churches), "Attorney General Mitchell ordered the Department of Justice to settle an anti-trust case against Pfizer, American Cyanamid, Bristol-Meyers, Squibb and Upjohn in return for $14.3 million given by the firms to President Nixon's campaign"; in 1972 similar charges were made in regard to anti-*

trust action against ITT. The list could be extended indefinitely.
There were, moreover, the increasingly pressing matters of civil
liberties, the government's overt attempts to intimidate the press,
its indiscriminate and extensive collection of dossiers on the private lives of nearly all Americans, the growing use of secrecy
and deception in regard to foreign policy, and the systematic
prosecution of political dissidents in the name of law and order
—even as the crime rate continued to rise. In the weeks after
Labor Day, McGovern began to sharpen his focus on these issues, spoke of workers "who gasp for breath because management put a lid on their factory and locked the pollution inside,"
or workers "who will never work again, because big business
cut corners on job safety," about special interests that "have a
friend in the White House," about tax loopholes and inflation.
After Nixon had gone to China and the issue of Vietnam was
officially relegated to a secondary position, he once told me that
he welcomed the opportunity to speak again about domestic
economic and social issues, "to talk about the things I talked
about when I first ran for office in the fifties." And yet the issues
of South Dakota were not the issues of America, the expectations
of the fifties were not those of 1972, and the tone of the plains
was not the sound of the city. In South Dakota they all talked
the same language. If you spoke about parity or price supports
or acreage allotments you could be specific: every farmer understood the figures, and since you were only running in an
agricultural state most of the people who would pay for those
supports had no chance to vote against you. But when, as a candidate for the presidency, you outlined the specifics of a minimum-income proposal of $1,000 for every American citizen or
proposed cuts in the defense budget, you had to satisfy the payers as well as the recipients, had to deal with workers in defense
plants who knew only too well what reductions in the military
budget could mean, and with millions of others who knew that
they didn't u..derstand the tax tables: Getting screwed on April
15 was as inevitable as, well, death and taxes, but giving still

more money to those bastards who didn't work was unforgivable.

Too often McGovern's solutions sounded studied and contrived—as if they had been learned from professors rather than experience (which, indeed, was often the case)—while his comprehension seemed distant and abstract. On one phone-in television program a caller asked what McGovern would do about "poverty and the slums," and McGovern replied that he would try to stop the flow of people into the cities; on another occasion a disabled black veteran from Vietnam came up to him to talk about guys who "died and bled fighting for a country ten thousand miles from home, and I can't get a job—what you doin' talking about amnesty for these hippies?" McGovern had no answer. In making his proposals concrete he created targets that he would then have to defend—the minimum-income proposal, the cuts in defense spending—and thereby permitted the Administration the rare luxury of playing challenger and incumbent at the same time. *They* were the sensible people, the people of reason, while McGovern was throwing up all those damn-fool complicated proposals, then revising them, and then dropping them altogether. "These goddam intellectuals," a Democratic politician said in Washington. "They think the average voter is a schmuck. The whole middle class is paying through the nose; they've got a shaft up their ass on prices and rates, they're as insecure as everyone else, and they're all thinking the same thing." Yet McGovern could never manage to turn that insecurity to his own purposes, was constantly groping for the right language, always seemed to be the friend of somebody else, and thus succeeded in defining himself as part of the problem. He had a penchant, as Nat Hentoff said, for hitting just the edges of a fat target.

Frank Mankiewicz, who had received his higher political education as Robert Kennedy's press secretary, seemed to understand. Perhaps they all understood—Mankiewicz, Gary Hart, Gordon Weil, all the people who were supposed to be managing

McGovern's campaign. Ted Van Dyk, who had worked for Humphrey in 1968 and was on McGovern's campaign staff in 1972, used to say that McGovern should "think Vince Lombardi"—should come on as the hard-nosed ethnic type, a winning-is-all football coach, and not as a WASP who "comes on as straight." But that was so clearly beyond the bounds of possibility as to be ludicrous. They could never get McGovern to stay on the attack, to come on as the man who knew, both from experience and from instinct, that nearly everybody was getting screwed. Mankiewicz had outlined McGovern's primary scenario months before the formal campaign began, knew that they had to do well in New Hampshire, take Wisconsin, and then, as "serious" contenders, win in California and New York and Massachusetts. It was not the best way to do it, he often said, it was the only way. More important, he had understood from the very beginning the importance of the George Wallace phenomenon and had pointed out as early as 1969 the significance of the fact that hundreds of thousands of Robert Kennedy's supporters had turned to Wallace after the assassination in 1968. Their allegiance had nothing to do with "Right," "Left" or "Center"—it had to do with alienation, with a distrust of all established, conventional politicians, and with a growing cynicism about both major parties. (Inevitably, the heir of the Kennedy appeal would also be the heir of the violence.) Mankiewicz could speak about the pervasive despondency about the conventional future, knew that a growing number of people felt that things were closing down, and understood that such a feeling could turn in any number of directions—in Wallace's, in McGovern's or in Nixon's. The country could turn toward status-quo politics, defining itself as a besieged middle class threatened by welfare, drugs, crime and hippies, and demand security, or it could define itself as an exploited underclass and demand a redistribution of power and resources from the people at the top. "If George McGovern had not been entered in this primary," Mankiewicz said the morning after McGovern won in Wisconsin, "Wallace would have swept this primary." There were always two parties, he said, paraphrasing Emerson, "the party of memory and the party of hope." McGovern would represent the party of hope.

The difficulty with redistributing power and wealth lay in the fact that it was always hard to persuade people one or two steps off the bottom that the biggest slice wouldn't come from them rather than from the Rockefellers and the Fords. The experience of the past generation had taught them only too well that equality meant opening up their schools and their unions and not the coffers of the Chase Manhattan Bank or the Pacific Gas and Electric Company. "If that black family is going to get its share of the American action, then other families are going to have to give up some," wrote Richard Reeves. "There is a real conflict of interest at the bottom of the American pyramid, between what new Populists . . . call 'poor blacks and working whites.' They may both dislike banks and Hottentots, and they may vote for a candidate who goes after bankers, but the day after election they're going to be on different sides about a lot of things. Government is still more real than campaigning." If a voter was going to support redistribution he wanted to make absolutely certain that the people who were doing it were his kind of people, and that in the end he would be left with more, not with less. The first lesson of any closing down—a lesson that Nixon reinforced at every turn—is that it was the people closest to you who did all the squeezing.

McGovern's background betrayed him. He could never shake the prophetic voice or the posture of the rural man looking with dismay at a scene of urban decadence that he could regard with compassion but not comprehension, and thus he seemed to be sitting in judgment on the very people he was trying to persuade. *Come home, America.* We were a flock that had strayed from the true path, and he was trying to bring us back. The so-called realists among the pundits continually accused him of misjudging "Middle America," of being to the left of the "Center," of missing the mainstream. And yet, as McGovern would be the first to point out, it was he who had come from the real Middle America and who had his roots in every genuine American tradition—the small town, the Methodist Church, the farm, the decencies, real or imagined, of another age, and the politics of a Jeffersonian liberalism that honored thrift, hard work and an enlightened independent citizenry. It was the very fact that these things no longer characterized the country which made him seem peculiar and off center, and which foiled his attempts to connect. His vision of the future, finally, lay in a vision of the past, and his idea of the good life implied the kind of vulnerability and honesty that was possible only in a setting of personal security and small-town familiarity. Because he believed in the past, his own special past, he could never quite accept the reality of the present, and because the country no longer believed in that past—honored it only with rhetoric and nostalgia —it had trouble believing in anything. In a setting where no one could be trusted—where you had to be tough, and where a certain level of unscrupulousness demonstrated toughness—McGovern was the wrong man.

In the end, true to himself, he reverted to the voice of the prophet: *"They that wait upon the Lord shall renew their strength. They shall mount up with wings as eagles. They shall run and not be weary. They shall walk and not faint."* He was back in South Dakota among his own, although even there he had been whipped, a man at once too "radical" and too old-fashioned, guilty by association and suspect of inconstancy, a loser of record dimensions. Isaiah too had been a voice of peace, a man charged with the duty of prophesying the end of Judah and Israel, a voice ignored. "We do love this country," McGovern said, "and we will continue to beckon it to a higher standard . . . The nation will be better because we never once gave up the long battle to renew its oldest ideals and to redirect its current energies along more humane and hopeful paths." If any of them in the Sioux Falls Coliseum or watching on television knew Isaiah as well as McGovern did, they would also have recalled more familiar lines, for had he not promised to "put Peace in as magistrate, and Integrity as the government," had he not spoken of a time when "there will be no more training for war" and had he not been sitting in judgment on the transgressions of his nation? *O House of Jacob, let us walk in the light of the Lord.* "God bless you," McGovern had said at the end of his concession speech. "God bless America," Richard Nixon had said at the end of his statement of victory.

There never had been a chance—only Goldwater and Landon had lost as badly in a modern presidential election—nor had there been any specific event or decision that made the difference. Nixon carried every state but Massachusetts (and the District of Columbia) and nearly every demographic and ethnic group with the exception of Jews, blacks, the poor and—just barely—the new young voters. But McGovern's most damaging losses were in the blue-collar vote, so called, once the backbone of the Democratic Party, where Nixon had won a substantial victory. On the day after the election, Frank Mankiewicz associated McGovern's defeat with "three names," Hubert H. Humphrey, Thomas F. Eagleton and Arthur Bremer, thereby refuting his own thesis that McGovern could have become the beneficiary of the alienated Wallace vote: McGovern, he seemed to be saying now, was not Robert Kennedy. (In electoral terms McGovern plus Wallace might have been Kennedy—maybe). But even that explanation didn't go far enough, for while each of Mankiewicz's three names had something to do with McGovern's defeat, even the three together did not constitute a critical mass. Nothing, finally, not even a combination of things, cost McGovern the election, unless one could say it was the candidate himself, or the lack of party organization and loyalty, or the mood of the country.

What Mankiewicz was talking about, finally, were not tactical failures, but the failures of the party system and the difficulties of creating consensus which helped produce those failures in the first place. Neither candidate could have been nominated had the old party establishments retained their influence. Nixon had been anathema to the old Eastern liberal Republican elites, a man originally tolerated on the Eisenhower ticket in an effort to neutralize the know-nothings of the McCarthy era, a two-time loser with a reputation for working the back alleys of the political system, and certainly not the candidate of those who regarded themselves as the custodians of the Republic; and McGovern, as everyone knew, was passionately hated by the Democratic Party establishment, by the city bosses and the union leaders who had, for a generation, dominated its councils, done its work and mediated its disputes. Both owed their candidacies to the defeat or default of the traditional party apparatus and the collapse of party cohesion. At Miami Beach people like Ronald Reagan enjoyed themselves by talking about the three political parties—the Republican Party, the "Democrat Party" (as they always liked to call it), and the McGovern Party. McGovern, someone said after the election, had received the largest vote of any third-party candidate in history. But there were, in fact, at least four parties, and perhaps dozens, among them the Nixon Party, and when the returns were in it turned out that the Nixons and the Democrats had won, and that the McGoverns and the Republicans had lost. It was not merely that Nixon had no coattails, but that his people often worked with local Democrats, especially in the South, or ignored local Republicans, as in Texas, in their effort to insure victory. After the election, McGovern suggested that perhaps there ought to be party realignment—meaning, in essence, a division of parties along ideological lines. The issues he had raised, and particularly the issue of income redistribution and social injustice, were not likely to go away; McGovern might someday turn out to be not the Landon or the Goldwater of '72, but the Stevenson. And yet McGovern had obviously not found the base of ideas and programs—the intellectual underpinnings—to make such a realignment work. More important, the lack of such underpinnings forced him again, as it had during the election, to assume the prophetic tone:

the issues themselves had not been perfected or articulated; he did not fully understand the failures of the liberal future and therefore could not yet propose alternatives. The vision was still a moral vision, but elections were not, after all, just moral confrontations. "There's lots of sons of bitches in this country," Coolidge was supposed to have said. "They're entitled to their representation." A party that had no room for sons of bitches might find itself a permanent minority. Jack Kennedy himself would never have been President if Mayor Richard J. Daley's organization hadn't helped him in Chicago in 1960.

The largest block of votes in 1972, of course, went to no one; forty-five percent of the electorate did not go to the polls (the highest apathy percentage since 1948), and even those who did vote often arrived at the polls with singular lack of enthusiasm: "That son of a bitch McGovern; he made me vote for that son of a bitch Nixon." Neither candidate had found the language or tactics of cohesion; where the parties had failed, they failed, too. McGovern had sought his strength in a coalition of alienation and frustration—the hard hats and the gay people and the freaks were supposed to lie down in the fields together—but could find nothing stronger than the moral message to hold them in place; the more apocalyptic his tone, it seemed, the more apathetic the national mood. Nixon, with the advantage of the White House, a weak opponent, and a record of twenty years of campaigning, did not need to campaign anymore, and he could proudly say after the election that he had won without offering the country any solutions to its social problems. (Presumably he owed no one anything—with the possible exception of Clement Stone, Elmer Bobst and a few dozen other millionaires and corporate fat cats who had contributed the bulk of the campaign money). While McGovern was rushing about the country trying to make the evening television news in every major city he could reach, the Republicans sent out surrogates and unleashed Nixon for a few carefully staged appearances, including, in Atlanta, a mechanically produced "ticker tape" and confetti shower operated by party workers. ITT, someone said as the paper floated down on the car carrying the Nixons, must have loaned them their shredder. Four more years.

In the final analysis, even the four parties were an illusion. Both the Republicans and the Democrats had historically been composed of disparate elements held together through the mediation of professionals—the arrangers of compromise—but their general lines, ideological and constituential, were clear enough. Beneath the differences there were integrating symbols and myths, a sense of historical continuity and, most significantly, a general confidence in the future of the country and the party. The whole system could function only—as many historians pointed out—as long as there existed agreement on fundamentals; in the one instance when that consensus collapsed, the majority party broke up and the country had civil war. Even the landslides that buried Landon and Goldwater could be interpreted as clear victories for the leadership of one party and clear defeats for the other. When they lost, their parties lost with them. In 1972, however, the results defied that kind of interpretation. The country had not shifted to the right or the left, no clear ideological direction was supported (and none was offered), and no policies were endorsed or repudiated. McGovern and Nixon agreed that rarely had the voters been offered such a clear choice on issues, yet the choice had been confused and ambiguous. They could think of themselves as an exploited working class subject to the power and machinations of corporate wealth, or they could think of themselves as overburdened middle-class taxpayers threatened by social revolt and moral decay; could regard themselves as masters and potential beneficiaries of change, or as its victims. Most of them, of course, were a good deal of both, yet neither party or candidate managed to offer arguments, policies or, indeed, a candidate to resolve the conflict. If you voted for Nixon you voted for big money and corporate management; if you voted for McGovern you supported drugs, amnesty, abortion and a man who deserted his friends. A bad President, the

Republicans seemed to be saying, was better than no President at all. Maybe Humphrey or Muskie would have done better than McGovern, but they would have done it without help from any of the constituencies of the New Politics. To many people they were the symbols of the failure of liberalism, the tainted relics of indifference. McGovern had always been likely to lose big; Humphrey or Muskie was certain to lose small.

In another decade, the analysts may conclude that 1972 was, in fact, merely the first step in a realignment of parties, a temporary dislocation in the movement toward a system which, while it might not pit the party of hope against the party of memory, would offer the choice between inclusive and exclusive policies of welfare and social acceptance ("permissiveness" against "character," the huggers against the spankers). Yet there was no certain indication, not in this election anyway, that such a realignment had begun. Breakdown was visible, but new alliances and programs were not. It was not simply that the "factions" were divided—kids, women, labor and all the rest—but that they also often lacked internal cohesion and power. Who could speak for the black vote or the women's vote, let alone deliver it? Who spoke for labor? Mayor Daley, for the first time in a decade, was unable even to deliver his own wards for his own candidates; the Democrats in New York had no leadership; the "liberal" wing of the Republican Party had no voice; the Left had no platform and the Right no principles. Nixon's campaign was conducted in an ethos of media manipulation and corporate management, McGovern's in a blaze of moral fervor. Where the hell were the politicians? There seemed to be no adequate political language left because that language had always assumed common traditions and a common future—elements which imposed a natural discipline on the divisive forces in society. You gave a little today in the expectation of getting something back in the future. The system worked as long as most people simply assumed, redundantly perhaps, that things would inevitably get better and, at the same time, that the powers of man and government were

sufficiently strong and their intentions sufficiently reliable to resolve problems, which is to say that it worked while the majority,
however cynical, still believed that with the right people in
charge it could work. You traded on a rising market, and since it
was rising, you could wait a few months or years for delivery of
the goods. But what happened when that natural discipline collapsed, when there might not be a future—not, at any rate, a
future when your debtors had the wherewithal to pay? For
nearly a decade the best and the brightest had been in charge, and
their most significant accomplishment had been the disaster of
Vietnam. Once the political market turned bearish, everyone
wanted to be paid at once or withdrew from trading altogether,
and everything that once constituted progress became a set of
non-negotiable demands. Both Nixon and McGovern had become national candidates as a consequence of the breakdown of
the old faith, symbols of that political bearishness, heirs of an
enervated national confidence and of demoralized political establishments, Nixon as caretaker, McGovern as miracle worker, and,
while they might yet leave a legacy on which new political possibilities might be erected, there was little in 1972 on which any
fundamentally new confidence could be built. The future was
four more years, no more.

TWO:

THE ALL-PURPOSE MIDDLE

I

By the time the 1972 campaign was fully under way we were supposed to be living in the renascent fifties, or even in the forties or the thirties. Rock 'n' roll was coming back into style, the leather jacket, even the Hula Hoop, and along with them the signs of a chronic stupor. Maybe somebody was putting something into the water supply after all and impairing our vital bodily fluids. "Our music," wrote Shana Alexander just before the election,

> has become more like Muzak. No more the excitement of the Beatles or Dylan; the beat is muted, soporific. At the movies only sentimentality sells. "The Godfather," "Love Story," "Butterflies Are Free." The seats are sticky with blood and tears. Listless porn bemuses the adventurous; the smug self-approval of Archie Bunker amuses the family trade. We all feel the languor. No fire burns within. It is twilight time in lotus land. Outside the window we watch the lilac air mattress drift aimlessly around the aqua pool. . . . A California bookstore has just published its best-seller list. Top favorite reading out here for the last 22 weeks has been something called *I'm OK—You're OK*. The book's only rival is a half-baked fantasy of a simple minded seagull. Sh-h-h-h. Don't disturb.

The country, said James Reston in the *Times*, had had enough of change and was "longing merely for a little calm and quiet." Meanwhile an apocryphal story was making the political rounds about a man who, after Eisenhower's heart attack in 1957, suffered a serious accident which left him in a coma for nearly fifteen years; in 1972 he recovers and asks whether Eisenhower is still alive.

"No," they tell him. "Eisenhower is dead."

"In that case," he says, "Nixon must be President."

The signs of the fifties were hard to miss. Nixon, in the White House, holding his prayer breakfasts; Norman Vincent Peale, Billy Graham, the big-band revival, the return of Elvis Presley and the disc jockeys of the fifties with their oldies-but-goodies, the resurgent privatism among the kids and the corresponding revival of college hoopla, beer drinking, fraternities and all the rest. Much of it, of course, was sheer nostalgia, a rummaging through closets and attics for things that might replace the exhausted artifacts of the sixties, and a good deal of it would, like everything else, represent another passing phase. There were signs, moreover, that a substantial portion of the culture of the sixties would never disappear, that drugs were here to stay, that the occult and the mystic and the nonrational retained their hold, and that the corporate enthusiasm of the fifties was not about to return. Yet if there was any certain indication of a new age, beyond the nostalgia and the nonsense, it lay in the rediscovery and resurgence of that amorphous social middle that C. Wright Mills called the white-collar class and that Nixon was trying to label as a new American majority. For three or four years people who called themselves "moderates"—Richard Scammon and Ben Wattenberg, Joe Alsop, Irving Kristol, Irving Howe—had been talking about America as a middle-class country, a country of people not given to what the writers regarded as excesses, people who had had enough of riots, assassinations, drugs, freaks, welfare, crime and upheaval. They took for granted the idea that what they saw as the "middle class" or "Middle America" was simply the successor to the middle class of the nineteenth century (which it wasn't) and that the virtues and values of that middle class were traditional and self-evident. Somehow all of them—Kristol and Reston, Wattenberg and Scammon—played to the Nixon rhetoric and finished by talking administration newspeak. They did not see the fear or understand that lack of confidence or analyze the pervasive cynicism, and thus accepted Nixon's assumption that apathetic majorities define moral imperatives. To his opponents Nixon had said during the campaign, "The will of the people is 'the prejudice of the masses.' They deride anyone who wants to respond to that will of the people as 'pandering to the crowd.' A decent respect for the practice of majority rule is automatically denounced as 'political expediency.' " By a happy coincidence, he pointed out, "what the new majority wants for America and what I want for this nation are basically the same." By a happy coincidence also, the majority refused to consider or accept the reports of the My Lai atrocities, to contemplate the impersonal destruction (for no military reason) of the Vietnamese landscape, to get exercised about Pentagon secrecy, to be concerned about General Lavelle's false reports to his superiors about his "protective reaction strikes" against North Vietnamese targets, about wiretapping and political sabotage, or about the criminally devious ways that Nixon reelection funds by the hundreds of thousands of dollars found their way into the hands of felons. For years we had been reading those polls of Americans which indicated that the majority would vote against the Bill of Rights or even the provisions of the Declaration of Independence. But never had anyone expected that, with the possible exception of a Joe McCarthy, any major politician would attempt to advance his career on these assumptions. Nixon, said Norman Mailer in Miami Beach, had managed to mine a certain "mediocrity of spirit" in America, was playing to the great wad sitting out there in front of their television sets. *There is only one freedom looked for by the American voter who votes for Nixon,*" Mailer had imagined Nixon saying, "*—it is freedom from dread.*" If Nixon won by a landslide, said Robert Townsend, the former whiz of Avis—he was then campaigning for McGovern— we would "have to face the fact that we have become a nation of 200 million used-car salesmen."

We called them the middle class, but that was often flattery and merely compounded the confusion, for, while there were elements of the old middle class among them, the definition was so vague and broad as to include almost anyone above the poverty level—and some who were below it—provided he wasn't on welfare or shooting dope, a sociological fiction composed of amorphous groups of undifferentiated and increasingly insecure people lumped together for political convenience. "Their rightful forebears," wrote Andrew Hacker, a political scientist at Cornell, "are not the old middle class but rather the peasants and proletarians of an earlier time." The artifacts of affluence often managed to conceal the distinctions: The horrors of meeting monthly payments and the gratuitous insults of the credit system remained a relatively private matter between a person and his bank or the Household Finance Company while the car and the furniture and the house were visible in the neighborhood and constituted items that could be recorded by the statisticians of prosperity. Employment figures were calculable (more or less), but the conditions of the job were not. Affluence had become a costume, an all-purpose fashion available at the discount store and the used-car lot, but the security and confidence of middle-class position was a relatively scarce commodity.

Whatever history they have had [C. Wright Mills had said] is a history without events; whatever common interests they have do not lead to unity; whatever future they have will not be of their own making. . . . In our politics and economy, in family life and religion—in practically every sphere of our existence—the certainties of the eighteenth and nineteenth centuries have disintegrated or been destroyed and, at the same time, no new sanctions or justifications for the new routines we live, and must live, have taken hold. So there is no acceptance and no rejection, no sweeping hope and no sweeping rebellion. There is no plan of life. . . . The broad linkage of enterprise and property, the cradle-condition of classic democracy, no longer exists in America. There is no society of small entrepreneurs—now they are one stratum among others: above them is the big money; below them, the alienated employees; before them the fate of politically dependent relics; behind them, their world.

As a mythic entity the old middle class had once represented the greatest of the American frontiers, certainly the greatest frontier of the period that lasted from the end of the Civil War to the beginning of World War II. It suggested mobility, respectability, convictions, energy, enterprise and, most of all, an abiding confidence in the security and sanctity of its own place and its own possibilities: the sprawling Victorian house on the wide, elm-shaded street, the sturdy father going to work, the stable family, the pride of place, the ritual of holidays and summer vacations and family reunions, and an expanding cycle of growth, progress and success. The middle-class kids of the sixties who were embarrassed by their origins and status and tried to rebel against them had rarely known such a life and were themselves confused by the terms, but they succeeded, however inadvertently, in giving to the undifferentiated amorphous middle that Mills described the illusion of a coherence it didn't deserve. The counterculture seemed to invest the wad with values, enabling it to define itself not by what it was but by what it wasn't. It wasn't taking welfare (not in the obvious ways), wasn't on drugs (not on illegal drugs, anyhow), wasn't using foul language (except maybe in the locker room or the Legion bar), wasn't demonstrating (except maybe to keep black kids from going to white schools), and it wasn't challenging the system. Thus the kids and the militant blacks helped give Nixon his constituency by associating a whole set of once vital (and now enervated) middle-class characteristics with people who had no convictions, no sense of place, and no confidence. "It is time," Nixon had said during the campaign, "that good, decent people stop letting themselves be bulldozed by anybody who presumes to be the self-righteous moral judge of our society. There is no reason to feel guilty about wanting to enjoy what you get and get what you earn, about wanting your children in good schools close to home or about wanting to be judged fairly on your ability. Those are not values to be ashamed of; those are values to be proud of; those are values that I shall always stand up for when they come under attack." On the political marketplace of American society, Mills had concluded, "the new middle classes are up for sale; whoever seems respectable enough, strong enough, can probably have them. So far, nobody has made a serious bid." In 1972, Nixon made the bid.

The forties and fifties were an obvious object of reversion and nostalgia; World War II represented the last moment in American history—with the brief and limited exception of the New Frontier and the Great Society—when the country seemed to be together, when the integrating myths and symbols of liberal Americanism held sway, and when it seemed that everyone, including blacks, Jews and Catholics, would be melted into the great WASP mainstream. The fifties were to be the realization of the dreams of the thirties and forties, the final end of war and depression, and the coming of the great affluent future that the middle-class frontier had always promised: every family in a little white house with a lawn and a picket fence, a station wagon, and a month at the beach every summer. The dreams of individual aspiration became collectivized in new developments, corporate jobs, pensions, security and universal white-collar status, the suburbs represented the all-purpose future, and society replaced the individual as hero. There was no race problem— the Supreme Court had already settled that in the *Brown* decision (it would be only a matter of time)—and no one spoke the word "poverty." "What can we write about?" a college newspaper editor had asked me in 1957. "All the problems are solved. All that's left are problems of technical adjustment."

The excitement—what there was—lay in the collective realization of the dreams of the war; by the end of World War II, as everyone pointed out in the fifties, the great age of individual enterprise—the age of the Protestant Ethic and Inner Direction —had come to an end. This was the time for accommodation, for cool heads, for corporate committees, and for staying on the track, no matter what. Although a good many people, especially people in the universities, were embarrassed, there were good enough reasons for loving the system, and even for feigning a stoic existential toughness—saying, for example, that it took more discipline and moral toughness to compromise than it did to allow one's romantic impulses to run wild. You did it for the kids or for the peace of the world; in a complex, technological, nuclear age people couldn't afford to indulge their passions or trust their instincts. If you were serious you read Hemingway and Camus, and if you belonged to the Book-of-the-Month Club you got *The Caine Mutiny* and *By Love Possessed*, but what you took from each (sometimes by twisting and stretching) was the same message. To be heroic was to endure; resistance, if any, was internal, and the system, though it might be capricious, either was immutable—could not be changed without total anarchy— or represented the best accommodation to a tough and often hostile world. Self-effacement was the highest moral duty of man, stoicism the highest virtue. Maybe you seemed to be comfortable on the outside, but how you suffered within! Everyone in a gray suit, a white shirt and a rep tie. Whoever heard of charisma in 1955?

The difficulty lay in the transformation itself. What was left after the suburbs had been created and the move was made? A row of ticky-tackies in Levittown or a ranch house in Park Forest or a split-level with two-car garage in Lexington—those things were not the equivalent of the respectable Victorian establishment which had first given this dream its content. Perhaps there was excitement in getting there, excitement in planning the new school or organizing the church (didn't they call themselves pioneers?), perhaps even an extended meaning in moving from one place to another, but it wasn't the same as being a member of a distinct and respected class that was not part of an all-purpose middle. The very universality of the new life helped deprive it of meaning. Dreams of individual success embodied in the old image depended on the idea that social distinctions would always persist, despite the egalitarian rhetoric. The Victorian house symbolized enterprise and property and values—the values of the countinghouse *and* the values of principle, the property of production and the property of the home. But the real estate of the suburb symbolized nothing except itself, suggested, indeed, a kind of fraud, since no real possession or control backed it up. How often did they mail their monthly mortgage payment to the bank and call it rent? Organizations had created this, and on organizations it would always depend. In the suburban fifties everyone could get himself a loan (or nearly everyone), a quarter-acre lot and a development house, and everyone (so it seemed) could find a slot in the organization, even if the job had no self-evident significance. You worked your tail off because you could never be certain that you had in fact made it, had produced anything of value.

No generation has been so well equipped, psychologically as well as technically, to cope with the intricacies of vast organizations [wrote William H. Whyte, Jr., in *The Organization Man*]; none has been so well equipped to lead a meaningful community life; and none probably will be so adaptable to the constant shifts in environment that organization life is so increasingly demanding of them. In the better sense of the word, they are becoming the interchangeables of our society and they accept the role with understanding. They are all, as they say, in the same boat.

But where is the boat going? No one seems to have the faintest idea; nor, for that matter, do they see much point in even raising the question. Once people liked to think, at least, that they were in control of their destinies, but few of the younger organization people cherish such notions. Most see themselves as objects more acted upon than acting—and their future, therefore, determined as much by the system as by themselves.

Most of that was familiar stuff by the end of the fifties—was the very thing against which the rebellions of the sixties were ostensibly conducted. You'll never know how bad things are until you've lived in Scarsdale, right? There had been a sort of unity about the period between 1929 and 1959—dreams and realization, frontier and settlement, depression and prosperity, unemployment and security—but by the end of the fifties there was indeed a new generation, children of the all-purpose middle who had only dim memories of the Depression, had been deprived of its fears and its particular version of the future, who regarded the new security as normative, and who didn't understand that there might, at least in the experience of their parents, be things worse than the rat race, the vapid jobs and the phoniness. *You'll never know how bad things are until you've lived in Scarsdale.* This is where the New Frontier and the counterculture had their common origins, and where they drew most of their recruits and many of their ideas. The new generation had not been raised on depression economics (or, if they had, couldn't understand how such things could have affected their parents' lives); their history began with Paul Goodman, C. Wright Mills, David Riesman and John Kenneth Galbraith, not with the UAW strike of 1937 or the bread lines or the plays of Clifford Odets. Whatever might have made the achievement seem heroic had begun to fade from memory.

What had changed toward the end of the sixties—or had anything really changed? Why the apparent reaffirmation of white-collar, suburban "values"—not in joy or confidence, but with a sort of grim defiance—and at the very moment when they seemed most vulnerable and, in the light of Vietnam, most shameful? Why this last rush to the barricades of exclusion, the determination to build enclaves, the spread of walled housing developments in Los Angeles and Houston and Atlanta and in dozens of other cities with gatehouses and checkpoints and armed guards? Why the success of books called *Safe Places*—regions supposedly immune from crime or freaks or blacks? Why the self-righteous vacuity of the Young Voters for the President that we saw in Miami and later in the Nixon campaign—this gaggle of mildly stunted minds, Mailer called them—who didn't want to know anything, spoke in clichés of contradiction, and were proud of their uncuriosity? And, most important, why the lack of embarrassment or guilt; in the fifties, it could be said, people were simply ignorant about poverty and racism, did not yet know of the brutality of their own country, had not been exposed to My Lai or the Pentagon Papers or Attica, hadn't seen the slums on television or read about Biafra or Bangladesh. By the end of the sixties there could be no illusions, no lasting fantasy about an American Century (as Henry Luce had called it a decade before), about how the world was becoming an extension of a middle-class American suburb, how everyone was drinking Coca-Cola and buying American goods, and how Pax Americana might last another thousand years. It was not only that the members of the amorphous middle saw themselves as "objects more acted upon than acting," but that, in the decade since Whyte had written those words, even the system to which they had committed themselves had shown itself to be confused, destructive and often helpless. We had helped to kill 1,300,000 people in Vietnam and destroyed the countryside, had watched apathetically while the Biafrans massacred the Ibos, had failed, despite all the promises, to mitigate domestic poverty, had watched our industrial superiority decline to a trade deficit, had seen the devaluation of the dollar, witnessed the assassination of the most promising leaders in our national life, watched the spread of drugs into the places that were said to be the safest, and seen the great WASP confidence shrivel to an apology before an eruption of cultural and political separatism which explicitly rejected the integrating heroes and mythology of American life. The fact that the system had shown itself to be limited, if not helpless (against Vietnamese guerrillas, foreign competitors, airline hijackers, presidential assassins, and urban crime) did not, however, create new confidence in the possibilities of individual action or personal freedom in that amorphous middle; it seemed, on the contrary, to make resignation all the more attractive and life that much more fearsome. The kids had taught a good many people in the middle class that it was now safe to wear your hair long, perhaps even to smoke grass, and to feel considerably more free in one's choice of personal style and expression. But alongside those enlargements of private freedom there was a new and pervasive fear growing from the failures of the system and the collapse of the old establishment. The dangers to "national security" had, in the sixties, been escalated from something relatively specific (like Communism or Russia or the missile gap) to something cosmic, had become a brooding and destructive omnipresence that might manifest itself in crime or drugs or black revolt or meaningless murder or simply in the indignities of a systematic foul-up of the computer at the bank, the credit office or the power company, but which, in the final analysis, was straight anxiety about a world that no longer worked or responded according to the instructions on the package. The more absurd and carpricious the system became, the more people wanted to trust it, and the less they seemed to trust themselves.

The conventional explanation for the resurgent middle was based on the idea that it had always been there and had simply been ignored by the establishment press. "All during those years [of the sixties]," wrote Steven V. Roberts in a piece about the Young Voters for the President, "while the nightly news recorded the exploits of Mark Rudd and Jerry Rubin and . . . Tom Hayden, things went on elsewhere. Few students emerged completely untouched by the sixties, but for a great many of them youth still meant fraternities, not communes; beer, not pot; allegiance, not alienation. Young Voters for the President is sort of a flowering of that other America." Agnew and Nixon had been saying those things for four years, and now the liberals were picking up the line. But the explanation wasn't sufficient, did not comprehend the vengeful screams of their parents in Miami—vengeance on freaks and hippies and badmouths—or the multiple edges of hysteria, apathy and indulgence that sliced through the surburban shopping malls, the cocktail parties and the meetings of the village board. It was almost as if the kids and the militant blacks and the counterculture freaks had taught the amorphous middle a perverse lesson about how bad things could be in Scarsdale, had purged them of a portion of their ill-fitting liberal guilt, had stripped them of their illusions (or, at any rate, their rhetoric) about the good life, and thus enabled them to imagine themselves as just another set of victims of conditions beyond the power of man to control. Maybe you were making

93

$60,000 a year and belonged to the country club and bought a new Buick every other year, but that didn't mean that life was carefree and easy; it imposed responsibilities that the slobs on the street and in the coffeehouses couldn't begin to understand— responsibilities for management and self-control, responsibility for the church and the hospital, responsibility for the PTA and the rearing of children, responsibility for the whole confounded structure that stood between this civilization and chaos. Cheers for Nixon, cheers for Agnew. They understood self-denial and obedience and service and hard work, understood Ortega's injunction that "if you want to make use of the advantages of civilization, but are not prepared to concern yourself with the upholding of civilization—you are done . . . Just a slip, and when you look around everything has vanished into air. The jungle is always primitive and, vice versa, everything primitive is mere jungle."

The multiple revolts of the sixties provided justification for the fears and aspirations that the fifties had almost forgotten, renewed the suburban rationale, and advertised the reasons for its existence. By 1969 people reading serious journals like *Commentary* or *The Public Interest* could find pieces about "The Myth of Affluence" or questions such as Robert Lekachman's "Why do we feel so poor?" This was not an affluent society after all; not everyone was living on a shady street or in a development house, and the laws of Darwinian survival had not been repealed. In the fifties, wrote Stephan Thernstron, an urban historian, "the myth of affluence encouraged the complacent illusion that poverty had been eliminated and that unequal distribution of income was no longer a problem. The problem was rather that the masses were lusting after the bread and circuses devised by the ad-men. Few of those who mouthed the clichés about American affluence felt *themselves* to be blessed with excessive income. The assumption was that others were not sufficiently spiritual to make proper use of their undue affluence." You could read that sort of thing —or could hear it from Agnew—and begin to relive proletarian fantasies, drift back into proletarian nightmares, and reenter that demonic mirror-world in which the possibilities of social hardship justified the behavior of private withdrawal. Every night you saw it on the tube—the ugliness, the violence, the poverty, the disorder—and it enabled you to remember just why you were there in the first place. The more conscious a man became of unemployment and welfare, the more certain he was that he didn't want any low-income housing in his community; the higher the taxes went, the more dubious he would be about welcoming more families with children. While the kids decided that suburban life was a drag or a rat race, their parents discovered that the idyllic conditions they had once imagined (and about which the myth of affluence might make them feel guilty) had often failed to materialize. The serpents followed the garden to Westport, and what had once seemed like escape felt ever more like a trap. If this wasn't it, what was? The marriage counselors proliferated, the shrinks prospered, and the schools worked overtime to churn out propaganda about the dangers of grass, speed and bennies. But the private hell of "affluence" was still better than economic destitution; some people might flirt with Consciousness III fantasies, running off to the woods, or trading an executive's desk for a pushcart in the park, but most simply built their fences a little higher and stayed put.

II

The more you looked at the amorphous middle, the harder it became to tell just what you were seeing. In Palo Alto, California, the parking lots of the military research institutes were dotted with cars bearing bumper stickers supporting McGovern and the passage of Proposition 19, the initiative making legal the possession of marijuana; in the hills of western Massachusetts the graduates of Harvard Law School renting the country house ("very responsible people," the realtor said) arrived with a couple of $1,500 stereo hi-fi sets, two pairs of Head skis, a wardrobe of Brooks Brothers clothes, satin cushions for transcendental meditation, two cats, three dogs, an aversion to vacuum cleaners and other power-consuming appliances, and a principled refusal to kill anything, including the flies that were feeding on the dog and cat shit that collected on the porch and in the attic; and in Westwood and Bel Air, California, "freaks" wandered into the local shopping centers in bare feet to pick up $90 sweaters, then drove home in Jaguars. In a book called *The Radical Suburb*, John B. Orr and F. Patrick Nicholson described such people as examples of "expansive man," an individual "devoted to the process of enlarging his experience, enlarging the number of perspectives within which his world can be perceived and felt, enlarging awareness of his own sensual and intellectual capabilities, and enlarging his ability to be playful with ideas and possessions." His time, they said,

is not spent in caring for the soul's state of health, but in playing golf, swinging from party to party, playing with astrology and ski equipment, and occasionally going to church. The usual question is not whether life constitutes a meaningful whole; it is whether the family has a rich, interesting schedule lined up for the next few weeks. . . .

That the expansive style is not simply hedonism is also shown by the fact that the radical does not retreat from rigorous, demanding commitments. He often devotes a burdensome amount of time to community organizations, including churches . . . He is occasionally active in politics, even to the point of assuming the ascetic disciplines of radical political communities. And he may be found spending hours figuring out studies on ESP, trying Zen puzzles, or plodding through technical material on astrology. He is not drawn to the esoteric to the exclusion of other areas of intellectual discipline, however, and he is rapidly turning adult education programs into a booming suburban business. The expansive man, when told that his intensive style shows a dabbling character devoid of serious commitment, can only disagree, because from his perspective, his style is motivated by an urge to be fully involved in his surroundings . . . Consistency appears to be anachronistic, a stale reminder of yesterday, starved for the richness that a freer style might produce.

In that kind of ethos, the frontier is internal; the soul is mobile, and the adventure is, in the final analysis, private. Far out is far in, and "Wow" is the ultimate accolade. Yet the more one looked at it, the more one was struck by the seamlessness of the fabric, a middle that extended from the uptight suburb created by the fears of the Depression right through the commune of natural-food freaks in the hills of Vermont. Often, though not always, they were inhabited by people with similar origins and attitudes, Protean types who could change face, dress and style to suit any occasion. The suburban parents of the fifties had told Whyte about how "they had to learn adjustment the hard way, without the benefit of an education anywhere near as contemporary, or socially conscious, as that the schools are now offering. If they have made their adjustment as successfully as they have, they wonder, how much more successfully may their children when they come of age?" Now those children had come of age, and while Spiro Agnew might regard them as the offspring of permissiveness and laxity according to the gospel of Spock, many of them also managed a remarkable adjustment that accommodated the styles of the counterculture to the politics of Nixon. By the time the employment crunch began in the early seventies, even the longhairs at Berkeley had started complaining about graduate-school quotas and job restrictions that seemed to favor blacks and women, and students who swore that they would never mess with corporate law firms or abet the construction of high-rise buildings took the jobs that were offered, and promised to do their own thing on the side. It was almost like the fifties again, when guilty WASPs bid goodbye to their Jewish friends at the door of the fraternity house and the country club with a vow that they would work for reform from within. If enough people changed their life styles the revolution would come without a shot being fired or a drop of blood being spilled. It was called the Greening of America and represented the consummation of the suburban–counterculture romance. Charles Reich was the Norman Vincent Peale of 1970.

What the children of the fifties had come to share with their parents was a sense of futility—"objects more acted upon than acting"—and the political cynicism it produced. The great era of their hope had seemed to prove that nothing made much difference, that you could bring a half-million people to Washington without affecting the course of the war, that you could march, picket, watch polls and register voters until the end of time and achieve virtually nothing. "The last chorus said it all," Pete Hamill had written about the March on Washington in November 1969—the one which Nixon had observed by watching a college football game on television:

Young kids, open and free about so many things, joined together, some of them swaying joyfully on each other's backs, a girl in a glossy black raincoat with her hands joined to other marshals and her head turned to watch the stage. Others crying, they were there to say farewell to the 1960s, a desperate and bloody era, one that had begun with John Kennedy standing in weather like this telling them the torch had passed to a new generation, and now, looking out at them, you remembered that when Kennedy was inaugurated most of them were only 10. The new generation was us; Thank God we had done better. . . .

At 5:52, on Nov. 15, the last chorus ended and the sixties were over. They had begun in hope, and ended with Richard Nixon in the White House and Spiro Agnew threatening other Americans with "separation," and when the crowd drifted away, there was no feeling left except remorse and loss and waste. The country had failed those children, and you could promise them nothing anymore except a dark and fearful future.

There was a ghostly echo about Hamill's words, an echo of the end of another era when youth had bemused the country, and when the beautiful people were supposed to be taking over. Even the cadences were familiar: "Now once more the belt is tight," Fitzgerald had written in 1931,

and we summon the proper expression of horror as we look back at our wasted youth. Sometimes, though, there is a ghostly rumble among the drums, an asthmatic whisper in the trombones that swings me back into the early twenties when we drank wood alcohol and every day in every

way we grew better and better, and there was a first abortive shortening
of the skirts, and girls all looked alike in sweater dresses, and people you
didn't want to know said "yes, we have no bananas," and it seemed a
question of only a few years before the older people would step aside
and let the world be run by those who saw things as they were—and it
all seems rosy and romantic to us who were young then, because we
will never feel quite so intensely about our surroundings any more.

Perhaps we were perpetually looking back on our lost youth, the
youth of a generation with its yellow submarines, its innocent
fantasies, its dreams of beauty, and perhaps 1969 had been a
crash similar to the one that took place, almost to the day, forty
years before. Yet 1929 and the Depression that followed had produced a concrete and common affliction; if they taught people
about the futility of individualism, they also generated a new
faith in collective action, and if they destroyed the old businessman heroes, they threw up other heroes in their place. Even in
the fifties people who survived the thirties could look back on
their youth with some nostalgia as an era of common purpose,
of battles won, and of excitement and meaning. The crash of
1969 had produced no such feeling; it seemed merely to confirm
the sense of futility, produced in its wake a rash of polls and
analyses confirming the cynicism, and gave the nearly forgotten
"privatism" of the fifties new justification. *The Greening of
America* did not simply reflect the co-optation of counterculture
styles by the upper middle class; it also indicated how profoundly
the styles and artifacts of the revolt had become the playthings of
the rich. Having been stripped of its political and economic content, the counterculture could safely become the material of nostalgia or for costume parties without end. Freak chic. "I think
I know what is bothering the students," George Wald had said
in the spring of 1969. "I think that what we are up against is a
generation that is by no means sure that it has a future." The
doubt, Wald believed, had produced the revolt; the nostalgia
which now replaced the sixties suggested that the doubt had been
resolved.

III

Even before Jefferson warned about the urban mobs of decadent
Europe, Americans had been ambivalent about cities and, in a
larger sense, about the meaning of progress itself. If the settlements of New England constituted the New Jerusalem, and if
the independent yeoman farmer of the eighteenth century was
the ultimate in a democratic civilization, which way was up?
The city was opportunity, growth and success, but it was also
temptation, sin and corruption. You could play the theology
both ways: going there was Good; being there was questionable.
Yet on one assumption the theology was (and still is) consistent:
the city was, all demography aside, the exception; the country
and its ethic were the norm, and every time you flew across the
country or looked at the ads on television, the vision returned:
Down there was the real America, on the wheat fields of Kansas,
in the small crossroads towns with their helpful banker and their
friendly Mutual of Omaha insurance agent, in the shopping
centers where the farmers congregated on Saturday afternoon
and the women came to have their hair set, in the new developments of Topeka or Quincy or Macon or Rapid City, neighborhoods clustered around cities of twenty thousand or seventy-five
thousand where they manufactured trailers or hardboard or
bricks or Thermopane windows, or where they refined beet
sugar, packed meat or milled flour, places where women ran
washing machines and men bought tires and where things always
went better with Coke. By the census definition, most of them
were "urban places"—meaning any town of twenty-five hundred
or more—and America was a nation that was seventy-five percent urban, but if one also understood that the census defined
places like St. Joseph, Missouri, Saginaw, Michigan, Billings,
Montana, Gadsden, Alabama, and York, Pennsylvania, as "Standard Statistical Metropolitan Areas," then the distinctions between

rural and urban became more complex and a whole landscape reappeared that had no comfortable place in any of the conventional categories of American sociology. The cliché was Middle America, but that suggested church suppers, clambakes, hard work and thrift, a whole network, indeed, of intrinsic "traditional" values, and not the concomitant suburbanization with its easy credit, its packaged food and packaged culture, or its near-total dependence on economic decisions and forces beyond local control. By the time the sixties came to an end, most of that country was simply defining itself as non-New York (even while it was buying the stuff that New York sold) and commiserating with anyone forced to live in a jungle where white people couldn't walk the streets after dark or sit in the parks without the risk of rape. Herman Kahn, the philosopher of thermonuclear war, echoed the conventional wisdom when he said that the American middle class had been split in two. "We are having a kind of religious war," he had said. "The upper middle class is forcing its religion—call it Secular Humanism—on the middle class, which is basically nationalistic and fundamentalist. The result is that the middle class has begun to feel it has lost the country." What the description ignored was the schizophrenia of each; the traditional values were there, all right, but anyone with half an eye could perceive that the newsstands of Main Street were doing better with *Playboy* than with *Church News* or *American Opinion*, the monthly magazine of the John Birch Society, and that while there were still local entrepreneurs, the big opportunity lay in a fast-food franchise or a service station or dealership dependent on the products and advertising of a national corporation. Every day you could see the salesmen and conventioneers from hicktown around the Americana or the Belmont Plaza or the Waldorf in New York picking up the hookers, every week you could see the ads in the swingers' magazines seeking compatible couples in El Paso and Tucson, in Albany and Joplin, and every morning you could hear the "California girls" on a San Francisco radio station or on similar phone-in programs on scores of other stations—housewives, thousands of them, in solid Middle American developments like Hayward and San José and Daly City—discussing their affairs with the milkman, the TV repairman, or their husband's best friend. They all had good marriages, they said (meaning that the husband was a good provider), but sex with the other guy was more fun. What you learned in Middle America was that it wasn't merely the kids of the Eastern upper middle class or the Ivy intellectuals who were smoking dope or screwing after the homecoming game, it was the high-school quarterback.

They had lost the country not because the elite had stolen it from them or because the media were prone to orgies of misrepresentation, but because they had chosen to live in a world for which they had no ethic. They lived neither in big cities nor in small towns, were not the sinful people or the crime-besieged victims of urban rot that they imagined the residents of New York to be, nor were they the honest yeomen of national myth. They were increasingly cut off from the security and motivations of the old middle class (and therefore deprived of its sense of the future), yet they retained enough of its ethic to be uncomfortable with the national culture which replaced it. Even in supposedly safe places people had started feeling besieged. New York was spreading. In Mason City, Iowa, the River City of Meredith Willson's *Music Man*, people were talking about Waterloo, Iowa, as an industrial place with a rising crime rate and a population of bad credit risks who couldn't be trusted to pay their bills; in Sioux Falls it was Minneapolis; in Tracy, California (pop. 14,000), it was Stockton, and in Stockton it was Oakland. Nearly all of them had their "urban problem"—slum housing, decaying business districts, ghettoes of blacks or Chicanos or Indians, drugs, unemployment, welfare—yet the idea that they were in fact urban, or that there was an urban problem, became a nearly unthinkable proposition. Not that they denied everything; the tax bills told them that something was wrong, even if nothing else did. Yet to make common cause with

New York, Chicago or St. Louis in confronting social decay was like inviting contamination. John Lindsay didn't speak for them. The big cities were hopeless—beyond repair or salvation—and the only reasonable policy was to diversify, to get the industry out of the big cities and back to the middle-sized towns. "The smaller communities need the plants and the people that are polluting the urban centers—not in large doses, but steadily, surely," wrote the editor of the Mason City *Globe Gazette*, and the words were familiar in other towns. "The small communities are geared up. They have comprehensive plans. They know they can't stand still or they will be passed by." It was a rare place, however, where local enterprise and local investors were able or willing to take the risk themselves. In places like Hannibal, Missouri, which was now trying to promote Huck Finn and Tom Sawyer into a tourist industry, the entrepreneurs of the nineteenth century grew prosperous by buying lumber in Wisconsin, floating it down the Mississippi, cutting it up in locally owned mills, and shipping it west on a locally owned railroad. By 1970 the barges passed most of the river towns by, the mills were closed, and the presence of the river as a great promise of romance and growth had become, on the one hand, an abstraction of international commerce and, on the other, a fading memory of the past.

You saw what you were supposed to see, and then you began to see things you were not: the Civil War monument in the square; the First National Bank; Osco's Self-Service Drugs; the shoestore and the movie theaters; Damon's and Younkers' ("Satisfaction Always"); Maize's and Penney's; Sears and Monkey Ward. They debated about the construction of a new mall or the possible renewal of the downtown business area, fought about one-way streets, and told you, depending on the region, that when the crops were good you couldn't find a parking space in town.

There seemed to be a common feeling that anyone, even a writer from New York, was, somewhere in his heart, a small-town boy come home. New York was something you put on, but Main Street was something you remained forever. They took you in, absorbed you, soaked you up; they knew whom you'd seen, what you'd done. In the back country of Mississippi, the sheriff used to follow you around; here it was the word. . . . Hannibal, Quincy, Keokuk, Sheboygan, Paducah, Sioux Falls, Rapid City, Mason City, Sandusky, Bristol, Haverhill, Greenfield, Bethlehem, Tracy . . . *Small towns co-opt, you told yourself, and nice small towns co-opt absolutely.* Nostalgia helped make the connections, for how could you be fully American unless you could be part of this? Yes, you were willing to come to dinner, to visit the Club, to suspend the suspicion that all this was some sort of Chamber of Commerce trick. Often they were delighted that you were not surprised that they had a local television station or perhaps two or even three, that there was a decent library in town and a community orchestra, and that you didn't assume that civilization stopped at the Hudson or (going the other way) in the foothills behind the Berkeley campus. They had heard about that other world out there—that's why they commiserated with you—yet they couldn't understand why the things that seemed to work here didn't work everywhere else, nor could they consider the idea that many times they didn't even work at home. The space, the land, the incessant reminders of physical normalcy made it possible to defer almost anything. Church on Sunday, football on Friday and the cycle of parties, dinners and cookouts remained more visible (not to say comprehensible) than the subtleties of cultural change or violence overseas or political repression. The answer to an economic problem, the official answer, was to work harder, to take a second job, or to send your wife to work, usually as a clerk or a waitress. On the radio, Junior Achievement made its peace with modernism by setting its jingle to "Get with It" to a rock beat, but the message of adolescent enterprise was the same, and around the lunch tables in places called the Green Mill or the Chart House or the City Café it was difficult to persuade any-

104

one that sometimes even people with a normal quota of ambition couldn't make it.

What they didn't discuss was what the president of one Midwestern NAACP chapter called "the secret places": the subtle discrimination in housing and jobs, the out-of-sight dilapidated houses on the edge of town or in places called the Bottoms, buildings surrounded with little piles of lumber, rusting metal chairs, and decaying junk cars once slated for repair; the lingering aroma of personal defeat; and the peculiar mix of arrogance and apathy that declared, "There are no poor people in this area." On Sundays, while most people were packing their campers for the trip home, or making the transition between church and television football, the old, who had nothing to do, wandered into the Park Inn for lunch (hot roast beef sandwiches cost $1.65) and discussed Medicare; while people talked about discipline and hard work around the high school ("Add umph to try and you have triumph"), the star quarterback was paying a brainy junior to take his college board tests for him so that he could get an athletic scholarship (a fact known to the school's college counselor, and to most of the students, who said nothing); and while the football-happy citizens celebrated another victory, the kids attending the dance after the game broke out the joints and turned on. There were, in many of these towns, ghosts of old patriarchs—the general, the founder of the mill, the people who donated the land for the park or built the YMCA —and, along with them, the remembrance, perhaps real, perhaps fantasy, of a lost heroic age when bank clerks became corporation presidents, the railroad workers boozed and brawled through the cafés on Water Street, and every year brought a new achievement, another monument of modern construction and another thriving business. The ethic remained, often the shadow survived the man, but only at the price of increasing tension and neglect, tension between the temptations of the national culture and the rhetoric of local belief, neglect of the secret places of destitution, poverty and frustration which underlay the illusions of local achievement. The sons of the founders were selling out to national corporations and exchanging control for shares in a conglomerate, and, while they spoke fondly about the wild times in the old days, they were not sure that even the state university was a safe place for their children. Sooner or later the world could come back here, they believed, because the cities were unlivable, and enough people had come—often for that very reason—to sustain the belief. In Mason City, Jack MacNider, the son of one of those local patriarchs, talks about the gradual movement of the "iron triangle," the Midwestern industrial region, into north-central Iowa (as if the movement of industry were a law of history but the accompanying problems were not), and in the old towns along the Mississippi the Chamber of Commerce promotes clean air and good hunting and fishing. Given enough time, people would come to their senses and rush back to places where life was decent and space remained.

So much for heroic visions and high ambition. The future lay in the past, and the big city was a mad aberration which was, at long last, coming to its unnatural end. The writers of the fifties had talked extensively about the lowering of personal ambition, about people more interested in security, pensions and a modestly decent life than in making it big or in taking big chances. But that older form of modesty assumed a general benevolence in the social order, or, at any rate, a continuing belief that the laws of nature and society were progressive. By the early seventies a great deal of that faith was gone, and, while the behavior of individuals often reverted to the patterns of the Eisenhower era, fewer people were talking about progress or the universal affluence just around the corner. The country had seen enough of the failures of social reform and had discovered enough of the dark underside of national "progress" to understand that segregation and inequality—economic and social—seemed to be the rule of history. (For many, of course, there was nothing new about that discovery; but once again it was becoming fashionable). The mythic Middle American was not only trying to

come to terms with change and complexity or to adapt his small-
town ethic to the realities of technocracy and bureaucracy; he
was also engaged in a paradoxical search to reestablish his historic
innocence, to flee from the appearance of *knowing*, and he tried
to use bureaucracy for precisely that purpose. Despite the official
rhetoric about the new federalism or the talk about decentraliza-
tion, the national response to the events of the late sixties and
early seventies was to try to enlarge the distance between the
decisions and their consequences, to make the old ethic viable by
restricting perspective to local concerns, and to "trust the President" on other matters. To vote for McGovern was, in a sense,
to accept some moral responsibility for those distant decisions and
become a participant in national affairs—the ethic of the small
town applied to Washington and the world; to vote for Nixon
was to sever the ethic from global applications—to preserve it
by keeping it local. Nixon offered his constituents the luxury of
maintaining their purity at home and getting the dirty work done
away from home. Official secrecy (in regard to the Pentagon
Papers, for example, or the war in Laos, or My Lai, or the in-
fringement of civil liberties at home) therefore functioned as a
means of keeping the moral illusion intact; brutality and repression could be delegated, and bureaucracies could take the rap.
The secrecy existed because most people did not want to know;
the President became stronger and the Congress weaker because
the amorphous middle, suspended between its old ethic and its
desire to live modern, was happy to delegate the responsibility.
The advantage of that middle world was in its double standard.
The old and the new coexisted, and one could change worlds
at will: big technology without slums, poverty or bureaucracy,
the amenities of modern life without the political and social complications that accompanied their production and use. Time
frames could be juxtaposed, like film running backward or
double-exposed negatives, the simple and the sophisticated, the
natural and the contrived. Here, too, people wanted the simple
life of the land without giving up their Head skis or their stereos

or their campers or their washing machines, and the affairs of Main Street became like the business of the commune, small decisions severed from the larger decisions of corporations and government that would, in the long run, make all the difference.

IV

"I take it as a fact of common experience," wrote the economist Robert Lekachman in 1970, "that we are all poorer than we are publicly told we are, but until the experts seriously apply themselves to measurement, we cannot know by how much we are actually poorer than the inflated national income estimates say we are." Lekachman was talking about the failure of the standard indices to measure disproduct—among them the disamenities produced by pollution, crowding and noise, but including also the declining marginal satisfaction of the goods people were forced or persuaded to buy through the simple lack of alternatives. If a man has to buy a car to get to work because public transportation deteriorated, does that purchase in fact represent a net gain in satisfaction or merely a frustrating accommodation to social neglect, another set of headaches, and another collection of repair bills (which will themselves become part of the gross national product)? Does the purchase of commercially bottled drinking water represent growth in GNP or merely the pollution and chlorination of the public system? As measured, gross national product includes all goods and services produced each year, among them the uncounted billions which the country spends to ameliorate the damage and deficiencies produced by "progress" itself: the price of cigarettes and the cost of lung-cancer operations; the cost of packaging and the cost of disposal (but not the "cost" of dirty streets and dirty air). Of the five million refrigerators produced in this country each year, nearly all represent replacements; the number of homes with a refrigerator increases hardly at all. If every car in America were produced to last a year longer, and people therefore bought fewer cars, GNP would go down but satisfaction would presumably go up. (Ralph Nader, on a television program, once asked a group of economists if inflation included the production of goods of declining quality at the same price—shabby cars, for instance. They were unable to answer.) "Our environment is sinking fast into a welter of disamenities," wrote the British economist E. J. Mishan, "yet the most vocal part of the community cannot raise their eyes from the trade figures to remark the painful event."

By the early seventies, such arguments were common; some people, at least, were raising their eyes from the trade figures. At MIT the social scientist Raymond Bauer had called for a system of social indicators—reliable indices of satisfaction and public well-being—and in the last months of the Johnson administration the Secretary of Health, Education and Welfare, Wilbur Cohen, had made the first attempt at a national assessment of social health and prosperity that went beyond the figures of gross national product and included such things as welfare, education, care of the aged, child care and similar items. Yet the recession and the growing unemployment figures that followed the Johnson years placed national attention right back on the trade figures; quite possibly the lack of better indicators made "inflation" and "recession" easy rationalizations for disaffections which transcended them. More important, the effort to revise reliance on GNP was soon swallowed up by discussions of the "environment"—meaning limited attempts to clean up the air, the water and the junkyards (usually by dividing the cost of such efforts between the consumer and the taxpayer)—without taking into account the effects of marginal satisfaction on the behavior and life styles of those who bought the goods or investigating the possibility of alternatives. Mishan had pointed out that statements about economic freedom of choice amounted to a myth where people were taught, among other things, that the price of affluence was a dull job whose nature was dictated by "technology" and where many options (even those beyond clear air and water) were no longer available at all. You had to buy a complicated outboard motor because the simple models you could fix yourself were no longer made, had to buy a new washer because no one had the ability or the parts to repair the old one. The pricing system and the market were not responsive to minorities who (for example) valued a quiet home free of the noise of jets flying overhead above the convenience of relatively inexpensive air travel, but who were nonetheless deprived of the air rights over their homes without compensation and were thus in effect subsidizing the airlines and the passengers, or to people who preferred to travel by rail or who liked their bread without preservatives. Freedom was a cart in the supermarket.

Among the most significant and least discussed of the consequences of growth and "affluence," however, was a phenomenon that Steffan B. Linder described in a book called *The Harried Leisure Class*. Rather than creating "satisfaction in the embrace of the fine arts and beautiful thoughts," he argued, the attainment of increasing affluence has produced a scarcity of time which drives "meditation and speculation" off the market and creates a misleading *partial* affluence.

A growing proportion of the labor force is employed in the service sector, but in spite of this, our resources are in fact less well "serviced" or maintained than ever. It is becoming increasingly difficult, for instance, for elderly people to obtain the special kind of service—care and attention—that they very much need. Our so-called service economy practices in reality a throw-away system at all levels, including the human level. We have long expressed hopes that the elimination of material cares would clear the way for a broad cultural advancement. In practice, not even those endowed with the necessary intellectual and emotional capacity have shown any propensity for immersing themselves in the cultivation of their minds and spirit. The tendency is rather the reverse . . . Our affluence takes only the form of access to goods. The idea of "total affluence" is a logical fallacy.

Most economists, Linder said, recognize the time factor in regard to matters of production, but they regard "consumption as an instantaneous act without temporal consequences." As incomes rise, therefore, "one would have increasing consumption (according to conventional economics) without any consequences to the time situation of the individual, other than a reduction in work time. This would give an increasing amount of 'free time.' The supply would be increasing on all fronts." In fact, he argued, nothing of the sort has happened, because the analysis is faulty. As incomes rise, time becomes more valuable: a man who might have "lost" only twenty dollars' pay by playing a round of golf now loses forty and therefore decides to spend the extra hours at the office, and a person who once could afford only the tennis racket or the golf clubs or the aqualung now has access to all of them but can't "afford" to use them. "Typically," he wrote, "we encourage . . . a myth that working hours are being steadily reduced. In this way we get both our consumption goods and a feeling that we have more time in which to use them. The statistics, however, give a different picture." Since World War I, he said with emphasis, *"there has been no further reduction in the work week.* There have been minor ups and downs, due probably to cyclical changes, but the movements have been around a flat trend line at just over 40 hours per week. . . . The reduction of work time has ceased."

Some people work long hours in order to become income oligarchs and to obtain access to those pleasures which . . . are necessarily reserved for a minority, no matter how much average productivity rises. Perhaps, to an even greater extent, long hours are the result of a fondness for work, rather than for the income which results. Compulsive work may be substituted for compulsory work. A still greater number of people, perhaps, are work maniacs, who try to keep haunting, disturbing thoughts at a distance. *However, most people will not curtail the work week, in spite of increases in productivity, for the simple reason that they are not satisfied with the increases in consumption that would then be possible* [italics mine]. This would mean that, owing to a declining utility of additional income combined with an urge to improve the level of well-being, people are lured into a misallocation of time, thus becoming the victims of growth obsession. The fact that we so ardently encourage the myth of the declining work week indicates that there is a vague feeling of uncertainty about the propriety of the present allocation of time.

Linder suggested that the declining satisfaction of increasing consumption created two apparently contradictory phenomena: on the one hand, a kind of cancerous acceleration of "growth mania at the individual level"—trying to acquire more and more but enjoying it less and less—and, on the other, the romantic, Consciousness III exasperation with the rat race and its rhetoric about a return to a simpler, less pressured existence. (It has also, of course, created the familiar middle-class combination of the two: busting your gut downtown so that you can maintain the quiet place in the country.) Both, however, derive from the same intuition of scarcity and, it seems to me, feed the hysteria that accompanies the already tedious debate about ecology and the preservation of the environment. It is not simply that people who *have* are becoming increasingly aware of the destruction of space—and therefore treat the environment as if it were a global zoning problem (ecology, needless to say, is no great issue in the ghetto)—but that historic time, like space, has come to be regarded as a scarce commodity. The ecology freaks are certain that both are about to run out, and the prophets of apocalypse are prepared to name dates—twenty years, fifty, a hundred at the most. If national growth mania is sustained by the pressures of "growth mania at the individual level" (as Linder suggests) the reaction to growth (as in ecology) is similarly sustained by the experience of personal dissatisfaction and frustration in the accumulation of more personal goods. The conservationists and the developers are fighting over the same hillsides and the same beaches: The country is leisure, the city is hurried, time is space and space is time. They run out (or on) together.

How the different elements of the amorphous middle respond to the GNP-ecology issue depends in part, of course, on where they fall on the curve. The issue of "environment" brings together those who already consume, not those who aspire to it. In the early days of flamboyant environmentalism (1968–70), when a group called Ecology Action buried a new automobile in California—presumably to show its contempt for pollution—a group of black militants demanded that the car be turned over to them for the movement; why should anyone destroy something valuable, however important the symbolism, when you can convert it into breakfast for five thousand hungry kids? The environment, in this case, was not simply a consumer good, but the ultimate item in conspicuous consumption for people who are so affluent that they can destroy cars that the lower classes are killing themselves to ride. Linder speaks about a "period of decadence" when, among other things, "there will be a curious combination of an increasing attachment to goods in general and, owing to a low degree of utilization and rapid turnover, an increasing indifference to each of them in particular." The indifference, of course, does not apply to people in the lower reaches of the economic order or, for the most part, I suspect, to anyone who has ever had recent personal experience with it, which is to say that it is essentially a second-generation phenomenon among people who have already made it. It may also be irrelevant to people trying to imitate aristocratic rather than bourgeois styles of consumption—Southerners and blacks, for example—where "indifference" to each particular good and "a low degree of utilization" may be sources of pride rather than dissatisfaction and where the most available commodity is precisely that element which the harried leisure class is supposed to lack: time to consume. One of the blessings of a feudal past (lacking almost everywhere in America except, perhaps, in the South) is the resistance it creates to the rat race and the importance it attaches to leisure time. What the American middle class has always lacked—even as it leaves most of its puritanical traditions behind—is the tradition of pleasure; it can still feel guilty not only about enjoying, but, in the world of *Playboy*, about not enjoying enough. The hippie imitates the black imitating the plantation owner imitating the aristocrat; while the final behavior tends to be rather distant from the model, it often retains its commitment to the sanctity of leisure and freedom of aristocratic expression. What the straights have always envied and hated most about the freaks and the "welfare chiselers"—beyond their bad manners or their aristocratic indifference to conventional opinion—is their apparently high ratio of consumption time to work time. Those are the lousy bastards who are always enjoying and never working.

Despite the aberrations of such aristocratic behavior, however, and despite its possible influence on the so-called expansive man of the radical suburb (either in liberating him or in creating still more anxiety), Linder's analysis makes a great deal of sense. Yet it may fail to take into account the sophistication of the people he describes. What Linder knows and analyzes with his mathematical models and his calculus a great many people were beginning to discover in their own terms and their own experience; they do not respond in quite the Pavlovian fashion that he assumes. Every vote for open space or against a new development, every suit against a power company—California's approval of a coastal conservation initiative and Colorado's rejection of subsidies for the 1976 winter Olympics (which were expected to bring more developers and more crowding)—suggested not only the mounting concern about the environment but also, I think, the growing dissatisfaction with the individual accumulation of goods and with the conventional GNP determinants of the good life. To date, the political terms of that dissatisfaction have generally been limited (or, at any rate, translated) to the language of ecology and thus have failed either to express the more subtle disenchantment that helps sustain ecology or to articulate the possibilities for class conflict it contains. Yet each of those votes for ecology was, in a sense, a vote against the conventional American future and another stumbling block—moral, psychological and economic—to the traditional aspirations of those who hadn't made it. The resulting parks and beaches may be available for everyone, and especially those who can't afford their own private preserves, but, since ecology was, at least so far, innocent of any corresponding policy for the redistribution of private resources, it would make existing economic divisions that much broader and existing deprivation that much more permanent. The hillsides that are taken away from the developers are also being taken away from people who require housing and from unions demanding jobs. As the curve of increasing material satisfaction flattens out at the top, the price of satisfaction rises at the bottom. Within such a context, modesty has a new meaning and the ethos of progress gives way to the standard of survival. "As a people," said Harvey Wheeler of the Center for the Study of Democratic Institutions in 1970, "we will never be as rich again."

Modesty, of course, always functioned as a valid ethical counter to ambition in American life. It was the common people that God loved, and it is the ordinary man that we have been celebrating at least since the age of Jackson. Yet modesty had historically been mitigated by two mythic elements: the expectation of the middle class, if not the fact, of general progress, and, along with it, the theology of personal independence and opportunity. If modesty was the counter to ambition (or, at any rate, to vulgar success), ambition was also the counter to modesty. This is what those Middle Americans were thinking about when they talked about the pitiful city dwellers coming back to the towns. Increasingly, however, the new modesty lacked such mitigation, and the middle class was therefore beginning to lose the essential choice that once helped to give it meaning, if not, in fact, its noble state. The pop cult of the lower middle class—the soap operas, the *Love Storys*—portrayed the individual as victim and his (or her) prime virtue as, on the one hand, love and affection, and, on the other, the ability to endure. The historic question "Which way is up?" was increasingly answered with nagging suspicion that said "No way." You couldn't go to the city anymore—it was a jungle, not a frontier; and even if the jobs and the industry came to Springfield or Lincoln or wherever, they would be just jobs, a living and not an adventure. The adventure would have to be found somewhere else. For nearly four years almost every scrap of political rhetoric had depicted the middle class as a lot of people having to put up with a lot of abuse, the most prosperous country on earth a nation of victims bravely enduring.

V

Americans have never been entirely comfortable with distinctions of social class or ethnic identity; our egalitarian prudery taught us not to talk about such things—though, God knows, we thought about them—and so class and ethnicity were largely relegated to the john walls of public discourse: fat Japs and dumb Polacks, grabby Jews and uppity niggers. When ethnicity required official recognition it was most often celebrated for its potential Americanism, for what it was giving up or what it shared with official WASP culture, and not for what it retained or what it refused to yield. The mainstream was defined, at least in part, as the antithesis of the cultural material from which it had presumably been forged, and its larger justification, if it needed any, was reinforced by the millions of people all over the world who wanted to join. Every immigrant was a testimonial to the success of the American experiment. We were all going to be WASPs, and we were all going to be middle-class; ethnicity, like poverty, was a state of incompletion or imperfection, a temporary affliction subject to the remediation of progress. "The public school taught us it was unpatriotic to be Italian," said Gino Baroni, who heads the Center for Urban Ethnic Studies, "and the church taught us it was immoral." There was only one complete American.

The process was supposed to have been completed after World War II; if the fifties celebrated anything, it was the idea that universal assimilation—ethnic, cultural and economic—

was at hand. The war brought the country together and reaffirmed how different America was from the rest of the world. The general prosperity which the war helped create indicated that affluence was possible for anyone and that the egalitarian absence of social distinctions of which the country had always spoken was now within reach. In fact, of course, the process had never been completed, and the rediscovery of poverty, class, race and ethnicity in the sixties indicated that the celebration had been premature. More significantly, the great assimilation—though partly illusory—was celebrated at the very moment when the convictions and style of traditional WASP culture had lost their certainty and when the historic assurance of American preeminence in moral and political spheres was beginning to wane. We found ourselves in a complicated, sensitive nuclear world in which romantic adventure was dangerous and where the frontiersman-cowboy-entrepreneur was quickly (and often necessarily) being replaced by a man who understood the sensitivity of things, knew the limitations of American power and appreciated the necessity for compromise. The WASP ethic had been the ethic of making it, as individuals and as a nation; it did not say much about the problems of having made it, about what followed when the country was developed and mature. What were we going to do after the orgy?

The implications of all this on the new, all-purpose middle class were enormous. In his study of changes in English working-class life after World War II, Richard Hoggart had pointed out:

It is probably easier to merge working-class people into a larger, culturally classless class when they no longer have such strong economic pressure as makes them feel the great importance of loyal membership in their known groups. No doubt many of the old barriers of class should be broken down. But at present the older, the more narrow but also more genuine class culture is being eroded in favor of mass opinion, the mass recreational product and the generalized emotional response. . . . The old forms of class culture are in danger of being replaced by a poorer kind of classless, or by . . . a "faceless" culture, and this is to be regretted.

Even though there never was official recognition of a class structure in America, something similar happened here: If the owners and managers of the textile mills of New England were middle-class, the factory girls were, at best, apprentices, people on the way, but not yet there, and if the lawyers and businessmen of the growing cities were regarded as the substantial people of place and community, the miners and steelworkers remained a subculture with its own language, its penny press and its own style. Harry Caudill pointed out, for example, that the coming of the mass media drained the Appalachian mountaineer of his indigenous culture—the folk music and the folk arts—and left him subject to mass music emanating from the radio stations of Cincinnati and Wheeling and Lexington. At the same time, however, something else took place. While pockets of class culture (or, even more often, regional culture) were "being eroded in favor of mass opinion [and] the mass recreational product" the mass product redivided and particularized itself into specialized magazines, underground radio stations catering to particular cultural and ethnic groups, and a variety of cultural activities and identities which tried to set themselves against the main current. The noble American label of "middle class" had simply become too broad and too enervated to retain its power to hold or to create meaning, and its very universality (or, at least, the illusion of universality) created the necessity for additional identification, including, as it turned out, the revival of ethnicity, the counterculture, and the elitism that Nixon and Agnew have managed to attack with so much political profit. "Middle class" was a term of satisfaction and honor for people who had struggled to join or struggled to remain put, but, like the material goods of affluence, it produced declining satisfaction for those who could take it for granted. The middle class, in other words, derived its honorable state from a consciousness of scarcity on the one hand and class distinction on the other. It could have substantive meaning only when there was an "other."

Everything that Nixon and Agnew have done has helped restore that consciousness. If the domestic policies of the Administration constituted a caretaker period—a political effort to protect the position of the taxpayer and the ordinary functions of government—its "moral" posture involved the far more significant task of investing new meaning into middle-class status. Henceforth, Nixon seemed to be saying, we were going to make Middle Americanism more valuable and honorable by making admission to its ranks more difficult, would reimpose discipline on the country by reviving the consciousness of scarcity that had historically given the middle class its meaning. "We have passed through a very great spiritual crisis in this country," Nixon told Garrett D. Horner of the Washington *Star-News* in an election eve interview (for publication after the 1972 election). "During the 1960s the war in Vietnam was blamed for it totally. It was only part of the problem and in many cases it was only an excuse rather than a reason. But we saw a breakdown in frankly what I would call the leadership class of this country." What was required, he said, was an end to the era of permissiveness.

"I am not saying that critically because many lost faith in many of our institutions. For example, the enormous movement toward permissiveness which led to the escalation of crime, the escalation in drugs in this country, all of this came as a result of those of us who basically have a responsibility of leadership not recognizing that above everything else you must not weaken a people's character. . . .

"The average American is just like the child in the family. You give him some responsibility and he is going to amount to something. He is going to do something. If, on the other hand, you make him completely dependent and pamper him and cater to him too much, you are going to make him soft, spoiled and eventually a very weak individual."

Beyond the patronizing, much of it was standard Republican doctrine, the gospel of small government and self-reliance that would allow people "to do more for themselves." "This country has enough on its plate in the way of new spending programs, social programs, throwing dollars at problems," he said, and it wasn't about to do more. "There will be no solutions of problems that require a tax increase." What the government would do instead was relieve the tax burden of the middle class, which, he said, had reached "the breaking point," by cutting back on those programs, to shift the privileges of consumption from the welfare client (one of the pampered children?) to the middle-class taxpayer and force the slobs to earn their way in. Yet, finally, it was not growth or prosperity that concerned him, nor was he talking about the morality of corporate subsidies or deficit spending; it was the American character and the matter of permissiveness, and what he proposed for a country that produced more than enough was the reimposition of the discipline of scarcity. The surveys had all indicated that the overwhelming majority of welfare recipients were as committed to the work ethic as anyone else—that, indeed, it was their very commitment to it that made unemployment so demoralizing—yet there were no proposals for full-employment programs. The shortage of jobs was not mentioned, yet clearly awareness of such a shortage would reinforce the policy. (Six months earlier, John Connally, then still Secretary of the Treasury, had pointed out that the six percent unemployment rate was misleading since it included a disproportionate number of blacks and women, who, presumably, didn't really count.) If decent employment were available to everyone, how could you build character? The whole ethic, as Nixon described it, depended on exclusion. If everyone achieved, what was the meaning of achievement? If all prospered in a system of guaranteed incomes, what was the significance of prosperity? There was no game without losers.

The legacy of the Depression left the postwar middle class in a bind. The new affluence had clearly been shaped from the dreams and fears of depression scarcity; its beneficiaries understood that it depended as much on social management and corporate organization as it did on individual initiative and personal ambition. It didn't matter how hard you worked in the plant if the company went bankrupt in the collapse of free enterprise, or how frugal you were if the government didn't guarantee housing loans and mortgage money. Yet if it was government action which helped provide the corporate subsidies, the jobs, the housing, and the social security, what justification remained for the exclusion of the minority that hadn't made it? The whole basis for the New Frontier and the Great Society, the social programs that Nixon disparaged, was to have government do for the residual minorities what it had presumably already done for the majority. The more successful those programs were likely to be, however, the more threatening they would become, not only in generating competition for jobs and housing and in bidding up the price of services on which the affluent depended (maids, hospital workers, gardeners, flunkies), but also in undercutting what was left of the belief that status and affluence had been earned. The social programs, in other words, were tampering with what was left of the class structure in America and, in their flirtation with quotas for minorities, were attacking inequality of result and not merely inequality of "opportunity." In that context, what Nixon proposed was to restore to the middle class the illusions the Depression had destroyed. Everything he said in his speeches and his election eve interview could have been used by a Republican of the thirties to oppose New Deal programs or by a conservative of the fifties to scrap Social Security, federal housing guarantees and corporate subsidies. Nothing, I'm certain, was farther from Nixon's mind. All he was proposing was the maintenance of the class structure.

"The 'humbling' of inferiors," wrote Richard Sennett and Jonathan Cobb in a study of working-class attitudes, "is necessary to the maintenance of social order." They were ascribing the sentiment to an eighteenth-century salonist, Madame de Sévigné, but, they said, "humbling" was also the "most routine of modern occurrences," a continuance, perhaps, "of the morality of caste, with its wounding image of the dignity of man, in a society without hereditary rights, without an aristocracy of leisure or kings." They noted what commentators from Tocqueville on had described as the anxieties of people caught in a system that had no rigid social classes, where men were never certain of standing and where "opportunity" itself made lack of success all the more humiliating. "If all men start on some basis of equal potential ability, then the inequalities they experience in their lives are *not* arbitrary, they are the logical consequence of different personal drives to use those powers—in other words, social differences can now appear as questions of character, of moral resolve, will, and competence." In theory, at least, those social differences were once regarded in America as temporary; the future itself was the open space where all invidiousness would be mitigated and all the humbling wounds healed. The more doubtful the future, however, the more permanent and necessary the difference. "The wide prevalence of a high standard of living," David M. Potter had written in 1954, "means that the individual is no longer required to become mobile in order to share the benefits which the economy has to offer. In proportion as this condition develops, mobility ought to become optional rather than obligatory. Where mobility was once the price of welfare, we now have a larger measure of welfare than any previous society in history, and this may enable us to relax the tensions of mobility, keeping it as an instrument for the self-fulfillment of the individual but dispensing with it as a social imperative." Perhaps that was true, but wasn't this also what had produced the "permissiveness" in the first place, and wasn't this precisely what helped to create the new anxieties of affluence? If there were, as Potter said, "fewer underdeveloped opportunities demanding to be exploited"—if, indeed, exploitation of resources might now be positively harmful—what would replace the discipline? The maintenance of social order in America had always depended not merely on "equality of opportunity" but also on inequality of outcome. In the age of Nixon, however, neither reform nor a mitigating future was offered.

THREE:
A PROVINCE OF HISTORY

I

In the fall of 1968, thanks in part to George C. Wallace, the American worker reemerged from a state of sociological limbo that had lasted nearly a generation. The bigot who refused to integrate his union, his schools and his neighborhood, and who, in the guise of "hard hat," was soon to start beating up on hippies and peaceniks, took his place with the other honorable figures of American alienation. He became the forgotten American, the blue-collar worker, the Silent Majority. "They call my people the white lower-middle class these days," wrote Pete Hamill in 1969.

It is an ugly, ice-cold phrase, the result, I suppose, of the missionary zeal of those sociologists who still think you can place human beings on charts. It most certainly does not sound like a description of people on the edge of open, sustained and possibly violent revolt. And yet, that is the case. Sometimes these brutes are referred to as "the ethnics" of the "blue-collar types." But the bureaucratic phrase is white lower-middle class. Nobody calls it the working class anymore.

By the early seventies that re-discovery seemed like ancient history. The books, the articles, the foundation grants and the political rhetoric had poured forth in torrents, and the white working class had begun to replace blacks as the most cliché-ridden element in American society. In our embarrassment for the original oversight—we were (remember?) supposed to have been a nation divided between affluent whites and poor non-whites, between slums and suburbs—we served up the American worker in patronizing colors so charged with anger or apology that he remained almost as invisible as he was during the years when he was blissfully forgotten. For what the speculations amounted to, despite the red-white-and-blue of the national palaver about his condition, was a great demotion. The independent yeoman of Andrew Jackson's age, the common man of the New Deal, the onetime "bone and sinew of the country" reemerged as Archie Bunker, the boobish protagonist of *All in the Family*. The once and future hero of the great democracy had become its chump.

We all heard the same things, heard guys in bars talking about how they worked their ass off and couldn't make ends meet, about the mounting resentment of welfare and hippies and students—people who "fart around and don't do no work"—and about how black kids weren't the only ones who didn't have a place to play or pools to swim in. A whole landscape gradually reappeared, gray, limited, a little out of style, bowling alleys and union halls, row houses and bus stations at five in the morning, dog tracks and roller derbies and hamburger joints. Between Harlem and Scarsdale, between Roxbury and Wellesley, between slums and suburbs, we discovered all sorts of forgotten places that never appeared in the magazines or the TV programs, places where the trains didn't stop and the mind never tarried: Astoria, Bay Ridge, Cicero, Daly City, Flatbush, Glen Park and all the rest. We found people hustling, working two jobs or even three, driving cabs in the evening, moonlighting as painters or mechanics, maintaining phony Social Security numbers, taking their pay in cash or in merchandise or free meals. "I don't think anybody has a single job anymore," a Teamsters Union official told me back in 1969. "All the cops are moonlighting, and the teachers and the truck drivers; a million guys moonlighting, holding a little back, hiding part of it so they don't get nailed by the IRS or kicked out of the housing projects that they live in. Every one of them is cheating. They're underground people —*Untermenschen*. We have no systematic data on any of this, have no idea about the attitudes of the American worker, the white worker, we've been so busy studying the blacks. And yet, he's the source of most of the reaction in this country."

Nothing quite made sense, and still doesn't. We knew a little about the resentments, about the sense of betrayal. Here, we believed, was a man trying to do all the right things, working hard, paying taxes, trying to keep his kids out of trouble, keeping up his dues, and finding that the nice, fashionable people who had taught him all those things in the first place had now started to hold him in contempt, made fun of his kitsch and his morals, and portrayed him as a beery slob whose greatest pleasures came in the homosexual cameraderie of the Legion Post and the bowling league. Meanwhile, they allowed *their* kids to break the law, smoke pot, dodge the draft and burn down the college campus. The Catholic Church itself, the stability of centuries, was revising the liturgy, was abandoning the mystery of Latin ritual and familiar saints, going liberal and rational, and beginning to doubt the authority (of church and priest and flag) which it once so stringently taught. Here was a man, we had said, who had a right to be alienated. He was doing the work while the spades and the welfare chiselers were getting the sympathy. *"You better pay attention to the son of a bitch," that Teamsters official had said, "before he burns the country down."*

But even that didn't explain very much; it only described what we observed—the middle class looking at the lower middle class, the anthropologist studying the native. There wasn't even a good definition. Blue-collar workers? People earning between $5,000 and $12,000 a year? Hard hats? At one end they merged into the ranks of the poor, people qualifying for food stamps, low-cost housing and Medicare, and at the other they vanished into the middle class—suburbanites, two-car families, property-tax payers, holders of mortgages. Perhaps the best definition we now have is that proposed by a couple of sociologists who labeled the lower middle class as those who live above the officially defined poverty levels and below that class of people who take it for granted that their children will and must go to college. But even that wasn't fully satisfactory. For what we had discovered was a class of people (some eighty million of them) who had outlived the mythology and assumptions that legitimized (and sometimes glorified) their existence. The heroic age of American production had come to an end; our era of socialist realism was over. We no longer admired the smoking factory chimney, had even come to question the almighty GNP, and retained only a nostalgic recollection of the days when the greatest of civilized achievements—when salvation itself—was something called work and production.

"Let the detractors of America, the doubters of the American spirit take note," said Richard Nixon in his Labor Day address in 1971, "America's competitive spirit, the work ethic of this people is alive and well . . ." Perhaps, perhaps. But if Nixon was right, how could one explain the thousands of auto workers who that year had chosen early retirement, the industrial sabotage, or the high and still rising rate of absenteeism on Mondays and Fridays (at some auto assembly plants it was close to fifteen percent before and after weekends), and the corresponding admonition not to buy Detroit automobiles that came off the assembly line on days immediately preceding or following holidays? How could one explain the wildcat strikes or the parties that the steelworkers in Gary and Pittsburgh held that August night in 1971 when the big layoffs were announced? On the one hand people were moonlighting to make ends meet; on the other they were walking off the job, telling the foreman to fuck off, taking every moment of vacation to which they were entitled, and a good many to which they were not.

"As the name implies," Nixon had said, "the work ethic holds that labor is good in itself; that a man or woman at work not only makes a contribution to his fellow man but becomes a better person by virtue of the act of working. The work ethic is ingrained in the American character. That is why most of us consider it immoral to be lazy or slothful—even if a person is well off enough not to have to work, or deliberately avoids work by going on welfare." It was a nice piety for the occasion, and it may well have corresponded to the convictions of some of the people some of the time, but as a description of national attitudes it said more about how we imagined the past than about how we felt in the present. A few months before Nixon's speech, a black auto worker at Chrysler who had been harassed by his foreman went home, got a gun, returned to the plant and shot the foreman and two other men dead. His lawyers argued that the stress of the assembly line had been too much, had produced a state of temporary insanity, that the man had flipped under the pressure of work. The jury acquitted him. Every day they were lining up at the gates of a thousand plants, like kids waiting to be let out of school, waiting for the whistle to blow, waiting to get into those campers, waiting for the day when their pensions would be sufficient to provide. Work was something you suffered, not something you enjoyed.

II

It is unlikely that American workers ever regarded themselves as heroic figures. We had our Paul Bunyans, our Joe Maggyars, our Joe Hills, had our hard travelin' roads and our union songs; but for the most part the triumphant moments, when they existed at all, came on the picket line and not in the plant, and what was won on that picket line was often lost in the contract. There was little about the mill or the assembly line that reinforced heroic illusions; the work was too dirty, too dull, too demeaning. But there surely was a time when the surrounding culture took work for granted, even noble, when the common faith assumed some direct relationship between work and success, even if it often failed in practice, and when the effort to produce was something of a patriotic exercise: we had our Sandburgs, our Whitmans, our Jack Londons. In a Darwinian universe the fact that the system worked for some was justification enough. Although the work might not be heroic, the factory was often regarded as a heroic place, a symbol of energy, a magnificence of brute strength. "The great bulk of these metal workers," wrote Bernard Karsh in a study of an Auto Workers local (1941), "have a high regard for their company and their union." Another writer, revisiting the same union thirty years later, concluded that while there have been no recent polls about worker attitudes toward the union, "the widespread grumbling and heckling hardly suggest 'high regard.'" At one time, he said, the workers blamed their own lack of education and training for their condition; "nowhere among the young white or black workers in Local 6 is this attitude discernible today: blame is now put squarely on the company, and often on the union." You could hear that sort of thing in every region of the country. There were still men with pride in the company, but they became scarcer every year. While the nation was still being made, in a society with an industrial rather than a post-industrial mentality, blue-collar work was legitimate without further argument; there existed a presumption of legitimacy about the company simply because it produced things. But in a consumer society even twenty million industrial workers—or a hundred million—constituted a minority, a class of outsiders, survivors of a creed that became extinct.

To think about such things at all, to try to understand, was to travel through a set of geographical and historical situations that ran from the abandoned textile mills of Lowell and Lawrence and Haverill to union offices in Bethlehem and Gary to airplane assembly plants in Seattle and Santa Monica; from a mythology of working-class aspirations to a demonology of reaction and fear, from the certainty of work as salvation to the equally certain desire for immortality in the ticky-tacky sunshine developments of the Southwest. Clearly the old Charlie Chaplin *Modern Times* imagery of all work as assembly-line drudgery and of all workers as struggling drones being gobbled up by machines no longer made sense. In the so-called continuous-flow industries, for example—plastics, petroleum, chemicals—where the process was highly automated and the work force relatively small, there existed a high degree of worker autonomy. The employees were there to check dials, to keep things from going wrong, and were not tied to the predetermined speed of an assembly line or subject to the filth and hazards of steel industry coke ovens. In electronics the work was generally clean, and in most high-technology, low-labor industries the employer could afford to make the conditions of work and the expectations of advancement relatively liberal. At the same time, the assembly lines and the coke ovens and the common labor pool were still there, and so there now existed, as David M. Gordon suggested in a recent issue of *Dissent*, a sort of "dual market," based on subtle but mounting distinctions between "secondary workers," people in jobs with no expectation of advancement, high turnover, little security and no pay, and "primary workers" who enjoy some expectation of mobility (though often not much), job security, union protection and stable wages.

But if *Modern Times* and Karl Marx no longer described the conditions of work and of the worker's life, neither did the facile American generalizations which replaced them. The "fact" that the nation's work force was now primarily "white collar" or that America had become a "service economy" was misleading. Even if those "facts" were correct, they would tend to make blue-collar workers (28 million of them) into a sort of historical anomaly, saying in effect that because they now constituted a minority, they really weren't of much concern, didn't really exist at all—but the facts were not correct. Those white-collar workers included the girls in the typing pool, the office boys, the messengers, the bank tellers and the insurance company clerks; and those service workers included, among others, firemen, garbage collectors, waiters, janitors and some 400,000 women in dead-end $80-a-week telephone company jobs. The "fact" that American workers were better off than ever before was equally doubtful. Between 1965 and 1970 the real wages of the American worker, after taxes and inflation, probably declined; he was supposed to be affluent (to be poor in America is to admit to being black, to be working *and* poor was, until recently, supposed to be nearly impossible). But affluent he was not.

Here too one had to confront generation gaps, places where, as one worker told you, "the whole night shift is smoking dope, not in the john or the cafeteria, but right on the line—guys stoned from the minute they report for work until the minute they leave," mills where the young workers spent more time hanging around the labor shack goofing off than they did on the job, and plants where the executives were, on the one hand, "praying for a good depression that could shape these kids up," and, on the other, realizing that such a depression "will kill us too." A growing percentage of the work force was composed of younger men—in some plants the average age was under thirty—who, by general agreement "aren't going to take the shit their fathers took," and who would walk off the job with little provocation. At the same time you could also see the kids of despair, schools where the sons and daughters of steelworkers (despite the rhetoric of working-class mobility) expected nothing more than a replay of the lives of their parents; unions where the constant struggle was between the demands for security of the older, Depression-conditioned members and the pressure for more wages—cash, please, not benefits—from the young, entire regions where the young could not visualize any future at all, where the gray present continued indefinitely, world without end. "The value system of patriotism, personal responsibility, self help, hard work, deference of gratification," wrote William Simon and John Gagnon,

all still co-exist with values of political cynicism, distrust of strangers, male dominance, demands for obedience from children and moral and personal inflexibility. In the midst of a rapidly developing and changing society, it remains a province, not of geography but of history. Its sense of personal accomplishment and success, having shared in the affluence after the Second World War, it still sees as precarious and hard won. The rising expectations of what it perceives as its inferiors by virtue of race or latecoming to the society are threats to their self-earned and visible new gains. The split between economic and social liberalism is nowhere more apparent than in this group. In this kind of world, both social change and the young, who are the necessary harbingers of change, are the enemy. Traditional ways continue to be preserved by the drifting away of some individuals and families into different worlds and perhaps by a drift of the working class culture away from the evolving life styles of the larger society. The very intact families and social relationships that continue to operate successfully are one of the elements that make the working class so invulnerable to change. . . . Its very capacity to survive isolates a large section of the society within these provincial value systems.

The trail went back to the very fount of the Industrial Revolution in America, to depressed textile towns and empty mills which once represented everything that was certain in America. In Lowell and Lawrence and Enfield, the watchmen sat in front of vacant lofts or in little gatehouses like museum guards, talking, if they were old enough, of days when these brick piles were jammed with looms and shoe machines, when thousands of people worked two or three shifts. It was not good work, and often parents warned their children that anything, even clerking in a department store, was better than going into the mill. But there was also the memory of something else, a remembrance of strength, something monumental, a sense of place and integrity. "Things are better now," says the man who guards the nearly vacant remains of the Appleton Mills in Lowell. He sits at the edge of one of the old canals; a few feet away is the silt-jammed intake of a millrace where the water spilled through to drive the looms and spindles and carding machines that filled the place. "Things are better now," he says again, looking at the darkening road across the canal. "I've got a car and a TV. I didn't have that forty years ago, when I was a steam fitter at Merrimack. But . . ." He stops for a moment to watch the automatic street lights come on, and marvels at this new form of magic, this electric-eye automation that throws its blue shadows on this ancient, unused monument; then he allows that it would be nice to have this rambling structure alive again, recalls that five thousand people once used to work here, and that the little machine shops and electronics companies which are now scattered through the buildings employ no more than two hundred.

It is a pile of huge factories [wrote a nineteenth-century European visitor to Lowell], each five, six or seven stories high, and capped by a white belfry, which strongly contrasts with the red masonry of the building, and is distinctly projected on the dark hills in the horizon. By the side of these larger structures rise numerous little houses, painted white, with green blinds, very neat, very snug, very nicely carpeted. . . . Here are all the edifices of a flourishing town in the Old World, except the prisons, hospitals, and theaters; everywhere is heard the noise of hammers, of spindles, of bells calling the hands to their work, or dismissing them from their tasks . . . of the blowing of rocks to make a mill-race or to level a road; it is the peaceful hum of an industrious population. . . . Lowell, with its steeple-crowned factories, resembles a Spanish town with its convents; but with this difference, that in Lowell, instead of working *sacred hearts*, the nuns weave and spin cotton. Lowell is not amusing, but it is neat, decent, peaceable and sage.

Some of the buildings were still there, the old Boote Mill with its magnificent courtyard, its copper cupola, its bronze weathervane and its ornate gilded clock (stopped now, stopped these last thirty-five years since the last man able to repair it retired or died), the Lawrence Manufacturing Company, self-proclaimed "monument to the birth of the industrial might of America," now employing a handful of people, many of them long-haired freaks, to knit the fabric used to back vinyl upholstery, a sort of demoted adjunct to plastics, renting what space it could to a handful of little entrepreneurs; the old sumptuous homes, now funeral parlors, overlooking the Merrimack; the grandiose First Congregational Church with its heavy paneling and its velvet-covered pews, now the headquarters of the local Model Cities Program . . . One could find places like this all over the East and the Midwest, decaying factory lofts and engine shops, multi-story buildings along murky canals ("Lawrence Manufacturing Co.," said the sign in Lowell, "is not responsible for the condition of the canal"), buildings no longer suitable to a technology that demands space to spread out, victims of cheap Southern labor and foreign competitors, temples of exploitation, places where factory girls from the farms and small towns worked for a couple of dollars a day, and where the patronizing entrepreneurs maintained chaperoned dormitories to see to their morals (though rarely to their health); yet places that, until one or two generations ago, also represented the strength of ages, a future which—despite recessions and layoffs and poverty—was not subject to doubt, a set of relationships not open to question, Puritan monuments to the Protestant ethic. It was not something to be sentimental about, but it was essential to some comprehension of the current ambivalence about the meaning of work, and about the growing sense that even those once strong enough to exploit, to live in those sumptuous homes, to construct canals and mills (and, later, power plants and assembly lines), people who once sanctified places of work into steeple-capped temples, even such people were not strong enough.

The old textile towns of New England were now suffering their second chronic recession, or perhaps their third. "The whole area," said a poverty worker in Lowell, "has gone down the rotten Merrimack again." The Second World War saved them once, and then the burgeoning postwar electronics industry around Route 128 saved them again. Now the new laboratories and the assembly plants for electronic components were in trouble themselves; the machine tool industry, the core of Connecticut's industrial economy (and once, as someone said, "the heart of the arsenal of Democracy") was weak; the old typewriter factories, Royal and Underwood, had moved their operations to Europe, the portable radios were all being manufactured in Japan, the shoes in Italy, the watch and clock mechanisms in Switzerland, and the SST, which might have helped support the big jet-engine manufacturers around Hartford, was not being produced at all. Unemployment in Connecticut rose to something over ten percent in 1971; in New Britain it reached twelve percent, and in Bristol it exceeded twenty-four. (It was equally high, of course, in Seattle, and higher in places like Gary, where it approached forty percent.) But statistics themselves were subject to doubt; they did not include those who had given up looking for work, those who had only part-time work, the welfare cases, the sick or the "retired"; they did include those who collected unemployment insurance even though they had no intention of taking a job if one were offered, and they said nothing about unreported moonlighting or about families with two or more wage earners in which only one person was laid off. "Unemployment" sometimes seemed strangely out of line with other symptoms of recession—houses for sale, families doubling up, foreclosures and all the rest. "This has to be the funniest recession I ever saw," said a union official in New York. "We've become almost civilized about people who are temporarily out of work."

But it was not simply the fluctuating unemployment figures that made the future appear bleak. Unemployment exceeded five percent in every year between 1960 and 1965, the era of the Great Society and the New Frontier, when the country was supposed to be full of optimism and no one had made it into a national crisis. In part, the explanation lay in a number of changes that the Bureau of Labor Statistics had made in its procedures. Categories of people who were counted among the unemployed in the early sixties were now regarded as employed or excluded from the count. Administration pressure on the BLS tended to produce figures that substantially underestimated the problem. Nonetheless, emphasis on the unemployment statistics for the early seventies—six percent, give or take a fraction—suggested something beyond short-range unemployment crises, a way of explaining something that we have just started to discover. They seemed to me to concretize a more subtle sense of decline, to give statistical substance to the line of junk cars outside the surplus-food distribution centers (where the men, too proud to enter, sent the wife and kids inside to pick up the month's supply of powdered milk and flour, the beans and butter) and reinforced the physical presence of the accumulating junk around the houses in the inner developments; and the old men, forced into an early "retirement"—often without pensions—who stood on the streets of small industrial cities, places where the old plant or the mill, now closed, gave life its only focus. What you came away with in these towns was a sense (mine surely, but how could it help also being theirs?) of historic stultification, of fixed limits, a European sense of class despair. "Maybe," said Ella Grasso, a Congresswoman from central Connecticut, "we're becoming Appalachia East. All this ingenuity, this skill, this talent that created industry in Connecticut is gone." Little companies that had started in some tinkerer's barn and later grew great had now become part of giant conglomerates and were being closed by corporate officers who knew nothing about the communities which depended on them, were judged in terms of tax losses, corporate profit and distant abstractions which no one understood. It was like living at the foot of a volcano subject to the whim of capricious gods.

Appalachia East. Increasingly the industrial cities of the Northeast had become invisible places inhabited by invisible people, places that the rest of the world flew over or drove around: Thompsonville and New Britain, Lowell and Manchester, Easthampton and Holyoke, Chicopee and Altoona, Easton and Bethlehem (not to mention Gary or Newark or Oakland), places where people might be angry or militant, but where they were—contrary to what writers like Hamill had said—equally likely to be despondent, to have been so conditioned by two generations of recession and uncertainty as to have no fight left. (What was the relation, you wondered, between corporate efficiency and the thing we liked to call "the problem of the aged," between welfare and automation, between "youth crime" or drugs and industrial anonymity?) Ella Grasso spoke about the eternal note of optimism, the pride of the older workers in their independence. "They keep thinking," she said to me, "that tomorrow will be better because, in their experience, tomorrow was better." But she also conceded that it was not true among the young and might not always be true about the old. "We're creating a new class of unemployables, people for whom there can't be a job, and we keep pretending that the problem will go away in two years." There was constant talk about opening up more service jobs; it was the all-purpose answer—this was going to be a service economy, but no one could make the connection between a new job for a $40-a-week carhop and an unemployed machinist who had been earning $4.50 an hour. People kept speaking about jobs in education, the arts and the so-called "health areas," but there were already too many teachers, and without some major economic reforms there would be no money for health. In Connecticut and Long Island there was brave talk about converting the aircraft industry to surface transportation. United Aircraft, it was said, already had plans to develop high-speed trains for mass transit, was waiting only for the government contracts; but no one was making any predictions about when it would happen, nor was there much mention of the fact that the technology already existed, that in this, as in many other things, the Japanese—or the Germans or the Italians—were ahead of us. Occasionally the workers knew, even if the economists weren't talking. In industry after industry—textiles, shoes, electronics, clock works, lenses, cameras—one could hear old hands recall their sense of shock when they first inspected the newer products of their foreign competitors. The stuff was not junk anymore, was cheap *and* good. And so there was a new fear. America had always been first, might still be first in many areas, but even here the certainty was gone. Ella Grasso, a liberal Democrat, voted for the federal $275-million subsidy to the mismanaged, inefficient Lockheed Corporation because scores of small machine shops in Connecticut depended on Lockheed subcontracts. "I can't watch these people get laid off," she said. Government subsidies to private corporations were nothing new, it had been done for generations, but the chronic uncertainty was. This was not assistance to a struggling infant, not an investment in the future, but (on Ella Grasso's part) a way of temporarily rescuing people with no other expectations. This is what had happened to the independence and ingenuity of American enterprise. The man who was supposed to be the most skilled, the most productive, the most resourceful, was beginning to confront a world where even the things at which he was supposed to be best were subject to question. More and more he was being beaten at his own game. At least in the realm of production time had always been on the worker's side. Now even that was no longer certain. "All this talk about a transition in the economy," said a labor official in Hartford. "All that talk is bullshit."

III

Doubt had become endemic. Doubt not only in personal possibilities, but in the system that was to carry one along. To hold a job in the expectation of growth and mobility is one thing; to maintain the same job for the purpose of survival is something else. In the mid-sixties Robert C. Wood, then Undersecretary of Housing and Urban Development, had spoken of the American worker as "a white employed male . . . earning between $5,000 and $10,000. He works regularly, steadily, dependably, wearing a blue collar or white collar. Yet the frontiers of his career expectations have been fixed ever since he reached the age of thirty-five, when he found that he had too many obligations, too much family, and too few skills to match opportunities with aspirations." Perhaps it had always been this way, perhaps things always closed down too quickly; yet, surely there had been a time when, even after personal mobility and achievement were no longer possible, there still existed the possibility of fellow-traveling, of getting a piece of the growing pie, of sharing not only in the common prosperity of the future but also in the reflected glory of America the triumphant. Now neither was certain: Increasingly (especially among young workers) the historic version of the future made little sense. There were still jobs of high morale: the iron workers and the bridge builders in high steel who could generate among themselves the intense camaraderie of a football team or a bomber crew; men who shared risks and who depended on each other, physically and psychologically, to make those risks bearable; truck drivers or cabbies for whom the job became a mental as well as a physical engagement, who prided themselves on their savvy—the way you got around load and hour limits of the Interstate Commerce Commission or around the cops, the places where you could make a quick buck and the places to avoid, the hustles and the traps; or the car salesmen who could play prospects the way E. Power Biggs plays the organ, knowing which stops to pull at what moment, playing it for the sheer contest and not just for the money. Here too one could get caught by excessive generalization: not all blue-collar jobs were dreary, not all white-collar jobs (God knows) were glamorous.

And yet the enclaves of excitement, the glamour jobs, may simply have highlighted those areas where little was possible. For a steelworker in Gary or Pittsburgh or Bethlehem or an assembly-line worker in Detroit or Flint, the choice was often between a dead-end job and no job at all. In Lordstown, Ohio, the young workers at the Chevrolet assembly plant were demanding a major voice in determining how the plant was run, resisting speedups on the line, first with sabotage and then with a strike, and talking openly about the limited possibilities of the job. In Gary a man who had spent six years as an officer in a local of the Steelworkers Union and then returned to his old job in the mill spoke about the place as a prison: "I'd forgotten what it was like—the darkness, the filth. The older guys look like they're wearing chains, and the young guys, the guys who aren't trapped by obligations, are ready to blow their stack. Of course there's sabotage. There are guys who heave firecrackers at the foreman, or take the bolts off his car, or louse up some piece of machinery. This equipment is getting more and more sophisticated, it's like this watch, and that means it's easier to stop. A lot of them never put in their forty hours—so they get to work at nine or nine-thirty; they don't give a shit." And in Richmond, California, a young woman who had been organizing workers in the oil refineries talked continuously about worker alienation. How many, you asked, still believed in the textbook version of what she calls the system? And she answered, "None."

There was no single set of responses, no consistency in how people talked about their lives; too much depended on the man, on his age and background, and on the place where he lives and works. Here too we lacked a language, for we now seem to have in this country a permanent, quasi-proletarian class without a proletarian ideology. Certainly there was still talk about a better life for the kids, some lip service to mobility, but the talk was hesitant and forced, like an incantation. "The older people who are here now," said Jim Balanoff, a steelworker in Gary, "came at a fortunate time, around the time of the war, when things were booming, when everything was good. You can't do that anymore. These mills aren't growing, they're letting people off. Twelve thousand were laid off by U.S. Steel in the last year, and a lot of those people will never go back. Everywhere you go, these guys will tell you that the country's in trouble, that it's all gone. At the same time, they don't want to hear the bad news. What they want is baseball in the morning, football in the afternoon and basketball at night. If they had to think about all those big issues they'd go crazy." People celebrated the lay-offs (with full benefit; in the steel industry a man figured he did as well while he was laid off as when he was working a four-day week). But vaguely, inarticulately, they also feared the end. What if the mills automated, as surely they must, and the jobs never came back? "A man is a damn fool to go into the mines," said a coal worker to a newspaper reporter in Virginia. "Sure, I'm a fool, but I don't expect my son to be. Breathe that coal dust and then hear Tony Boyle (the then president of the United Mine Workers) up in Washington say it ain't gonna hurt you. No, buddy, a miner's nothing but a slave." It was the same in steel, on the automobile assembly lines, in textiles. You hated the job, but you also feared that it would disappear and nothing would replace it, felt the old guilt and anxiety when the layoffs went into their eighth week, or their tenth, hung around the bars and talked about another hunting trip or a day at the races or about how you cleaned your wife's rug; hoped for a new defense contract or a general increase in government spending (which inevitably means defense), but understood also that all defense work was unstable, that the flag itself was vulnerable. Again and again you asked what would happen when the unemployment benefits ran out, and again the answers came in shrugs or in words like "relief." In steel towns like Gary, the mills along the lakefront were a gigantic, red-brown-and-yellow-smoke-belching presence, monsters that made pronouncements—about jobs and taxes and sales—subject to no review. If the pollution regulations got too tough, they would have to move; if their taxes were raised (they were assessed for about one third of what their plants were worth), they would have to close down. Their books were not subject to inspection by municipal officials, their sales expectations were clouded in corporate newspeak, their intentions mysterious. They moved according to their own impulses and announced their decisions like Olympian gods. (And beyond them there were still other forces: Japanese steel, "the economy" and the never-defined calculus of profit and loss). "The unions," said an assistant to Richard Hatcher, the mayor of Gary, "should have been blowing their stack about the new federal investment credits. They're going to automate like crazy out here, and the union guys tell you—privately, of course—that at places like Inland Steel in Hammond one third of the jobs will be eliminated in three years." Somewhere, some-how, according to the rumors, a deal was made. The industry signed a new contract in the summer of 1971, a good contract, and signed it without a real fight in return for a union promise not to scream about automation and layoffs. The unions, they said, were in cahoots with the Lake County political machine, which was in cahoots with the mills. Attack one, they said, and you are suddenly hit on the blind side by one of the others. But the great presence remained the mill itself. No ordinary person could comprehend it; it was too huge, too complex, too much a mystery. It could overwhelm the confidence of any man. Start a rumor that it might close, that smaller, modern mills were more efficient, and all the fixed points of existence began to tremble.

The issue here was not the accuracy of the rumors or the im-pressions, but the impressions themselves. The union, the com-pany, the political system were all stacked against you, and so the community and the company became a sort of single entity. (It was not the same everywhere, of course, but there was enough of it in the steel and coal towns and in other one-indus-try communities to make it significant.) In Gary they said that there was no point in going to union meetings, because every-thing had already been decided in advance; things were arranged and gerrymandered in such a way that the blue-sky locals, locals with a small membership, could dominate the whole organiza-tion. (As in other areas, the young and the black were under-represented. In the plant they got the dirtier jobs; in the unions the older white men held most of the offices.) "At the union meetings in the thirties," said a man in Gary, "there was all sorts of excitement; people thought they were going somewhere, and there were causes all over the place, not just our own: Spain, the South, the New Deal. Now at the union meetings they rule everything out of order." And so the resentment, overwhelmed by the Great Presence, was directed against individual foremen, against blacks or welfare recipients, against the young or against oneself. There were all sorts of flaws in the caricature of Archie

Bunker—the missing tolerance and sense of decency, the moments of insight, the timeless sense of bearing up, the intuition, I suppose, of tragedy; but the omission that struck me as most significant was the system itself. Outside the door of that row house in Flatbush or Astoria was the unthinkable, the unmanageable—the plant, the economic structure, the political system, overwhelming in size and complexity—elements for which there were hardly any symbols, let alone a language, for which there were only surrogates and scapegoats, a system in which a man no longer really believed, but which he feared too much to fight. "It might be good for the country," said a community organizer in Lake County, "if things really got tough. As long as the guy gets his check, he's happy—no, not happy, but not angry enough to overcome his apathy and his fear." The one imponderable was the potential for militancy among the young, but, with a few exceptions, that potential had not yet been tested.

The element that was common to all the inconsistencies—the flirtations with militancy on the one hand, the apathy on the other, the hatred of the job and the fear of losing it—was what struck me as a pervasive class inability to perceive much of a future within the existing system; even when people were pressed, they were reluctant to think about it. Of course, there was the lip service of last resort. The national compulsion to call oneself affluent leaves very few people untouched. Not to be affluent was to be a failure, was not to be American at all. Not to say something about your expectation of making it was to declare yourself less than a man. And yet there was a strange dourness, a discontinuity with what most of us would call conventional middle-class aspiration. "The predominant value climate with reference to achievement and mobility in the working class," wrote Simon and Gagnon in a study conducted for the National Institute of Mental Health, "is one that consoles and justifies the non-mobile. By forswearing the largely theoretical chance that they might have toward the easy way to success, the normal response of this population is the earning of possession through hard work. Since much of the work is intrinsically empty, it is the daily round of going and coming and spending time in the workplace and the possessions that result from the paycheck that are the rewards." Simon, who is now conducting a major study of working-class youth at the Institute for Juvenile Research in Chicago, spoke about a "culture of resignation" which had always regarded upward mobility as faintly immoral and which took for its heroes those people who stayed put. (Capturing respect in the larger America, wrote Richard Sennett and Jonathan Cobb in a profile of a blue-collar worker turned bank clerk, "means to Frank getting into an educated position; but capturing that respect means that he no longer respects himself. . . . He believes people of a higher class have a power to judge him because they seem internally more developed human beings; and he is afraid, because they are better armed, that they will not respect him. . . . He has felt compelled to put himself up on their level in order to earn respect. All of this, in turn . . . is set against a revulsion against the work of educated people in the bank, and a feeling that manual labor has more dignity.") "For a lot of them," said Simon, "the idea of prosperity is absolutely unnerving," and the idea of moving up into a higher class was yielding to temptation. "These people never expected much." Which is to say that the last great vestige of Puritanism in America, the sense that life was tough and bleak, the resentment of what Spiro Agnew called permissiveness, and the suspicion of everything that smacked of self-indulgence, from *Playboy* to the hippie, was not necessarily associated with a belief in mobility, but with its difficulties. It was the consolation for accommodation. The American working class, in Simon's terms, had become an "urban peasantry."

All of that may be too pessimistic. There had clearly been a time in the thirties when there existed, despite unemployment and depression, some sense of class solidarity, a sense of possibility in reform; and there clearly was a time in the fifties and sixties when most of the measurable conditions of life seemed to be visibly improving, and when the possibilities of middle-class life—the possessions, the vacations, the college education for the kids—appeared within the reach of most whites. At the very moment that the postwar generation of college students was beginning to read Marx and C. Wright Mills, the affluence of the fifties seemed to refute them. (It was the possibility itself that made us declare ourselves an affluent society. We noted that some children of janitors and stevedores were going to college; we forgot that most did not.) And yet, at least for the present, Simon's assessment spoke to that lack of expectations, to the resignation and the resentment; it also raised questions about the larger American ambivalence about the thing called the working class: Did we admire the lower middle class for what it was or for what it might be? Did we want to celebrate its qualities, as Nixon did, to reinforce, as Simon said, "the self-image of the American working class, i.e., that it represents those values and life style commitments that are essentially valid and fundamental to the preservation of the American way of life," or did we want to transform it, to get people out of their traps, to organize them, to give them the language and political techniques necessary to make organized claims on the rest of the society?

IV

For the ultimate hope, we always had the young. When all else fails, said the conventional wisdom, turn to children. They would all do better than their fathers, would go to college (or to junior college, or to a trade school), would move out of the inner cities, away from Mechanic Street and Railroad Avenue, and into the suburbs, would make more money, work in pleasant surroundings and lead more comfortable lives. The kids were the future.

Often enough it had been true. Travel through the small towns of the Midwest and the South, or through the white ghettoes of the major cities, and they would tell you, over and over, about the daughter who was teaching in Oregon, the son who became a chemist in California. The bright, the ambitious, the hopeful were leaving, following the ancient pattern that associated economic with geographical mobility; following the familiar tilt to the west, to the suburbs, to the shining tomorrow. The American dream was still coming true. What they did not speak about in the small towns or the larger cities were those who did not leave, who didn't move, economically or geographically—people who were not supposed to exist at all, were not even supposed to believe in their own existence. We had all seen them: the kids on the corner with their ducktail haircuts, the canvas-bag-toters, lonely and lost, lining up at the induction centers at eight in the morning or being led through airports and bus stations on the way to basic; kids in knocked-down junk cars with sagging springs, shuttling between Hamburger Heaven and the Burger Chef, a whole generation of certified losers, kids who would not become affluent, would not go to college, would do no more than relive the lives of their parents. (The majority of those who did go to college were children of the middle class. The majority of the children of blue-collar workers did not; and of those who did, more than half dropped out by the end of the first year. There was, moreover, no way of calculating the amount of fraud that went on within the junior colleges—courses in "secretarial science" or "pre-nursing" which, at best, constituted nothing more ambitious than remediation for the failures of the high school.) Coming out of school in the afternoon, the boys already resembled their fathers when the shifts changed—rows of dark, tufted mail-order-house jackets, rows of winter hats with the earflaps laced above the head, crossing the road from the plant to the parking lot, from the high school to the waiting buses and the bare-wheeled Chevies. The girls, not yet stretched by pregnancy, often in short skirts and bright sweaters, would catch up with their mothers, would be married at eighteen or twenty, would often be engaged before the tedium of school was at an end. In a sense they did not exist for themselves, but rather to define and give meaning to the position of others, academic and social losers whose prime function was to reinforce and substantiate the position of the winners. What was an A without an F? What was the point of being in the top of the class or going to Harvard if there wasn't someone at the bottom?

They learned early, learned that every person had his place, and that there were mysteries of style, background and language which they would never understand, that, indeed, the very attempt to learn, and therefore to move a little higher, could be corrupting and dangerous. What their parents demanded (of the schools, and of them) was obedience and conformity, adherence, as the sociologists would say, to class norms. Again and again the girls were enjoined to be "little ladies"; again and again the boys were impressed with the unmanliness of excessive sophistication. A command of language itself could become a demonic threat. Let the kids from the fancy side of town work their heads off, let them corrupt themselves with ambition and high living, let them grub for grades and go off to distant institutions of immorality; for us the proper life is the humble life, a life free from temptation, a life that responds to complexity in a set of moralistic terms that, lacking any other language, don't admit shades of gray, deny irony and shun ambivalence. "I know this is a dreary place," a high-school senior told me in Bethlehem, "but I like dreary places." By the time they come to high school, the patterns were already established; they may, indeed, already have been established before the kids started school at all.

The fact that defeat was not nearly universal, that many kids did make it, did nothing to mitigate the impact; in many ways it sharpened it, made it more personal and ugly. Since the schools legitimized success and failure and gave them the sanction of "objectivity," they taught even the losers to accept the idea that their status was justified: it was not the school that failed, it was the individual, and it thus trained him to accept the low esteem in which the system held him. He didn't work hard enough, or he failed English, or he couldn't handle mathematics. At the same time, the school also extended its small rewards to its underclass, patted them on the back for being good boys and girls, for not causing trouble, and for accepting the system's judgment. It is hard to find schools which do not arrogate to themselves some sort of distinction: the state championship marching band, league leadership in football or track, a squad of belles who twirl, hop, bounce or step better than any other in the country. A girl makes her way from pom-pom girl to cheerleader or majorette, a boy comes from the obscurity of an ethnic neighborhood to be chosen all-state tackle. There is vitality and engagement and, for the moment, the welding of new common-interest groups, new friendships, new forms of integration. It is the only community that adolescents have, and even the dropouts often sneak back to see their friends. And yet, most of these things come to a swift and brutal end: a note in the yearbook, some clippings, a temporary sense of value and distinction convertible into an early marriage, a secretarial job, an occasional scholarship, or into permanent fat. The most prestigious activities of high school have no lasting value. Next year, or the year after that, there will be no band, no football, no pep club. Too often, life reaches its highest point at seventeen.

You kept looking for those aspirations, that sense of the future, and you discovered that they hardly existed at all. The heart of ambition was to get away from home, to have a place apart. The automobile thus became not only a vehicle but a place to be, a fortress against the impositions and demands of adults; a place to drink, to smoke and to neck. We had heard all this many times before, had heard about the hot rods and the drag races, sometimes in amusement, sometimes in indignation, but we hadn't come close to understanding how much it meant.

The car, quite simply, was everything. It was the only place where adult experimentation was tolerated: experiments with sex, with self-realization, with independence, with courage, with change, with death. The car shuttled within the city limits—the drive-in, the pizza parlor, the game—but rarely beyond, rarely even to the next town. People didn't grow up with cars, they grew up *in* them.

For many kids there was no place to go, not now, not ever. "The essence of higher class position," wrote Melvin L. Kohn in a book called *Class and Conformity*,

is the expectation that one's decisions and actions can be consequential; the essence of lower class position is the belief that one is at the mercy of forces and people beyond one's control, often beyond one's understanding. . . . Conformity—following the dictates of authority, focusing on external consequences to the exclusion of internal processes, being intolerant of nonconformity and dissent, being distrustful of others, having moral standards that strongly emphasize obedience to the letter of the law—this is the inevitable result of conditions of life that allow little freedom of action, little reason to feel in control of fate.

All of that might be obvious, but when it was reinforced by institutions, by schools and political structures, and by an ideological vacuum that had little place for a working class, it could suggest—at least to a middle-class mind—attributes of unspeakable horror. In such a world the school served as a sort of waiting room where people sometimes arrived or from which they sometimes left, but where the majority always remains. From class to class, from home to school and back, from the job to the parking lot to the home, there was a sort of passing through. What was learned was to defer—to time, to authority, to events. One kept asking, "What do they want, what do they do, what do they dream about?" And the answer was almost always institutional, as if the questions no longer applied: "They go to school, they have jobs—in the diner, at the dime store, over at the filling station—and they ride and repair their cars." Ask the kids themselves about major issues, the economy or the war or the future itself, and they would tell you (in the tones of a text they wished they could remember with more confidence—a lesson badly learned and now to be regurgitated on demand) that the war was a mistake, or that we had to resist the Communists, or how there should be better jobs. You heard about someone's cousin or brother over in "Nam" who talked about how those crazy gooks even had kids throwing grenades at our convoys, or how soldiers were just being asked to sit around waiting to get killed, but the agony of the reply, the painful speech, made it hard to press too many questions. The hard line, or any line about the war or jobs or whatever, played back no better than a Shakespearean sonnet or a Euclidean theorem never worth learning. You did what you were told. Propaganda and schooling were the same thing. You felt things in your gut, and the unexpressed anger might someday explode, but more often than not the feelings were still encapsulated by a sense of incomprehension and impotence, by a detachment from time, and by a life that seemed strangely severed from the abstractions of the larger world.

No place to go. For the girls there were connections to the national passion for consumption: the sociologists had pointed out that the girls could respond to the consumer roles depicted by the media; they were in training to become "homemakers" and were therefore, however tenuously, in touch with current styles and trends. For the boys, the business of growing up tended to be discontinuous with what would come after school was over. There was no training for family life or heterosocial relationships, few ways to learn how not to go crazy (with guilt or boredom) if you had to stay around the house—go to the parties and the men talked to the men, the women to the women—and no preparation for dealing with (or even talking about) the complexities of the larger world around. In school you learned that the book is an instrument of torture, not of liberation, and that words are means of obfuscation and deceit, ways of putting people down. The joy came from the honesty of *things*: an engine works or doesn't work, a joint holds or it doesn't. There was no evasion there, no prevarication; but increasingly the world demanded language, mathematics, abstractions, and increasingly it rejected those who could manipulate only things.

No place to go. The old landmarks disappeared, the certainties of old ethnic neighborhoods, family relationships, churches, social clubs became more tenuous, and few sources of strength replaced them. Work was no longer heroic, perhaps it never had been. Although the stories of the past remained—remember the Great Strike, the shootings, the marches—there remained few socially acceptable ways to establish one's manhood. At one time a boy could join the Army, could go to war, and thus prove something, to himself, to his friends, to his father, but Vietnam and its doubts had diminished even that possibility, had turned even that corollary of socialist realism into a terrible joke. Listen carefully to the response to the My Lai revelations, to the unspeakable confusion, the denials, the anger, and what you heard were people who went to war (or allowed their sons to go) in the belief that this was the moment of connection, the flash of distinction, the path to something, and who were now being told that the connection was to the brutal, the ugly and the inhuman. Make the fraud large and personal enough, and none of us is able to confront it.

Of course there were exceptions, there were triumphs and moments of high success. There was the steelworker who told Studs Terkel that "when you're living on green apples, you want to give your kid red ones whenever you can. Whatever you got, you want to make it better. Otherwise we'd be back in the cave . . . Every time I see a young guy walk up with a shirt and tie and dressed up real sharp, I'm lookin' at my kid . . ." There were all the classic stories of janitors and dishwashers saving so that they could send their children to college or to medical school, and there were the regular moments of joy and celebration in everyday life: the weekend at the lake, the

bowling league, the hunting, the camper, the workingman's resort. A whole landscape, nearly as invisible as the factory towns
themselves, where people with limited means went to Have Fun:
acres of tar-paper beach bungalows at Revere and Rockaway,
weekend package plans (sometimes called cabby specials) at
hotels in the Poconos or the Catskills, Clint Eastwood at the Pal-
ace, MacDonald's on Friday night, Old Orchard Beach on Sunday, the Legion Bar on Tuesday, and the trotters and the dogs
any day—Connaught Park, Roosevelt, Yonkers, Rockingham
and forty others where men came not for sport and beauty, not
to watch horses, but to read numbers on charts and electronic
boards, to study and dope. If you won you had figured something, had in a small way controlled your world, had surmounted
your impotence. If you lost, bad luck, shit, "I'll break his goddam head." Baseball was not the national pastime (or football
either); racing was. For every person who went to a big-league
ball game, there were four who went to the track and probably
four more who went to the candy store or the barbershop to
make their bets. (Total track attendance in 1965: sixty-two
million, plus another ten million who went to the dogs.) Most of
all, there was the family, the people one clung to or fought with
or loved or ignored in the harsh blue light of the television set,
but who, after everything else went crazy, remained a norm
against the world outside.

What the middle class took for granted the workingman and
his kids had learned to regard as special: dinner at a restaurant
downtown, two weeks at the beach, a cabin by the lake. Even
these things had a tendency to turn sour under the special stress
of a marginal budget: the place was too crowded, the kids
screamed too much, sitters were for the affluent, the rides got too
expensive, the lines too long. Forty years ago George Orwell
wrote about the special expenses incurred only by the poor: a
man on the street on a cold day must buy himself a cup of coffee
he doesn't want in order to get inside to warm his hands and feet.
What few people have considered is the existence of a whole

economy structured specifically to exploit people too poor to get a better buy: credit, housing, clothes, furniture, automobiles, toys, entertainment. People in the black ghettoes complain incessantly that the prices in Harlem or Hough are higher, the cuts and quality poorer, than they are in middle-class neighborhoods. But beyond that there are simply those items that the affluent don't have to buy at all or can buy for less: household loans and finance charges of sixteen or eighteen or twenty percent per year, clothes that wear out after three trips to the laundromat (and, indeed, the charge at the laundromat itself), junk cars and junk furniture and junk toys. No one, as Ralph Nader reminded us, has calculated the inflationary effects of goods that become shoddier and wear out faster every year; any price freeze is especially likely to encourage shortcuts in production. Nor has anyone calculated the trade-off between the liabilities of Japanese competition in the job sector and the advantages of cheap foreign goods at the discount store. The same man who screams about foreign shoes and textiles sends his wife to Bradley's or Zayre's to buy the children clothes made in Hong Kong or Formosa. In such an economy, descriptions of life sometimes become almost Chaplinesque. Life was humble but not simple; the terrors of insolent bureaucrats and contemptuous officials produced a demonology that lost little of its horror for being partly misunderstood; a man gets a raise which puts him into a slightly higher bracket which causes the Housing Authority to raise the rent by an amount roughly twice what the original raise in pay is worth; you want to get a sink fixed but don't want to offend the manager; want to complain to someone about the teen-agers who run around breaking windows and harassing women, but get no response from either the management or the police. "You're afraid to complain, because if they don't get you during the day they'll get you at night." Automobiles, windows, children, all become hostages to the vague terrors of everyday life; everything is vulnerable. Liabilities that began long ago cannot possibly be liquidated. "You try to save for something better; maybe someday we can get out of here, and then something always comes along that knocks you right back. It's like being at the bottom of a well waiting for a guy to throw you a rope."

Dreams were to be denied. You learned to accommodate, to dilute, to dream small. *"Imagine," says a school counselor to a group of lower-track high school students, "that you could become an animal, any animal. What animal would you choose?" The secret heart would choose freedom: eagles soaring over mountains, mustangs roaming the plain, greyhounds loping through fields. Freedom.* But freedom itself was demonic, a temptation to be repressed in oneself and to be put down in others. It, too, offended the puritanical sensibilities: get the hippies, the fags, the freaks. What remained was the acceptable residue: you dreamed about the low accretion of small comforts—another room on the house, a converted basement, a better car or a better camper, things that were thinkable, the burdensome possessions of a freedom that often restricts nearly as much as it liberates. The car and the camper were what remained of the eagle and the mustang. If you were not worth very much, you had no right to make excessive demands, and so you learned to celebrate small things, to celebrate repeating cycles—weddings, anniversaries, confirmations—each of them the end or the beginning of something that repeated other ends and other beginnings. Each started another cycle, perhaps a little better, perhaps not. The middle-class people celebrated at least the illusion of movement, departures to other worlds and other realms. Here you celebrated another round of something similar to the rounds that preceded it. Thank the Lord that the kids made it, that they didn't get into bad trouble, that they finished school, that they have a job, an acceptable husband or a competent woman, and the prospects for a stable life.

V

By now we have heard no end of speculation about what will become of the working class (or the lower middle class, or the forgotten American), about the consequences of its alienation, and about its political and social volatility. *You better pay attention to the son of a bitch before he burns the country down.* We know that a disproportionate share of Wallace's labor support came from young workers, people for whom the old liberalism of Hubert Humphrey held no charm (for whom, indeed, all establishment politics was unappealing and irrelevant), and from lower-income people generally. Every presidential candidate in 1972 learned part of that lesson: Ivy League patricians began to call themselves populists, "tax reform" became a political staple, and busing—whatever it means (and obviously it means a great deal more than the pundits appreciate)—became the universal issue. In the Florida primary things came to such a pass that John V. Lindsay was moved to suggest that he, and not Wallace, was the true man of the people. (The fact that Lindsay could run against Wallace for anything, anywhere, and that neither of them was associated with the Democratic Party in 1968 indicated just how bizarre American politics had become, and how far we had moved from the old mainstream.) Wallace was therefore correct in claiming, as he did through the campaign, that the "issues" he had raised in 1968 were helping to shape the political discourse of 1972.

Yet it was still a swindle. Because Wallace had discovered a constituency that conventional rhetoric had neglected in the two decades after World War II, it was assumed that he had his finger on some secret nerve, that he understood something about America that others failed to perceive. The fact that he received something like thirteen percent of the vote in 1968, and that, but for a heavy anti-Wallace campaign by the unions, he might

154

have received more, clearly demonstrated that he appealed to more than simple racism. But what that appeal was, how it related to the general frustration of the people who appeared at his rallies, never became clear. Yes, they were "protecting" their neighborhoods, were resisting elitist injunctions from the likes of Lindsay that they should integrate their schools while the nice people on Park Avenue could send their kids to Exeter and Groton; yes, they were complaining about welfare and hippies and campus disorder, but how much did all of that explain? Was busing itself not merely a code word for racism, but also a surrogate for a cluster of inexpressible and, at least for the time being, politically covert dislocations that not even Wallace really understood? Who was conning whom? After the 1968 election some of us were saying that if Wallace had been smarter, if he had worked the populist issue harder (had run, in effect, against banks, corporations and the rich in general), he would have done considerably better. But the fact was that he didn't, and that when he had the chance, in 1972, to try again, he still didn't do it. Neither his record as governor of Alabama, which has one of the most regressive tax structures and one of the most backward social-welfare programs in America, nor his presidential campaign rhetoric belied the suggestion that he was as much of a Southern redeemer as he was a populist; with the spread of the race issue into a national rather than a regional concern, people in Flint and Pontiac and San Francisco were beginning to behave remarkably like those in Jackson, Montgomery and Memphis. That, of course, was also part of Wallace's argument: wait a few years (he might have said in 1963), and you folks in Michigan will be standing in the schoolhouse door yourselves.

And they did. All through the last months of 1971 and into the spring of 1972 we saw those pinch-faced women haranguing Congressmen and television commentators in the great crusade against busing, saw the whole soggy debate about neighborhood schools being chewed over again. Usually they called it "forced busing," which suggested rape (a suggestion not belied by the tone of near-hysteria in which it was proposed). There was no consideration of the parallel issue of forced schooling and forced attendance, or of the sorts of forced thinking which they often produced. (How would the same people react to "forced patriotism" or "forced Bible reading" or "forced prayers"?) But who, or what, was being raped? Was it the Mothers for Neighborhood Schools, or the kids, or was it, finally, the fear that the last barriers against the hostile and unthinkable world were about to be broken—not by integration necessarily, but by a simple disruption of familiar patterns? Here, after all, were many of those same girls who had been married at eighteen or twenty, who had had three kids by the time they were twenty-five, and who were screaming at those same kids before they were old enough to understand. What was the connection between those women, the assembly lines at Pontiac and busing? Anyone who had ever witnessed the trauma of parents when they learned that their children's lunch hour had been changed or that the kids would have to come home at a different time or by a different route could recognize the hysteria. Life at the margin had its special terrors—a chain of minuscule frustrations that would not bear escalation into debatable political issues. Only women's liberation had turned its attention to those frustrations, but, like other forms of middle-class radicalism, it had not yet succeeded in making broad connections with the exploitation and alienation of the lower middle class. (Women, I suspect, make the drudgery bearable. A man who works all day with his back or his hands is in no position, physically or psychologically, to come home, take care of the kids and start cooking dinner. Liberate the woman, and the man's job becomes untenable.) Busing in this context became a double imposition: the imposition of the outside world (the "federals," Wallace would say) on the province, and, simultaneously, the imposition of another disruptive nuisance into a women's world that could not tolerate the impositions that already existed. *"Unwanted kids," a school administrator once remarked in Bethlehem, Pennsylvania, "kids of guys who got girls in trouble, kids of Korean War veterans and veterans of World War II, who didn't want the first child, and before they knew it, they had two or three. There was a recent survey that indicated that seventy-two percent of the first children of this generation were unwanted."* The kids were a nuisance, shopping was a nuisance, housework was a nuisance, and the shortage of money, as the kids accumulated, became a consuming horror. In 1971 some 55,000 cases of child abuse were *reported* in America, and the authorities estimated that that represented only a small fraction of the incidents. Perhaps the pill (and ultimately the availability of legal abortions) would help change that pattern, but for the moment the child could be a fearsome nuisance—a mouth to feed, a set of clothes to wash, an endless series of risks to run—in a technological world that had few places left for children, and where, all wars aside, it had become dangerous for children and other living things.

Busing symbolized that nuisance: it was a reminder of the kid's ambivalent presence. You wanted him out of the house, but not far enough out to have him contaminated by others. The school, for the lower middle class, was more a perpetuator of the culture, a teacher of order and discipline, than it was a vehicle for mobility. At the same time, the issue of busing also served as a link to middle-class behavior, a taxpayer's, property owner's issue. (How much was there in antibusing of an illusion—or a pretense—that one had made it, the pride of capitalist possession? To what extent did the respectable middle-class consumer-home-owner, especially in the South, set the style for lower-middle-class resistance to school integration nationally?) The fight therefore served both the purposes of middle-class behavior and the anxieties of lower-middle-class frustration. You were protecting your child and your neighborhood (just as you once protected him—and, presumably, the neighborhood—by sending him on an hour's bus ride across town to a segregated school or, as many still did, to a private or parochial school). You were saving him from the social engineers in Washington, and from the spades, and you were, most of all, trying to protect yourself from still another liability in a world where nearly all changes were liabilities. Busing was a corollary to law and order, an attempt to restore the illusion of normalcy, to protect what you think you have. When the trip to school became more significant than the school program, it was fairly clear just what was expected of education. What better symbol than busing for the fear of negative social mobility? You had just escaped one set of horrors, and now they wanted to ship your kids right back to it. The politicians couldn't resist the pressure because they were unable to offer any confidence in positive mobility as compensation. It was more bearable to be accused of bigotry than of not caring about your kids, easier to be called a white racist (or a black nationalist) than to confront the inexpressible fears of life outside the village, or to express the growing doubt that neither the school nor the economy could offer much beyond what already existed. Turn the cliché around: racism made the fear of busing respectable.

Wallace—and to a lesser extent Nixon behind him—made busing into the great national distraction, a code word for a closed world. Yet clearly that closed world and its fears and frustrations would survive the yellow bus, and so the original question returned: What would be the political and social consequences of working-class alienation? It had often been said that things could blow to the right or the left, and that, especially among the young, the tendency to radicalism was more likely to be reactionary than liberal. But none of that was very revealing. Right and left didn't mean very much without specifics: a man might vote like a frightened property owner in a local election—going for a tough cop, a Frank Rizzo in Philadelphia or a Charles Stenvig in Minneapolis—and like a "liberal" in a national campaign where employment or social security were primary issues. More important was the likelihood that, with isolated exceptions (like busing, for example), nothing would happen at all, that the capacity for sustained political action in the lower middle class was limited, that, indeed, its cynicism and apathy about politics (often similar to that of the middle-class kids who had dropped out) was the most significant measure of its alienation. Those who worked for Frontlash, the union-sponsored effort to register eighteen-year-olds and get them to the polls, and those who had tried to organize local coalitions around school or housing issues spoke incessantly about that apathy. In a nation that included an estimated eighty million people who might loosely be classified as working-class, there existed not one major politician and not one permanent organization (with the qualified exception of the trade unions themselves) that had articulated the frustrations of the working American.

The attempts were being made, attempts to organize workers, students and minorities, attempts to forge community coalitions, or ethnic coalitions of "Pigs" (Poles, Italians, Greeks and Slavs), attempts to rediscover or reinvent some form of national populism. "The American worker," wrote Michael Harrington four years ago, "is not servile; he does not carry himself like an inferior. The openness, frankness, and democratic manner which Tocqueville described in the last century persists to this very day. They have been a source of rudeness, contemptuous ignorance, violence—and of a creative self-confidence among great masses of people. It was in the latter spirit that the CIO was organized and the black freedom movement marched." Since Harrington wrote those words there had been other reminders of the possibility for forging new coalitions around workers. We had Jack Newfield and Jeff Greenfield's *A Populist Manifesto*, had seen countless pieces in *The New Republic* and *The Nation*, had seen the efforts of Fred Harris' short-lived "populist" campaign for President, the studied populism of John Lindsay and the endless search for the fountain of youth by the Polonius of American liberalism, Hubert H. Humphrey. After a prolonged strike against the General Electric Company in 1969, a group of labor leaders, university professors and students had met at the

Harvard Faculty Club in Cambridge to organize what they hoped would be a permanent "alliance." Among those who attended were Leonard Woodcock of the Auto Workers, Harold Gibbons of the Teamsters, Abe Feinglass of the Meat Cutters, George Wald of Harvard, Noam Chomsky of MIT, Richard Barnet of the Institute for Policy Studies, the president of the National Student Association and a number of student leaders from various campuses. The immediate spur for the meetings was the happy coincidence of a pair of speeches. Victor Reuther of the UAW and Wald had been reading each other's material. "There are people in this country," Reuther had said, "who are trying to divide the workers from the students. It is as cold and calculated a strategy as the Southern Strategy, but there are no two groups that have more in common than working people and students." Reuther had also read Wald's famous speech in which he had described the young as "a generation that is by no means sure it has a future."

The upshot of the Harvard meeting was the creation of a plan to establish university-labor-student task forces to study certain issues: conversion of the economy, health care, welfare programs, the war, education. "The most urgent concerns of American workers—among them peace, racial justice, job security, decent environments in which to work and live, adequate medical care, housing, schools, stable prices—all represent equally the needs of students and faculty members," said a statement issued after the meeting. It was not to be a political organization, would not support particular candidates or a particular party. Rather, it would "encourage programs directed toward increasing the cooperation between the university community and labor organizations to foster our common interests, and in this way promote the political health and social and economic welfare of our nation." What the statement did not confront was the more fundamental problem of growth and mobility, the question of whether the basic system itself had broken down to the point where no one in the lower middle class—or his children—had much prospect of improving his condition without radical changes in the economic structure.

No one had confronted those problems: neither the politicians nor the unions nor the intellectuals. They had missed the connections not because they missed the issues—although they sometimes did—but because they lacked a language, because the acceptable terminology of American politics itself failed to touch those with whom it was supposed to be concerned. What had been required was not another round of studies based on New Deal assumptions—on the idea that the system must be restored to its productive potential, or on the notion that "workers" or "the common man" constitute the great majority—not another set of sermons about "productivity" and "competition" and "free enterprise," not another round of social-welfare measures but, rather, a more fundamental confrontation with the problem of defining and organizing people who had become a new (and often inarticulate) minority, a group of people for whom no existing political ideology would serve. "The American system had been fairly flexible," said Mike Barnes, a community organizer in Gary. "The economic structure was pinned to higher wages, higher prices and higher taxes. That whole system is breaking down." The system had become something that got your kid and put him on a bus.

There were still possibilities, left, right and undefined. You saw them in little storefronts or on the dark residential streets of industrial towns, heard ordinary unexpected people talking about how "the kids were right" about the system, and witnessed an existential capacity for resistance that, in its own American translation, was strangely reminiscent of the essays of Camus. We didn't yet understand very much about the politics and the attitudes of the younger industrial workers; the apathy was there, often in overwhelming doses, but alongside it there were also the increasingly numerous indications that the young in the factory shared with their contemporaries outside a mounting hostility for (and not just apathy about) the institutions, the system and whatever went by the name of establishment. If the Puritan in the American worker felt betrayed by establishment "permissiveness" (about kids or drugs or morals), there was also a side of him that must have been sorely tempted. And so the hair got longer, the drugs became more prevalent and the hostility more vocal. "More and more," said Cindy Amiotte, a twenty-year-old Frontlash organizer in California, "the antagonism gets turned against the industrial bureaucracy; it's decreasing at the personal level—it's not turned so much on fuck the foreman—and increasing against the institution." Whether any of that would amount to anything was hard to know. As usual, a few people were doing the work while the majority remained a mystery. Most of the polls and the informal estimates indicated that the younger workers—perhaps because they were better educated or less security-conscious, or because they had caught the scent of dissent from their middle-class contemporaries— tended to be less establishment-oriented than their parents; their politics were more centrifugal, and they were less willing to take shit from anybody—the boss, the company or the system. George Wallace obviously seized on a piece of that anti-establishmentarianism and brought people to the polls who had rarely if ever participated in a campaign before; by appealing to them as parents, property owners and taxpayers, he confused the issue (why not call them mortgage and interest payers or wage earners?), but he nonetheless demonstrated that even a candidate with the most tenuous credentials as a "populist" leader or a workingman's candidate could make anti-establishment politics work.

Possibilities: "Our white worker," said Gus Tyler, an officer of the International Ladies Garment Workers Union, "is ready for battle. But he does not quite know against whom to declare war." Tyler, like most of the old New Left, to which he does not belong, suggested that he fight the system: "If there is a devil, he is—as he always is—invisible, ubiquitous, and working his evil through the way of all flesh. In our case he is the inherent imperative in a culture that has badly distributed its wealth and people: the devil is still the system." The hope was that success in a limited battle—getting garbage collected, or getting rid of a neighborhood nuisance—could create a sense of power, that "the ability to act is transferable," and thus could generate a new confidence in political possibilities: the gospel according to Alinsky. And yet the question, both about the premise and about the solution, was whether the system was still too pervasive and powerful to fight, whether the worker, of whatever age, was too much locked into that system, economically and psychologically, to resist with anything but occasional outbursts of sabotage and guerrilla warfare. "It's surprising," said a sociologist in Chicago, "how much dissonance working-class people can bear." One night, on one of those dark streets in Gary, I spoke with a man named George Sullivan, a tough old boy from southern Illinois who had become one of the organizers of the Fraternal Association of Steel Haulers, a group of truckers who own their own rigs and had split from the Teamsters Union because the union was not representing their concerns. The battle had turned into one of those bare-knuckled labor struggles. There had been fist fights, shootings, dynamiting and continuous intimidation, and in the process Sullivan became a radical. "I'd never thought about things," he was saying. "I thought the kids were crazy." Then he became involved with FASH and with the Calumet Community Council, a coalition of community organizations oriented toward the problems of blue-collar workers—housing, utility rates, neighborhood improvement and political action—and discovered what he and other CCC members regarded as the cozy relations between the union and the local political machines. There had been a fight in a parking lot outside a union office in East Gary, and Sullivan, in self-defense, had slugged a Teamsters Union business agent. A year later, while he was checking voting records in the courthouse, he was arrested on charges of assault. "I don't approve of the methods of the kids, they're not effective," he was saying now, "but they know what they're talking about." There was only so far you could go in fighting the system, "only so far and they'll get you. Lots of un-known people get themselves killed besides Kennedy and King and Yablonski. If I disappear, nobody would read about it in the papers. Still, you have to use what's there. We elected those guys. I don't believe in nonviolence; violence is the way things have always been. They send guys after you, and then you have to go after the guys who sent them. There's no place to go, no place to run to. You have to stand and fight where you are. Hell, I see them coming back here from California." So you lived on that dark street, a few blocks from the mills, and tried to organ-ize—against the Teamsters, against the steel industry, against the big truckers, against the whole political system. There were other men, especially the young, who were ready to fight; maybe if the word got around . . . "The motto of U.S. Steel—you know what it is? It's 'We're involved.' I'd like to show people how." *"This is my place," you remembered someone else saying in another city. "I can't just watch TV and pretend there's noth-ing happening. These are my people. They're not just looking for better jobs, but for a better life. But they're also scared. Maybe if we can organize, if we can find some leadership, they won't be scared anymore."*

The radical hope had always rested on the possibility that the system would be seen for what it is, that people would discover a language and thus a set of tactics to deal with it. But if you pressed hard enough, you came up flat against a sort of existen-tial despair; heard people like Sullivan saying that you could go only so far and they'd get you like they got Kennedy or Ya-blonski; and you began to understand that the issue, at least for now, was not between the politics of the Right and the politics of the Left, but between despair and alienation, on the one hand, and a belief that something could be done. The pressure for bet-ter conditions and for improvements in the general quality of life—not to mention the incalculable possibilities of women's lib-eration (which by itself could upset the entire economic struc-

ture)—was, at least for the moment, on a direct collision course
with the limits of American industrial growth.

American manufactured goods [wrote Daniel Bell] are pricing themselves out of the world market. From the view of theoretical economics,
in the inevitable "product cycle" of goods production, a more advanced
industrial society finds itself at a price disadvantage when a product becomes standardized, inputs are predictable, price elasticity of demand is
higher, and labor costs make a difference, so that less advanced but competing nations can now make the product more cheaply. . . . In the
world economy the United States is now a mature nation and in a position to be pushed off the top of the hill by more aggressive countries.
. . . At a time when workers may be asking for more control over the
conditions of work—which will inevitably increase costs—the squeeze
may be greatest because of the changed condition of the economy.

None of this was terribly new. What was new was that many
American workers now knew it, and this fact alone constituted
one of the great imponderables about the political future. But
there was more: the limits of the economy were compounded by
the technical, psychological and (just perhaps) the genetic
limits of mobility itself. If it was true that there was a historic
tendency, however circumscribed, for the most ambitious, the
most talented and the most energetic individuals to move up
from the working class into more prestigious jobs and life styles,
then was it also true that the possibilities for mobility among
those who remained—despite increasing educational "opportunities"—became smaller every year? Would Gary and Lowell
and New Britain and Duluth and Detroit become extensions of
Appalachia, residue communities of millions of never-made-it
blacks and whites? And would behavior in those communities
come increasingly to resemble behavior in the hills and hollows
of eastern Kentucky and West Virginia, alternating between
explosions against the most obvious and immediate manifestations
of oppression and injustice—blowing up a train or a trestle or a
mine, starting a wildcat strike, walking off the job—and a sort

of chronic apathy about a distant system that people felt impotent to change? (The real possibilities for effective sabotage, of course, were in the service sectors, and not in production. A hundred men could and had, tied up most of the bridges leading into New York City; and a few thousand could cut off the milk supply or the collection of garbage. There was no comparable power on an assembly line or in a steel mill.) It would not be Appalachian poverty, not all of it anyway; for most there would be enough middle-class amenities—refrigerators, television sets, development houses (and the debts that go with them)—to maintain an "affluent" façade and to foster bourgeois caution and "responsibility." At the same time, the system—the schools, the welfare structure, the finance company, and the job—tended also to teach that political silence, however unpleasant, was better than anything else: enough to deter desperation, but too little to create confidence. It was an uneasy balance, and opportunists like Wallace would constantly try to work those situations where it broke down. But there was also a chance that (for the next few years, at any rate) it would be maintained. As I think about that possibility, I am constantly reminded of a remark I heard along the way: *They are not that vastly discontented out there.* What looked like despair or alienation to one man might just be accommodation to reality to someone else. Law and order, busing, and all the rest were, to be sure, the responses of people whose faith in mobility was limited, but just as surely they were also expressions of that greatest of desires, the desire for stability, a demand that things remain reliable and intact. "God bless the squire and his relations," said the old English chant, "and keep us in our proper stations." "God bless the establishment," proclaimed the hard hats of New York. Things were not good, and were not getting any better, but you took it as it came, adjusted to what you had, and even took some pride in the hardships. *A cultural predisposition to pessimism,* Simon had called it.

The limits of populism. Clearly there were issues on which

the middle class and the lower middle class (plus several million individuals who vaguely belong to both or to neither) could unite: closing tax "loopholes," tightening the regulation of utility rates, enforcing or strengthening antitrust laws, providing better medical services, requiring "truth in packaging" and so on. But most of these issues focused on consumer or community problems and had little to do with the conditions of work, or with the matter of working-class identity, or with the re-creation of a credible future. More important, such issues quickly became "technical"—the calculation and assessment of the rate structure of AT&T was too much even for the staffs of the federal commissions, let alone a factory worker who came home exhausted every night—and thus tended to intimidate people in the very place where the system had taught them they were most vulnerable. The kids learned from the beginning that they had no right to an opinion, and that if they expressed it they would quickly be shown up as stupid and inarticulate. It was a lesson they would never forget. *They*, the system (or fate or whatever), might get Yablonski with hired thugs, but more often they could get anybody with words and bureaucratic complexity and legal complications. The very essence of contemporary middle-class politics included a pervasive tendency to define the citizen as a consumer rather than a worker, and thus to relegate most of the lower middle class (as workers and as marginal consumers) to a secondary role. Here again the worker could choose between the political semantics of affluence and the language of poverty and welfare. "The labor problem," wrote Bell, "has become 'encapsulated.' An interest conflict and a labor issue—in the sense of disproportionate power between manager and worker over working conditions—remains, but the disproportions have shifted and the methods of negotiation have become institutionalized. . . . The crucial fact is that the 'labor issue' *qua* labor is no longer central, nor does it have the sociological and cultural weight to polarize all other issues along that axis." The middle class defined the issues.

For the worker it was a double trap: what you had was insufficient; but what you were—politically and culturally—was insufficient, too. It was in this sense that the person in the lower middle class, despite four years of agitation and "rediscovery," remained the forgotten American, a potential recruit for other people's causes. Three sets of invitations were out: he could join the middle-class liberal reformers (Muskie, Lindsay, *et al.*); he could join the bigots (Wallace); or he could join the poor (welfare rights, community action and all the rest). I am mindful that all these things and the people who represented them tended occasionally to overlap. But in no case could he be himself, and in no instance had anyone articulated even a reasonable future to replace the closing (and perhaps mythic) frontiers of the past.

FOUR:

HOW THE WEST WAS LOST

I

We had all been born with the same gyroscope. Long after all the doors were shut, all the frontiers declared closed, the tribal instinct was West. West and East themselves were not neutral directions of the compass—nor were North and South—but qualities of politics, moral values, points of commitment. Mark Twain's irony in the last line of *Huckleberry Finn*, that declaration about lighting out for the territories, was turned on its head, and then turned again. There *were* territories out there, there would always be territories—if not of sage and prairie and virgin land, then of cities and the accumulated mythology of the good life—because they had to be, because identity demanded it, because the whole national sense of time and motion carried one in that direction. Without it there would be no future; without geographic mobility there would be no economic or social mobility either, and without those, by God, there would no longer exist the America that we knew.

There were always two Wests: The West of the East and the West *in situ*, the dream and the achievement. The distinction was not so much between myth and reality (or between literature and "fact"); so much of what we perceived as the West (or the South) was literary anyway. The distinction, it seems to me, lay more in the differences between innocence and experience, between different conceptions of time, and between different versions of the future. It was striking how much of the best California writing—Nathanael West's or Joan Didion's or, in its own way, Raymond Chandler's—was alternately Eastern in its perspective and apocalyptic in its vision: the West of the East, the mythic West, had order; the West *in situ*, the West of experience, enjoyed no such luxury. This, I suspect, is what accounted for the peculiarly lobotomized quality of so many young native Californians: they were heirs to a myth that could only remain plausible somewhere else, the children of a future of which they were supposed to be the preeminent examples. Whenever people talked about how the young no longer believed in a future, the culprit was supposed to be technology or the atom bomb or the depersonalization of society. But nowhere was that attitude more obvious than in the place that the future was supposed to be. California, as the cliché goes, was the birthplace of the counterculture, the breeding ground of hippies, the haven of the commune. If any of that was true, then surely it was also true that California gave the counterculture its peculiar sense of time, its apocalyptic vision, its peculiar despair. "The city burning," wrote Joan Didion in 1967, "is Los Angeles's deepest image of itself: Nathanael West perceived that, in *Day of the Locust;* and at the time of the 1965 Watts riots what struck the imagination most indelibly were the fires. For days one could drive the Harbor Freeway and see the city on fire, just as we had always known it would be in the end." Charles Manson would have been inconceivable anywhere else.

Clearly more distinctions were required. Los Angeles was not the West, not all of it anyway, nor were the inflated expectations of the first generation or the apocalyptic visions of its most sensitive writers completely satisfactory descriptions of what the experience of the West does to the West of the East. Steven Arkin, an Easterner who teaches at San Francisco State, speaks about the phenomenon of inner weather and outer weather, allusions to a poem by Frost, a Californian gone East, and a man who therefore might understand better than others about tensions between the climate and the spirit. What Arkin was saying had to do, most simply, with the question "If it's so beautiful outside, why do I feel so bad?" I think this was a compulsion that many Western immigrants shared. Jesse Unruh, the onetime big daddy of the California legislature, once explained that it was the warm weather that produced so many fruits and nuts; the frustrated dream itself created the compulsive perfectionism of the sects and cults and movements that California became noted for. But the dynamics of that compulsion involved a sort of hedonistic guilt, the conversion of the Puritan into a man gone wild with his inability to comprehend frailty and imperfection, tragedy and death in the midst of so much sun and beauty. The man who lived in the Great State of Now was deprived of past and future and therefore had to choose among identities unaffected by time itself. The utopian and the apocalyptic resided together and shared the same clothes; the children of people who asked too much would often be the very people who expected too little. "California," Didion wrote, "is a place in which a boom mentality and a sense of Chekhovian loss meet in uneasy suspension; in which the mind is troubled by some buried but ineradicable suspicion that things had better work here, because here, beneath that immense bleached sky, is where we run out of continent."

In California, she might have said, we ran out of time, and were thus forced to confront the unresolved ambiguities of the national imagination itself. Was the virgin territory of the West the essence of American perfection, the antidote to urban corruption and European civilization, or was it the beginning of something else? Was the mythic West composed of open space and the simple life, or did it represent something that resembled Los Angeles or Phoenix or Dallas? In the late sixties, for the first time, the gyroscope showed signs of disorientation: the outmigration of people from California was now almost equal to the immigration; smog, they said, or crowding, or simply lack of jobs. In the early sixties they were arriving at the rate of a thousand a day; now the net growth of California's population from new arrivals amounted to barely twenty-five thousand a year, and a number of communities, especially in northern California, were passing regulations that would, in effect, shut growth down forever. It was California that spawned the great ecology craze and which constitutes the locus of the national movement against development and the unchecked spread of people; the Friends of the Earth, the Sierra Club, ZPG, and scores of others not only were based in California but had taken on—often, if not always—the peculiar fervor that the country always associated with the children of the golden dream. Although all of them were worrying about space and resources and people, what they were really talking about was time: *This is where we run out of time*. Since everything once seemed possible—nature and civilization, clean air and cars, space and development—it was assumed that everything could be simultaneously achieved. What was surprising was how much had in fact been accomplished: a whole new civilization was created out of orange groves and aquaducts, out of plastic and glass and air conditioners. What could not be achieved was the resolution of the ambiguity itself: Was the West the beginning, or was it the end?

To anyone who thought very much about the West, the most striking fact was not its immensity (nor the sprawl of Los Angeles, the provincialism of San Francisco or the irrigated lush of the Central Valley) but the brevity of history itself. In North Dakota they began constructing silos for intercontinental ballistic missiles eighty years after the United States Army fought its last engagements against the Indians, and in El Paso the German rocket scientists who were captured at the end of World War II began to perfect their technology (and to stimulate business for German restaurants) a scant thirty years after the last raids of Pancho Villa. As a consequence, all dimensions of time became distorted and all expectations turned surrealistic. This was in some ways an old country: there were Spanish missions here long before the Pilgrims landed at Plymouth, and Francis Drake sailed into the harbors of California nearly a generation before John Smith explored the coast of New England, but those events left no more of an imprint on the tribal memory than the Vikings left on the traditions of the East. The names were Spanish, and some of the older settlers in southern California could trace their landholdings to royal patents from Spanish kings, but the collective memory was innocent of the sense of time that such traditions suggest. The West of the East began thousands of years ago, began with Platonic reveries about continents lying beyond the Pillars of Hercules, with medieval dreams of gold, and Renaissance visions of El Dorado, but the West in place—the West's memory of itself—went back no more than a hundred and twenty-five years. Anything that smacked too much of history or of permanence was systematically eradicated: the past was recreated to suit the needs of the present, the whims of the Native Sons of the Golden West, the entertainment of tourists, or to sustain the momentary desire for a mythology that could be reinvented, changed or discarded like any other cult. The past—what there was—got in the way of the present. Sooner or later the whole thing would go in one apocalyptic moment anyway—in a fire or, more likely, in an earthquake. "California," went the pun, "is going to lose by default."

We all knew about the transience, the impermanence, knew about people who built $100,000 houses that hung suspended over space alongside canyons, structures so precarious that, in this country of earthquakes, no insurance company would accept the risk of protecting them, knew about people from Iowa or Kansas or Wisconsin who moved from subdivision to subdivision, year after year, trying to find perfection, had seen the sprawling freeways and the California statistics on automobiles (one car for every 1.6 residents, or was it 1.8, or did it really matter?), had seen or heard of the rootlessness, of the kids in their vans and their Volkswagen buses shuttling between the beach and the camp grounds and the rock festivals, and of the adults in their campers, people who lived in mobile homes too large to move and parked the camper alongside had heard the whole liturgy of the search for beauty and belonging, for meaning and stability. In the absence of history and tradition, they had created a land of façades, the life of the West trying to imitate the art of Hollywood, had become actors playing out the script of the West, performing for their memory of the dreams of the past, bit players in the scenario of the good life somewhere else. Heaven itself, one might imagine, was a place where the lonely, the lobotomized and the terrified played the role of Perfection for the benefit of the jealous sinners still on earth. It was no wonder, then, that, as one writer suggested, "sympathy for the Devil was everywhere."

Some of it was easy to explain. Since there was virtually no history (and since the history that existed was swamped by people who knew nothing of it and couldn't care if they did), little life intervened between the dreams of the West and the realization of something that resembled, but didn't feel like, fulfillment, and so nothing was ever worked out. Nothing, in fact, could intervene, because that intervention would have denied the magical properties of the place itself, would have suggested, contrary to the myths and to the Chamber of Commerce, that this place, like any other, required work to make it what it was. It is often said that there are several Californias—one north of the Tehachapis (the Bay area), another south of it (the sprawling region that reaches from Los Angeles south almost to San Diego and north toward Santa Barbara), and still another in the Central Valley—but it can just as surely be said that there are several Wests. The differences were not important before we became fully conscious of the West as a settled place: before that the only West that mattered was the West of the East, the unexamined myth, because the other West (Ohio, or the plains, or California itself) still remained, unsettled, beyond the frontier. But now that we had indeed run out of continent, the differences were crucial. The last frontier had, in fact, consisted of conflicting visions. There had been the familiar American desire for land and freedom and opportunity, the dream of the farmer and the immigrant, the vision of the hungry and the land-poor. But there were also the remains of the medieval vision of sunshine and gold, the dreams of Spanish explorers chasing across the desert in pursuit of fantasies told by half-starved, half-crazed Indians who knew of places where the natives adorned themselves with silver and jewels and where the streets were made of gold: El Dorado, the Seven Cities of Cíbola, the utopian ultimate, the alchemist's revery, places that had once been drawn on the medieval maps and had never quite faded from memory. No wonder, then, that where there was sunshine there one would also find magic and witchcraft, that this was the land of healers and spiritualists, of cultists and kooks. The dream of gold and eternal life, moreover, could easily become a dream of death, Charles Manson's dream, the dream of Forest Lawn and perpetual care, the dream of a future become the present and therefore deprived of all futures, all dreams. Here, in the West, one could find the ultimate guilt: not the guilt of indolence and idleness, the fear of not working hard enough, but its very opposite, the guilt created by the sun itself. The façades reinforced it: all around were the beautiful people, the tans, the beaches, the seeming availability of it all, and all through the core there lurked the possibility, if not the fact, of nothingness. *If it's so beautiful out there, why do I feel so bad?*

II

For fifty years it was the entertainment capital of the nation. Not just Hollywood, certainly not just the movies, but all of southern California from the John Birch Society and the religious fundamentalists on the right to the Los Angeles *Free Press* way out there beyond everything. Clichés were spawned faster than they could be published: the America of the future; couch canyon, forty suburbs in search of a city, the dream factory. Everything seemed available, and every half-sensitive writer and journalist was overwhelmed by it; yet most of us would also come away unable to reduce it to anything more than a list:

You could live out your entire life on Ventura Boulevard [wrote John Clellon Holmes in *Playboy*]—be born, get married, die and be buried from it. You could eat in a Taco Belle, a hard boozing Kansas City steakhouse or a chic French restaurant. You could furnish an apartment in Swedish modern or a mansion in fine antiques. You could learn karate or how to swim. You could bowl, dance, ice-skate or ride horseback. You could buy, rent, wash or repair a car—or a motorcycle, or a camper, or a mobile home. You could go to movies, saddleries, nude entertainments, jazz clubs, lectures, or even church. It was the ultimate bazaar, and driving its length three days before—the temperature up in the high 80s, everything two blocks away unfocused by a shimmer of heat and exhaust, the glare off cartops, chrome, neon and aluminum piercing even my Polaroids—I had one of those premonitory hallucinations that a man who had been quits with cities for some years occasionally experiences: Eventually this street would lengthen, store after store, mile after mile, state after state, all the way back to the other ocean—the vast signboards walling out the trees, the leveled concrete denying the contours of the land, the towering neons creating a perpetual hour that was, eerily, neither night nor day. At last, the continent would be conquered; its ability to disturb us, enlarge us, depress us or arouse us finally annulled. And the valley that had given birth to this incredible street—the valley that was over 100 square miles of tract houses and subdivisions where no down payment and instant financing made the split-level paradise of leisure living and wife swapping available to all—the valley would finally leap over the mountains that circumscribed it here and *become* America. The meanest aspect of the democratic dream would be achieved at last: Everything, in this land founded on the idea of diversity, would become *one thing.*

We all made lists, or even lists of lists: the names of crazy organizations, ads in the *Free Press,* radio commercials for Forest Lawn, conversations at dinner parties in Westwood or West Hollywood or Malibu, the voices of old men sitting at the corners of Pershing Square late at night (discussing, among other things, the question of just who were the social engineers), the behavior of the gum-chewing, rye-and-ginger-drinking hairdressers at their annual banquet at the Ambassador, the expressions on the faces of the Hollywood relics wandering in and out of the Beverly Wilshire, stories about Aimee Semple McPherson or Edgar Cayce or the Mighty I Am, or the names of other endless streets chained together with neon and glass and cars with 400-horsepower engines.

SAN PEDRO, Calif. (AP) Jolene Gearin says she was poor before she inherited $200,000 four years ago. Now she's poor again and cheerfully admits "We blew it."

Mrs. Gearin was living in a $75 a month apartment when she learned she would inherit $200,000 from the estate of her father. With her husband, Leonard, a merchant marine seaman, and their four children, she waited through two years of court action for the money. Then taxes took part of it. "But when it came, it really wore us out spending it," she recalls. "We were just exhausted. We couldn't spend it fast enough. . . . We bought cars and motorcycles for the boys, and a truck, and a $2,000 hi-fi . . . and clothes, and we put a down payment on a house, and the girls and I all had our teeth capped, and I had my breasts lifted. . . .

"And, oh yes, we bought ski equipment . . . and we travelled . . . we put 200,000 miles on one of the cars in one year . . . and we all saw a psychiatrist . . . I invested $10,000 in the stock market and lost $4,000 of it . . . and we spent $5,000 on new furniture, a washer and dryer, small appliances . . .

"We paid cash for everything . . . You can sure waste a lot of money on cars and the stock market is a bad investment . . .

"When we found out about the money, it brought the family together. It was the first time in our lives that we really worked and planned together.

"After the money was gone we started fighting. They kept saying 'Why didn't we spend it this way?' But they were all there to spend it and we all had fun . . ."

Sexually Deviated Games Our Specialty   789-0476   12 to 12

Hey Guys. I'm the Foxiest thing you've ever seen!! I dare you to call me for a date. Mary: 851-0486   24 hours

The federal disaster program, designed to help citizens caught in the aftermaths of earthquakes, floods, storms and fires, has become a source of scandal as well as social service. . . .

More than 100,000 [Los Angeles area] quake victims filed applications for SBA loans. To date, 55,000 loans have been granted for a total disbursement of $211 million. . . . Millions of dollars of public money were improperly spent. Some homeowners took the forgiveness money—those $2,500 grants—to repair damage not caused by the earthquake. Others got more money than the actual damage warranted. Money was given for repairs and to replace personal property without any proof of loss or that repairs were made. . . .

Getting fucked? Don't. We pay the most for TV's, cameras, stereos, jewelry, musical instruments . . . most anything. For fast cash, call Swap Shop, 465-4797

Helmut C. Schulitz, an assistant professor of urban design at UCLA, declares that billboards are "collages of the commercial vernacular . . . unself-conscious and dynamic expressions of urban life. . . . If we want an architecture which is not remote from life," he adds, "we must accept the vernacular in its vulgar form as part of architecture. We will have to integrate it, not transform it."

Black Girls Only: W/M, 32, will satisfy you orally. I love it. You'll love it. Lips, 11325 Blix, Holly. 91602

It was the ultimate spectacle, the greatest show anywhere. Everything could be played for laughs or as tragedy, the people who had come to die or to live forever, the fast-buck operators and the perpetual optimists, the developers and the entrepreneurs. There were people who, like the climbers of Everest, were challenged to drive every mile of freeway in record time— some five hundred miles of road, it was said, crossing and recrossing the city—and occasionally one read about them in the papers, usually for laughs, but there were also those who saw in the same freeways the ultimate horror of Los Angeles, or perhaps, indeed, of the future itself. None of the specifics mattered, unemployment in the aircraft industry, the number of health spas, the names of denominations, or the shifts of population. Even the matter of power didn't seem very important here, because all standards were somehow unworldly and the politics unreal. You learned to suspect very quickly that this place itself might have been responsible for saving the country from a violent revolution in the thirties, that Hollywood—not just films, but the place, the idea—was the opiate of the masses, and that if it didn't avert what the political reactionaries in Orange County would describe as a Communist takeover, then it certainly prevented the rise of some national madness that might well, even by Orange County standards, have been worse. What it did was preserve the promise, the concept, of beauty and glamour, even while it vulgarized both. For finally all of Hollywood was about itself, which is to say that the lights were most often turned on its own glitter, and that the vulgarity which was institutionalized in the streets and canyons of Beverly Hills became the safety valve of the Depression. Hollywood resurrected the dream of gold and turned half the nation into a society of Spanish grandees, got waitresses in Indiana and farm boys in Iowa dreaming of stardom, and succeeded in transforming that older American vision which concentrated on making it into a revery about life in Egyptian palaces, New York night clubs, Oriental temples and Arab harems. The furniture of those reveries was all there: the phony exotic, the imitation plush, the cut-rate elegant. A simple Marxist mind could quite accurately portray it as a capitalistic trick, but the final joke was on those who believed in it too much. To see Los Angeles as entertainment was one thing; to try to live it quite another. This is why we were all stuck with lists and found ourselves unable to create metaphors. There was no way to summarize it because it was originally designed as entertainment—was meant to be taken seriously only at the box office. Bathing beauties, colored fountains, overstuffed hotels, lush gardens, glittering premieres, cheap sex, quick divorces, Western saloons, Continental frippery, fancy cars—they were all part of the set and were not intended for people to live in, were not supposed to be *that* creditable. As showpieces they could all be equal, were not subject to some larger scale of values, and would be immune from moral judgment. Stay outside all that and you could still see it as a joke, or as romance, or as drama. But once you were inside, having to treat it as real, it became unmanageable, literally unspeakable, because the real imitation of the imitation real can impose no more order and no other set of values than the costume designer or the studio prop department from whom this style was derived. In Los Angeles distinctions between fact and fantasy were no longer possible. The Sharon Tate murders, someone said at one of those dinner parties, represented the end of a cultural era, the final corruption of something that might have been beautiful and positive. Yet in a different sense wasn't the Sharon Tate–Charley Manson episode simply another illustration of the region's inability to make distinctions between fantasy and action? I am speaking not only about Manson's demonic imagination but also about the setting, the surroundings, the response. By what other than simple murder could Los Angeles judge Manson's act without also judging itself? It was, after all, in perfect taste. Recall Nathanael West's hero in *Day of the Locust;* he is painting his masterpiece, "The Burning of Los Angeles":

Across the top, parallel with the frame, he had drawn the burning city, a great bonfire of architectural styles, ranging from Egyptian to Cape Cod colonial. Through the center, winding from left to right, was a long hilly street and down it, spilling into the middle foreground, came the mob carrying baseball bats and torches. For the faces of its members, he was using the innumerable sketches he had made of the people who come to California to die: the cultists of all sorts, economic as well as religious, the wave, airplane, funeral and preview watchers—all those poor devils who can only be stirred by the promise of miracles and then only to violence. A super "Dr. Know-All Pierce-All" had made the necessary promise and they were marching behind his banner in a great united front of screw balls and screwboxes to purify the land. No longer bored, they sang and danced joyously in the light of the red flames.

That was written in 1933, long before the hippies or the counterculture, yet Manson would have been just as appropriate to that setting as he would be forty years later: Here was another face for "The Burning of Los Angeles." From without, the scene could be placed in judgment—judgment, at least, about its success as a work of art, judgment about aesthetics. But from within everything was reduced to the same existential equality, avenger and avenged subject to the same holocaust, clinging to the sides of the same canyons, and locked in the same bond of mutual disregard and timeless indifference.

One kept asking why—asked intelligent, sensitive people why they lived in Los Angeles, asked what it was like; you didn't really want reasons, but merely some kind of order from within, wanted a statement, anything at all. More teenagers in America, wrote a columnist in the Los Angeles *Times*, want to live in Los Angeles than anywhere else. "Maybe," he suggested, "it's our openness; our optimism; our innocence. We're not hopelessly cynical, like New York, nor vain, like San Francisco. We're really naïve, just as they've been saying all these years." But that wouldn't do, nor would the expressions of amusement or the talk about easy access—to sun, or beaches or sex, or whatever. To understand, one had to stop believing that Los Angeles was a place at all, or even a series of places, but rather a collection of stages and costumes, a place of roles. New York was regarded as cynical because it prided itself on its ability to detect phonies (false pride often), and San Francisco *was* vain, believing itself highly civilized when, in many instances, it was simply shallow, humorless and apathetic. Los Angeles did not care about phonies; it was not interested in making such distinctions. Sentimentality was its most common public emotion and performance its most significant social standard of judgment. (CHAPLIN OVATION, screamed the banner in the L. A. *Times* the morning after Hollywood, in an orgy of forgiveness, honored a man, now half senile, whose political and personal sins had always been regarded as excessively embarrassing during the years when he was still really alive.) The real heart here was private, the most private place in America, where each person was connected primarily to his own gods and his own hell, and where fervent belief—belief in witches and fairies, belief in belief or nonbelief —could thrive free of social interference or of the impositions that a normal community might interject. Whatever common holocaust lay ahead—fire or earthquake or fog on the freeway— was beyond social remedy anyway:

"This morning," said Senator Ribicoff of Connecticut to Mayor Sam Yorty of Los Angeles at a hearing on urban problems, "you have really waived authority and responsibility in the following areas of Los Angeles: schools, welfare, transportation, employment, health and housing, which leaves you as the head of the city basically with a ceremonial function, police and recreation."

"That is right, and fire," the mayor answered.

"Collection of sewage?"

"Sanitation, that is right."

"In other words, basically you lack jurisdiction, authority, responsibility for what makes a city move?"

"That is exactly it."

To live in Los Angeles was to live beyond the limits of conventional time, and to accept it one had to break through barriers where ordinary forms of hope and despair—social and personal—were relinquished. (Most Angelenos, of course, would never say they live in Los Angeles, anyhow; they live in "the Valley" or at "the Beach" or in Beverly Hills, become part of the whole through their common severance not only from time but from place.) In one sense it was like living on borrowed time, existence within a sort of science-fiction noncontinuum where salvation, damnation and pleasure all become equally pressing matters. But that wasn't saying enough (or perhaps it was saying too much), because it suggested a universal sense of doom. That sense of doom was there, but it remained, for the most part, a literary perception, something for Didion or West, not something for the mayor. What one said at those dinner parties was that Los Angeles was crazy, or that it would someday disappear in a great disaster, but that one didn't really live there, was not part of either the city or its madness. Malibu was a nice place, Westwood was pleasant, West Hollywood was a wonderful area to live. If one became private enough one might even be exempt from social disaster: the rest of the world might be subject to growth or deterioration, to war and riots and fires, but to be genuinely a part of Los Angeles was, in a sense, to have left that world altogether. One could, at least for a time, continue to live in one's own private beauty, in the sun, in the sea, to maintain, as long as possible, that suspension from time, and to hold the future motionless. In other cities the common problems of life were generally unavoidable, at least for those who were not very, very rich: the dogshit on the sidewalk, the breakdown of commuter trains, the bus strikes, the crowding, the noise, the ugliness. But in Los Angeles the only public forum was the freeway and the air, and one could continue to exist without connection to anything but the anonymous car ahead, the commercials on the radio, and one's most private thoughts. To live *in* the future was to be detached from time, and only the ubiquitous billboard advertising Japanese motorcycles constituted reminders of what perils such detachment may incur: "Suzuki," they said, "Conquers Boredom."

III

California, someone told me in Sacramento, is closing down. In the State Capitol, the freaks were assembling to present petitions calling for the elimination of the marijuana laws—they now had enough signatures to put the issue on the ballot—and in a corner committee room the feminists were about to try to blast the Equal Rights Amendment to the Constitution, already ratified by a dozen states, through the resistance of a collection of reluctant pigs. But the issue of the moment was something called Assembly Bill 200, the California Coastal Conservation Act, which would provide "a comprehensive, coordinated, enforceable plan for the orderly, long-range conservation and management of the natural resources of the coastal zone"—in effect a huge plan to control further development—and beyond that there was the growing and nearly universal sense that, as

183

Didion said, this is where we run out of continent. "Each time," the California Coastal Alliance had declared, "that a 'special interest' sells a local government one more freeway, a power plant on a spectacular headland, a housing development on an eroding cliff, a non-water-related industry, a super sewage outfall, another beach dies. The public interest is scorned." But it wasn't only the beaches or even the shore that people were worried about. It was the whole state, perhaps the whole universe. There was Proposition 19, a referendum item which would, among other things, ban the use of all DDT, sharply reduce the emission of all pollutants, and block the construction of nuclear-power plants for at least five years; there was the battle over the development of Mineral King, a recreation area in the Sierras that had been betrothed by the National Forest Service to the Disney interests; there were the familiar battles in San Francisco against freeways and high-rise buildings (more or less successful in the first instance, more or less futile in the second); there was the endless talk in Los Angeles about smog (which seemed in itself a symbol of the corruption in Eden); there were new ordinances in towns like Livermore which would, if they survived in the courts, block all further development permanently; there were serious discussions at the Marin County Water District about stopping all new water connections altogether; and there was the battle of Bolinas, a relatively isolated coastal town north of San Francisco where unknown local residents had started destroying Highway Department road signs in the hope that strangers would no longer be able to find the place. In the northern areas, where a larger proportion of the residents were natives and where there was more of a proprietary attitude about the region, people were prepared to fight; in the south, which was dominated by immigrants, the disenchanted simply moved out.

In fact, of course, nothing was closing down, not yet anyway. They were still clear-cutting the redwood forests, consolidating farms in huge corporate organizations, throwing up developments, building shopping centers and planning freeways. In the same legislative corridors where the feminists and the freaks were now so visible, the lobbyists were still plying their trade: the oil people and the Growers Association, the truckers and the insurance men. Yet all these things were proceeding with the kind of deference which indicated that the resistance was mounting, that the Forces of Stagnation were all about: development *sotte voce*, against increasing opposition, and with what I took to be a sense that this won't last forever. The big boom was over, and even the folks at the State Chamber of Commerce were speaking softly, saying now that the expansion of the sixties had been "artificial," that the stimulus of increasing defense and aerospace budgets had pushed things along too fast, and that the day of reckoning had come. They were keeping a nervous eye on the businesses which had been moving from California to Nevada and Utah, where taxes were lower, talking about the flight of unemployed aerospace workers back to the East (which meant anything beyond the Sierras), and projecting state unemployment, which had reached 7.0 percent in 1971, to 6.8 percent by 1975. It was getting too expensive for some companies to do business in California, they said, people were asking too much, too much in pensions and benefits, too much of everything; now they were even demanding dental care and prescription drugs in their union contracts. And on top of everything there was Proposition 19, which, in the unlikely event that it passed (it did not), would seriously cripple further growth and perhaps stop construction altogether. The opponents of Proposition 19 were taking no chances; they had prepared a blitz of slick television commercials suggesting that the consequences of ratification would be dark streets, power failures, rape, murder and chaos. California was big on catastrophes.

Clearly this had become the national hotbed of ecology and conservation, and those things, in turn, had evolved into the latest and most universal of the California cults. Down in Palo Alto, Dr. Paul Ehrlich and his ZPG acolytes had achieved such monumental importance that the doctor had become harder to see than the governor himself. Everyone was saving something: the Bay or the Sierras or the Santa Monica Mountains, or the condor, or the fox, or the view from Russian Hill, and there were times when you felt that if you didn't faithfully recycle your cans and bottles, cutting the tops off the cans and flattening them, World War II-style, and then deliver them to a schoolyard where someone would pick them up and take them somewhere else—that if you didn't do this in the spirit of saving the planet, your baby-sitter or some neighborhood snoop would denounce you to the Movement, and the Friends of the Earth would come in the middle of the night and take you away.

And yet the sense that things were closing down was both subtler and deeper than ecology or conservation or the belief that the interests, whoever they might be, are ripping off the land. Plunder had always been one of the great traditions of the West: timber in California and Oregon, copper in Montana, lead and uranium in Colorado, real estate and railroads everywhere. In Assembly Bill 200 there was a phrase which said that "the California coastal zone is a distinct and valuable natural resource belonging to all the people . . ." As the bill went through the processes of amendment, the words "belonging to all the people" were deleted—socialistic, no doubt, but also suggestive of something else. Perhaps the land did not belong to all the people, but certainly the romance of the land was a common possession, an intangible but vital resource, and that romance was coming to an end. Here again the brevity of history had become vitally important: to belong in any sense to the West required association with that romance because, until yesterday, give a day or two, there was nothing else.

All that is constant about the California of my childhood [Didion had written] is the rate at which it disappears. . . . It is hard to *find* California now, unsettling to wonder how much of it was merely imagined or improvised; melancholy to realize how much of anyone's memory is no true memory at all but only traces of someone else's memory, stories handed down on the family network. I have an indelibly vivid "memory," for example, of how Prohibition affected the hop growers around Sacramento: the sister of a grower my family knew had brought home a mink coat from San Francisco, and was told to take it back, and sat on the floor of the parlor cradling that coat and crying. Although I was not born until a year after Repeal, that scene is more "real" to me than many I have played myself.

We all have "memories" like that, and we all come from places where landmarks are systematically bulldozed or rebuilt or converted: the Brownsville where Alfred Kazin grew up, the Lower East Side of New York, or the West Side of Chicago. The difference lies, rather, in the feeling that the West began with perfection. "My own childhood," Didion wrote, "was suffused with the conviction that we had long outlived our finest hour." It was not just that the past was better, but that it had been flawless. That there was a fatal contradiction here—that history itself had been rewritten to suit the purpose—didn't seem to matter. Even the books of Upton Sinclair and Frank Norris could be read as tales of romance.

You heard it again and again, variations on a theme. In Jackson, which lies in the gold country of Forty-Niner days, a twenty-five-year-old printer talks about packing up for Alaska. The gold was long gone, of course, and the most successful man in town—said to be a millionaire now—was a twenty-two-year-old entrepreneur named Mike Spinetti, who, in four years, parlayed a back-street motorcycle shop into one of the largest Honda dealerships in the West. Things are all right here, the printer says, there are jobs in construction (building vacation homes for people from Sacramento and Stockton and San Francisco), but there is no future, no space, no romance. His father had worked in the mines before the gold ran out, and then for the county road department. Eventually the old man retired, at $120 a month, on a civil-service pension. "There's no future in that, in any of it," the son was saying. "You can't depend on the state or the federal government; one of these days the whole damn country is likely to turn belly-up on you. Alaska is the only frontier left." And in Sacramento a legislative assistant to a state representative, a young man with a law degree, is about to leave the country altogether; sooner or later he may join his friends who are settling in the woods of British Columbia, but for the next year he and his wife will explore India and Afghanistan to see what life could be like out there. There is a future, he tells you, but it lies in new dimensions, lies inside, in talents and resources of spirit that have yet to be explored.

We had heard a great deal of this before. But in the context of the Sierra foothills or the Western ranges of South Dakota or the slopes of the Rockies the thing that struck you about this romance of a new future—indeed, about this whole generation of nomads and would-be nomads—was how much the mythology of the Old West and the aspirations of the counterculture coincide. You couldn't tell the freaks from the cowboys. In Rapid City, kids wearing jeans and denim jackets were going off to the Black Hills on spring weekends to smoke grass and to talk about living in a cabin in the woods, and in Tuolumne, California, not far from where the prospectors once scratched for gold, the café pool tables were occupied by four longhairs who might be hired hands in the nearby lumberyard but who turn out, on closer inspection, to be just another vanful of welfare-collecting hippies. Everything flowed together, the restored Wells Fargo Express offices, the saloons, the abandoned mines, and the craggy hillsides where the semicivilized and the antisocial won the West for what the books called Progress. All of this had now been cleaned up, was being purged of its scruffiness, and was on the way to "restoration" in accord with the highest ideals of John Wayne. Yet history, because of its very brevity, might yet defeat the effort. It had been only twenty years since Pat Brown, then attorney general of California, and later to become governor, closed the whorehouses in Jackson; until that time they had been in continuous (and overt) operation since the gold rush. Ten years after the closing, a group of local entrepreneurs, tongue partly in cheek, succeeded in installing a heart-shaped bronze marker in the sidewalk:

BOTILLEAS BORDELLOS

WORLD'S OLDEST PROFESSION
FLOURISHED 50 YDS EAST OF
THIS PLAQUE FOR MANY YEARS
UNTIL THIS MOST PERFECT
EXAMPLE OF FREE ENTERPRISE
WAS PADLOCKED BY
UNSYMPATHETIC POLITICIANS

The marker didn't last long; in the only episode in Jackson's history to receive international attention, a bowdlerizing majority of local citizens, many of them said to be newcomers from the Middle West, stormed the offices of the mayor and the council and succeeded in having the plaque removed. It was not the way they wanted to think of their town or their West; it was all right to mark abandoned churches, mines, assay offices, banks, stage depots and hotels, but this was something else, and it required cleaning up. Rowdy yes, bawdy never. The West began in perfection.

All over the West there were new façades. In Sacramento, a major restoration project called the Redevelopment was turning what used to be an area of cheap hotels, flophouses and saloons into an imitation-gaslight revival of a Western movie set, and in the once flourishing town of Columbia, also in the gold country, a restoration operated by the State Department of Parks and Recreation offered, among other things, a chance for every visiting Boy Scout to "pan" gold in a sluice fed by a garden hose. It was all good, clean fun, but it began to suggest not only how history was being retouched but also something of the meaning —beyond ecology and conservation—of the Closing Down. The romance was becoming a museum piece and the pioneer a clean-living, hard-working, God-fearing antecedent of Ronald Reagan; at the same time it was hard to believe that the scruffy, the bawdy, the freaky and the antisocial, so close to the surface of Western life, could be completely wiped out by a restoration project or an act of the town council. What, after all, were Leatherstocking and Daniel Boone and the frontier scouts? Were they the advance agents of civilization making the territories safe for the Methodist Church, or were they, in effect, freaks and hippies, people forever running farther West from a society which they didn't suit and couldn't abide?

It is clear that there were no territories left, no place to run to (except perhaps Alaska or British Columbia or Afghanistan), and that history itself had been declared off limits to the rebellious and the antisocial. And yet here, more than anywhere else in America, the strain formed of the romantic, the hyperbolic and the violent remained just barely below the surface. The counterculture, such as it was, was still anchored here; at its best it had probably been no more optimistic and beautiful than the historic romance of the West now being enshrined in those restorations, at its worst it was probably no more vulgar or vicious than one might imagine the real Jackson or the real Columbia to have been in the golden era. What fantasies were articulated in those Mario Savio speeches, during the early days of the Berkeley Free Speech Movement, about throwing your body onto the machinery to keep it from functioning? Captain Ahab striking the sun? Moonshiners and revenuers? What wishes were preserved in levis and buckskins? What frustrated dreams in the endless contemplation of a commune in the woods? When a man imagined that the only alternative for a nation likely to "turn belly-up on you" was the frontier of Alaska, you could not be sure whether you were listening to someone supremely contemporary or to a voice of the Old West (or to Huck Finn), and when you heard the rhetoric of a California ecology debate you could not be certain whether they were choosing up sides for the apocalypse or whether you were witness to a replay of the ancient quarrels between the homesteaders and the "interests"—or the farmer and the cowman. Too much land, I heard someone saying during one of those debates, is fenced in. What you knew for certain was that everyone was valiantly trying to preserve his own version of the romance, and that without the romance the West would be just another place.

IV

Ever since World War II, and most apparently since the late fifties, the West had been divided by its own Mason-Dixon line, a line that demarcated a region almost as distinct from the rest of the area as the Old South was from the East. Draw a rough parallelogram, one side between Dallas and Houston, the other between Santa Barbara and San Diego, connect the top and bottom of each, and you had it: Phoenix, Tucson, El Paso, Palm Springs, Fort Worth, Dallas, Houston. To some extent all those places shared something with Los Angeles, or, rather, Los Angeles shared something with them, but among themselves they also constituted something unique—a certain style, an outlook and, most essential, an absolute dependence on modern technology. All of them were made possible by automobiles and air conditioning, their infatuation with gadgets remained undiminished, and their reliance on the defense industry could not be matched by any other region in the country or, indeed, in the world. It was the land of NASA and heart transplants, of McDonnell-Douglas and Texas Instruments, of oil and electronics, of airbases and missile factories. It was also the land of Barry Goldwater, Paul Fannin, John Tower, Lloyd Bentsen, of two Congressmen who belonged to the John Birch Society—the only two in the House—and of a collection of other political reactionaries who made their colleagues from the so-called conservative Middle West resemble radicals of the left. In each instance the conventional wisdom offered *sui generic* explanations: Tower and Bentsen were explained by Texas oil, the old frontier and some

mysterious (and largely nonexistent) legacy of conservatism;
Goldwater and Fannin were said to be representatives of all those
rich retired people from the South and the Midwest in Scottsdale, Arizona; the Birchers of southern California were supposed
to be the voices of first-generation right-wingers recently arrived
from Indiana and Iowa (which, in turn, were represented by
Birch Bayh, Vance Hartke, Harold Hughes and one lone conservative, Robert Miller). There had been—and perhaps still was
—a frontier in this region, but it was not only made of cowboys,
pioneers and homesteaders, but also—and, I think, more significantly—of sunshine, technology and government contracts. The
first made the region attractive, the second made it livable, and
the third paid for it.

The Southwest, as everyone knew, had been the fastest-
growing region in America. Houston was probably the only
boom town left in America; El Paso grew from a population of
96,000 in 1940 to something approaching a half million in 1970;
Dallas–Fort Worth, once jealously competing towns forty miles
apart, had simply flowed together into a single metropolitan
area; Orange County, California, largely farmland before World
War II, tripled in population during the fifties, doubled again in
the sixties, and now had a population of nearly 1.5 million; San
Diego County, with 1.3 million people in 1970, had doubled its
population in each decade since 1940. Clearly all of these cities
had been *places* thirty years ago—regional commercial centers,
army towns, clusters of banks and office buildings with big ambi-
tions, few traditions and little money. What had freed them were
technology and the government. The Southwest, in a sense,
began with technology; its very existence was tied to it, and so
technology itself had become a sort of mythic element, an article
of the common faith. While the national romance with the machine—always ambivalent anyhow—had been attenuated in other
parts of the West, just as it had been everywhere in America, it
remained undiminished in the Southwest, despite the filth in the
Houston ship channel, the smog over Phoenix and the ticky-

tackies flowing down the lower valley from El Paso. This Eden had not been defiled by the machine; it was created by it; it *was* the machine. The Southwest was the Spaceship Earth of Bucky Fuller's imagination, and very few people there would be able to survive without its gadgets.

The consequences of a miraculous technological birth were obviously enormous. Technology itself created the illusion of modernity; it seemed to define its own relevance, and, since it was the most obvious element of the environment, the mythic, quasi-religious qualities of existence could appear perpetually up-to-date. Certainly there had been, and there remained, strains of old frontier lore, of cattle trails and bandits, of Mexican War battles and the glorious days of the Lone Star Republic, but the land itself—the land from Dallas twelve hundred miles west to the California desert—had always been a harsh land, not a land that one could ever regard in any terms but those of contention. One surmounted the elements; one might even become sentimental about the beauty of the place, about the Big Sky and the tumbleweed and the mesquite. But it had not been the sort of place where one could ever imagine lush bottom lands, or small farms or magnificent streams. It had not been made to be part of the scenario of virgin land and yeoman farmers or of tall timber and majestic mountains, and was not in that sense part of the dream of the West. Water itself had usually been a trick; there was rarely enough of it, and so even here technology was required. Every victory had once been a one-shot proposition: another summer without drought, another herd sold and delivered to market, another rancher (or oil man) got lucky or gone bust. Fundamentally nothing would ever change; there would be no real growth without machines, and so when the machine came it seemed like a gift from God. It was the only place on earth where anyone might have the imagination, let alone the will, to buy London Bridge, ship it from England, stone by stone, reassemble it in the desert, and then build a river to flow under it.

In the beginning were the transistor, the car, the airplane and the air conditioner. In Dallas people were constantly speaking about how someone parlayed a few thousand acres of boondocks left him by his father into a multimillion-dollar real-estate windfall. Some of those people, of course, had made money in cattle or in oil before, but the real-estate deals would have been impossible without people, and the people would have been impossible without the technology that, on the one hand, provided the jobs and, on the other, made the climate bearable. Familiar stuff, but it explained a lot. It explained, for example, how the word "environment" could have an entirely new meaning, how existence within a B-52 six miles above Vietnam could seem like a perfectly reasonable extension of life on the ground (or, for that matter, how life on the moon itself might not be so different from life in Houston), or how the future itself, whatever the problems, could still be regarded by many people as a relatively simple matter of engineering and finance. If the environment of the Southwest had any precise model, that model was the Astrodome.

Ten years ago John Bainbridge, in a *New Yorker* magazine profile-turned-book, called Texans "the Super-Americans." Texans, he wrote, bore the same relationship to other Americans as Americans bore to Europeans. They were more open, optimistic, ebullient, vulgar, ill-mannered, friendly and enterprising than the rest of us, just as we were more of all those things than the majority of Europeans. People came to Texas to make money; it was the place for everybody's second chance (and therefore somewhat different from other parts of the Southwest—Arizona or Orange County—to which most newcomers came in quest of what had been generally described as the Good Life). To some extent those observations were still true, yet the gaps seemed to have shrunk since *The Super-Americans* was published—the gaps between Texas and America, the gaps between America and Europe. Despite the region's abiding ebullience and its continuing love affair with technology, it was just possible that the boom was ending even here. The great era of growth in the defense business was coming to an end, NASA had been cut back, the aircraft industry was in trouble, and the national supply of oil was becoming increasingly dependent on foreign deposits. Defense helped fuel the boom: Texas and California (meaning southern California) had been the nation's two leading states in defense and NASA contracts; together, in 1970, they received nearly $15 billion from the Defense Department alone. For twenty years that curve had been rising steeply. In the late sixties it leveled off.

The boom couldn't have continued indefinitely, in any case, at the rate it had been going. Curves didn't rise forever, and so the question was likely to become, for the Southwest and, in lesser proportions, for the country, What are you doing after the miracle? There were strong signs during the 1972 election campaign that Texas liberals were once again getting themselves together—that the old politicians of the boom era, the Johnson and Connally people, were in trouble. In Houston Barbara Jordan became the first black Texan to be elected to Congress since Reconstruction; Bob Eckhardt, another liberal from Houston, was elected to his fourth term, while the old guard, among them Ben Barnes, former lieutenant governor, and the hand-picked gubernatorial candidate of the conservative Democrats, were badly beaten. Some of those changes had been clearly attributable to a series of stock scandals (which, like insurance scandals and oil scandals, constituted the Great Entertainment of Texas politics), but there may well have been another factor, and that a subtly revised estimate of the future itself. In Orange County, California, the children of right-wingers were registering as Democrats and talking about McGovern; in Los Angeles the school system was busing ghetto children into schools in exclusive neighborhoods because the once-affluent engineers and technicians, now unemployed, could no longer afford to live there; and in Dallas, which had, until a few years ago, been in the control of a business elite called the Dallas Citizens Council, people were talking about "things opening up." Not that local politics were wildly democratic, but that the liberals, the newcomers and the minorities—blacks, Chicanos and Indians—were less intimidated. The old boom spirit was fading, and the younger generation of business and professional people, who represented the technocracy and not the old commercial boosters, tended, like their counterparts everywhere else, to be less romantic, more dispassionate and, most important, less committed to the place itself. "The DCC," said an old Dallas liberal, "was certainly a crowd of conservative curmudgeons. But they were, in their own way, deeply interested in the city. It was their town; they made money off it, and they wanted to see it grow." A love affair with technology was one thing, but the infusion of technocratic thinking tended, ironically, to dilute the booster mentality that had helped produce it in the first place. It was more romantic to build Astrodomes and air-conditioned cities than it was to live in them. After a while one modern shopping mall looked like another, and after a certain time in any hermetic, technological environment it would be difficult to remember whether the place was called Midland, El Paso or Tucson.

The religion of technology persists, of course, despite the political changes, and the reactionaries (if that is the proper word) are still there. The mixture of sunshine and money created some powerful illusions and tended to attract the sort of people who were likely to succumb to them. It was not simply that the Southwest was full of people from the South and the Middle West (Geritol Gulch, they call it in Scottsdale), but that it had drawn a certain kind: individuals and families fleeing from "problems"—meaning crime, blacks, noise and social complexity—and individuals pursuing the "opportunities" that the technology made possible. They were either coming with money or for money, were going for gold and sunshine. The welfare state had made it all possible—the insured savings, the Social Security, the vast water projects and the Defense Department contracts—and, like all those recipients of foreign aid about whom they liked to complain so much, they hated the welfare state for it. What Uncle Sam had provided Uncle Sam might also take away. Nothing was stable or permanent or reliable: the region floated in its own transience—pot-smoking kids, militant Chicanos and blacks, changing neighborhoods, sections and towns. The assassination of John F. Kennedy might have been secretly welcomed, but it nonetheless traumatized Dallas; if the President wasn't safe, what was? Even now, after a decade, the first place visitors wanted to see was the old Texas Schoolbook Depository building and the freeway that passed below it.

In the end, all one could really love was the technology itself. And yet that hardly constituted a frontier, not anymore; it was, indeed, its very opposite. Technology can create its own time, can speed it up, slow it, and perhaps stop it altogether; it can create days without nights, nights without days, can leave sound behind, and may someday, without too much stretch of the imagination, overtake history itself. As an idea it represented a perpetual future, a never-ending newness, but as a fact it constituted its very antithesis. There are few options in a spaceship, and most of the surprises were likely to be fatal. Once, perhaps as little as a generation ago, it was the territories that were supposed to be unsafe; now it was civilization itself, and yet without civilization there would be nothing but the sun and the too-harsh land. Perhaps the Southwest did represent the patterns of the American future, but what were the patterns of that future? The miracle had happened, and now it was coming to an end.

V

Manifest Destiny, the American version of *Lebensraum* and the *Drang nach Osten*, was not supposed to stop at the water's edge. The dreamers of the nineteenth century imagined that the West was not only an empire to be conquered and settled but also a route to the East, the Passage to India. "An American road to

India through the heart of our country," said Senator Thomas Hart Benton in 1849, "will revive upon its line all the wonders of which we have read—and eclipse them. The western wilderness, from the Pacific to the Mississippi, will start into life under its touch." The consequences of such dreaming were still with us; they had been with us when we "lost" China to Mao precisely a century after Senator Benton spoke—a century after the gold rush began—and they were with us now in the legacy of Vietnam. The American frontier would go beyond the eastern shore of the Pacific—would extend all the way to the coast of Asia. Twenty years ago, California was represented in Congress by a man sometimes known as the Senator from Formosa; in 1972 it was his onetime Senate colleague Richard Nixon who declared that era at an end.

And yet the impulse survived even the *de facto* recognition of the Chinese Communist government. Nixon's declaration that he would not become the first American President to lose a war— another of his ironic Churchillian echoes—was, after all, a declaration of machismo: we were still tough enough to do it if we really wanted to. We didn't want to, of course, never having sought territory, but no President, despite all that, could preside over the liquidation of the nation's symbolic empire, even if no territory was involved. Out there we still maintained a vicarious frontier with vicarious Indians, a vicarious cavalry and the fear of a vicarious General Custer. It was less than ninety years between Little Big Horn and Tet.

There had been—and still were—other vicarious frontiers. There was the moon, and there was inner space, and there was the continuing Western tension between transience and permanence, between civilization and territories yet to be explored and conquered. You tried something—a place, an idea, a movement—and then, literally or figuratively, you pulled up stakes and went somewhere else: straight people turned into radicals or junkies, then into Jesus Freaks, and then they came out of the hills to register as Republicans and to demand stronger enforcement of the drug laws. "The conservative Republican view-point," one of them said, "is the closest to the laws of God." Conventional families turned into communes and then back into conventional families; scientists became astrologers, and mathematical economists emerged as food freaks. There was the Portola Institute and Esalen, *The Whole Earth Catalogue* and the Glide Church, where the homosexuals were married, and there was a judge in San Francisco who agreed to drop the drug charges against the fifty-seven-year-old leader of a commune if all his cohabitants agreed to get married. Meanwhile, half the population seemed to be on the road; you met them on the highway or in the trailer camps, and as they spoke about how it was nicer in Mendocino or in Boulder or in the woods of Oregon, their talk was strangely reminiscent of the dialogue of the Okies in the thirties, stuff from *The Grapes of Wrath* or from Studs Terkel's tapes in *Hard Times*. One learned entirely new geographies, the geography of the hitchhiker and the panhandler, places where freaks get hassled and where they don't, camp grounds that were still relatively uncrowded, places where the land was cheap and the neighbors hospitable. In some vague way they were always looking, always thinking of moving on. It was as if, having reached the Pacific, they could no longer trust the compass: On this shore everything bounced, rearranged itself, and began to move in random directions. This is where the gyroscope broke down.

Transience and permanence. Nearly a million Californians lived in mobile homes. *"In Manteca,"* said the brochure, *"it's El Rancho Mobile Home Park . . . convenient mobile home living in a resort atmosphere!"* It was like hundreds of other such parks. One could find them everywhere in America, but in the West and the Southwest the climate and the inhabitants combined to give them an intrinsic quality entirely foreign to other places. Across Route 120 from El Rancho there was a used-car lot with a huge neon sign, next door was a motel, and behind it the fields of the Central Valley flowed on toward the south, toward Modesto and Fresno and Bakersfield, one huge flat irrigated fruit factory extending for two hundred miles. At El Rancho, as in most of the others, you rented your space and received in return the use of an air-conditioned community center (kitchen, meeting rooms, pool tables), a swimming pool, laundry, playground and car wash. At the same time you also had to abide by the rules. The "adult community" was segregated from the families with children, you agreed to keep your mobile in good repair, to install skirting and awnings within three months of the day you moved in, to get approval before installing an air conditioner (so as to minimize noise for the neighbors, who, after all, lived just a few feet away), to clean up after your pet—and to get permission before you got one in the first place, and to refrain from hanging laundry outside at any time. It was the best of all worlds, and the worst. To move a mobile twenty feet wide and sixty feet long is a major operation; it is not something you hitch to your Buick for a run to the next town. And yet it preserved the illusion: if you really wanted to move on you could do so. This was not something that was rooted in the ground, a place subject to block busting or to the permanent misfortune of unpleasant neighbors or to a stagnating economy. With a minimum of fantasy you might even imagine that these mobiles were, in fact, a community of prairie schooners pulled in a circle around the campfire, people who had gathered temporarily for mutual protection and sociability but who were nonetheless expecting to pull up stakes at dawn in their search for the golden tomorrow. You were surrounded by the symbols of transience, by the cars, the motel, the road, and there was hardly a landmark in sight to suggest that this would ever be something other than a place to camp. A few miles down the road the migrant agricultural workers, coming north with the spring, were moving into a camp very much like it. It was smaller and meaner, of course; each unit had three rooms with a couple of cots in each, and the johns were outdoors, but there were no rules against hanging your wash outside (or about air conditioners), and the state of California, which operated the place (with the help of federal funds) provided day care for young children so that all the able-bodied could go off to the fields at 5 A.M. Yet it provided no more or less permanence or community; in the fall, you knew, everybody would get back in his car and turn south again—to another field, another territory. One American in fifteen makes a major move each year (one in five moves within a local area); many of us were, in that sense, transients. But most of us still clung to the illusion of permanence; to live in a mobile must, in a very deep way, require the illusion of change. The parks were all the same, but the need for new territories dies hard.

The land itself suggested that the territories would always be there, that Manifest Destiny still lived. Driving east from San Francisco toward the Sierras—across the Mount Diablo range, through the fruitlands of the Central Valley—one sometimes got the peculiar sensation that one was, in fact, driving west, going from the city to the farm to the undeveloped land, from the end of something to the beginning. There was a West behind you, across the Pacific, toward the islands, toward China, but there was also a West ahead, toward the mountains where the sun rises. You couldn't trust the compass. In those hills or beyond the snow-capped peaks or along the slopes from Montana south all the way to New Mexico it was hard to deny some projection of possibilities. The hard data told you that much of the land was useless, it was too steep, too cold, too rocky, too dry, and that where it had been settled the inhabitants were more dependent on the Martin Company or the Atomic Energy Commission or the Coors Brewery than they were on land or cattle or timber. And yet the romance was undeniable: the sounds and pictures that one was raised with, and the lyricism that went back to the first settlements on the Eastern shore kept playing back and became a reality that made the hard data seem like abstractions; crowding, pollution, unemployment, decay—it all seemed distant. Maybe, you told yourself, there were possibilities here, possibilities stemming not so much from physical space, but from the fact that all the commitments hadn't been made, that the burden of history was light, and that the mirage of the West still remained more or less intact. In 1971, when interviewers from the California poll asked disenchanted Californians why they wanted to leave—and about twenty-nine percent did—more than a third spoke about smog and pollution, and another twenty-seven percent about the crowding along the Pacific Coast. But of those who wanted to go, a majority listed another Western state as first choice; to go East was apparently unthinkable (New York was first choice with four percent of those interviewed). Perhaps, just perhaps, those territories wouldn't be settled until we had come to terms with the ambivalence in ourselves, had decided how we would deal with technology, how we could use it without having it destroy us, had grown beyond Vietnam, and beyond the various utopias which had driven so much of California to the brink. Clearly the lessons were there: Los Angeles had not repealed death, San Francisco and San Jose and Phoenix couldn't control development, and no one had yet fully come to terms with the price of growth or with the social shocks that followed after growth came to an end. Could we confront ourselves not out of innocence but from understanding? "The price of civilization, civility and living together," wrote Howard S. Becker and Irving Louis Horowitz about San Francisco, "is not getting everything you want." It might not have been an entirely applicable "lesson" about San Francisco, but it was clearly a reasonable statement about the excessive and contradictory expectations Americans held about the West itself.

What San Francisco had done was make peace with time. Clearly the tolerance was there—tolerance of hippies and freaks and homosexuals, tolerance of the classy and the schlocky, tolerance of tolerance and even of intolerance. While the rest of the state voted to restore the death penalty, San Francisco voted no, and while other Californians opposed the legalization of marijuana, San Franciscans voted yes. San Francisco was, in many ways, a Mediterranean city; it took a lot of things seriously, most of all itself, but it had rarely tended to think in absolutes. San Francisco too might one day lose by default; when he was asked about the city's casual attitude about earthquakes, Mayor Joseph Alioto replied that living six months in San Francisco was better than a lifetime in Whittier. Yet there was nothing fatalistic about it, as there was in Los Angeles, no sense that one was living on borrowed time. San Francisco had simply slowed down the clock; every provincial place tried to do that, but when the climate, the scenery, the mixture of races and styles and the national polls all told you that this was the place to live, then the provincialism turned into cosmopolitan reverie and life could go on without the vaguest sense of inferiority or guilt. Sooner or later there would be an earthquake—not to mention high rises, school busing fights, and racial conflict—but, like everything else in San Francisco, that too could be postponed.

There was a price for that kind of civilization, but it had little to do with "not getting everything you want." It lay, rather, in the willingness to accept too much that was second-rate, in a cheerful readiness to avoid harsh distinctions between high standards and things that were merely pretentious. "If you took the city's three art museums and combined them," one visiting curator was quoted, "you would have one bad museum." Everything got the fancy labels, the opera, the theater, the baseball fans, the conversations, even though much of it was minor-league stuff. "This city," said someone who had been in San Francisco three years and was preparing to leave, "is full of losers. Everybody who doesn't make it somewhere else ends up in San Francisco sooner or later." When the Giants traded the aging Willie Mays to the New York Mets, thereby losing the greatest baseball symbol of a generation, New York gave him the key to the city and indulged in orgies of self-congratulations. San Franciscans merely shrugged their shoulders. The team, they said, had lost a man who was getting to be a liability; moreover, one sportswriter explained, the city had never gotten over its attachment to the minor-league clubs that used to play there. In a provincial town that basks in its own beauty it was the fear of liabilities that became the governing impulse, not the dream of greatness.

The important lesson, however, had to do with time itself. The myth of the West—the Old West of the East—simply assumed that time was on your side. The clock was man's best friend. When the serpents began to appear in the garden, therefore, it was just as easy to begin thinking that the clock was your worst enemy, that the inexorability of the westward movement and Manifest Destiny was also the inexorability of crowding, pollution and war. The opposite of a future that promised everything was a future that promised nothing. Once the cowboy ceased to be a hero it must inevitably follow that the hero was really the Indian. Once the machine was seen as a thing of liabilities all technology became negative. "A system which revolved about a half-mystical conception of nature," wrote Henry Nash Smith in *Virgin Land*, "was powerless to confront issues arising from the advance of technology. Agrarian theory encouraged men to ignore the industrial revolution altogether, or to regard it as an unfortunate and anomalous violation of the natural order of things." The unresolved conflict between the legacy of that "half-mystical conception of nature" and the issues arising from technology still explained a great deal of the West; it explained its crazy mixture of styles and sects and attitudes, its beauty-craving façades, and, most important, the apparent paralysis of a generation of people who were either drifting from one form of salvation to another or—and this may amount to the same thing—simply waiting, in a sort of stupor, for something to happen. Sometimes it was even possible to imagine that California had produced a new ethnic type, blond, tanned, easygoing, a creature of sunny disposition, little ambition and no particular commitments, a composite of all the American virtues and therefore a model for none. A living doll.

Perhaps all of that was inevitable. This is where all the streams and tributaries ran together, where things which originated elsewhere—through time and history, through myth and imagination and wandering—came to rest. It was the final evolution of Western man. The West got its meaning from the East—its several and often contradictory meanings—and it had never been able to develop a consistent meaning for itself. Thus one lived beyond time, or by slowing time, or with the crazy apocalyptic fear that time was running out. And yet, despite all those things, or perhaps even because of them, there remained the search for possibilities. Geographically this was the end of the American future, but it was not yet the end of American identity or of the search for something new. We were, of course, all hooked on the romance of this place: if you wanted to be a big-leaguer you returned to New York, but if you clung to the hope that life might again be worth living, you voted with the majority who wanted to stay. California was the place that killed George Jackson and that experimented with drugs and "psychosurgery" on prisoners to make them more compliant, but it was also the place that acquitted Angela Davis and that thought seriously about making marijuana legal (and might, eventually, become the first state to do so) and that would, after the last large generation of immigrants from the Midwest come to their final reward at Forest Lawn, be the first state fully to outgrow the Puritan curse. The very fact that fantasies were still possible, however crazy or confused, suggested that another future may yet be invented. Perhaps this would be the primordial ooze of which new cultures were made. For better or worse.

FIVE:

THE NEW SOUTH
SHALL RISE AGAIN

I

The need to identify possibilities with particular geographical regions dies slowly; we adapt old myths to new requirements, shape them for the occasion, and create the semblance of new hopes. Somewhere there has to be a generic West, another place to go, a region of alternatives and new opportunity. At the same time, and for related reasons, we need connections with history, the more proximate the better; where the past is close, there the future may be closer also. And so, as the West began to fade under the excesses of its own success, its frustrations, its dreams removed, the most historical of all American regions began to reemerge, buttressed now by a strange mix of old and new, of liabilities become assets, of tradition transformed to change.

Old ghosts kept coming back. Again it was the New South, the *New* New South, looking away now from the dusty crossroads and the men in the white sheets, looking now to suburbs, electronic plants, country clubs and *moderation:* Talk progress, talk new attitudes, talk change. New men, new faces, new rhetoric. But the old myth survived, became part of progress itself, and each time we tried to destroy it or explain it or debunk it we seemed to give it new life. Perhaps the myth of the South was still necessary to our image of America, was something we needed to establish connections with the tragedy and darkness that shaped the experience of other men in other places; through the South, through some Faulknerian Reconstruction, perhaps,

207

we might join the rest of humanity—might make common cause with Greeks and Frenchmen and Italians. We spoke about the New South, read the statistics, listened to the rhetoric, said the clichés, mentioned the names of new men—Carter, Scott, Bumpers, Askew—yet each time the scent of honeysuckle and reprocessed magnolias returned as strong as ever.

Returned enlarged: By God, maybe the South would save us all. Maybe the South contained the real American future. "I would see among blacks a new commitment to Mississippi *as a place*," wrote Willie Morris in 1970, "expressions of a love and loyalty to Mississippi as a society worth working for, as a frontier for redeeming some lost quality in the American soul." The less romantic among us would say it in other ways, more *hardheaded* ways: Southern progress without Northern mistakes, growth without pollution, integration with courtesy and understanding, a chance even for a new Progressive Era in American politics. The South as redeemer. "It may be the South," wrote Marshall Frady in *Life*, "where the nation's general malaise of racial alienation first finds resolution. Not in the order of division prophesied by the old segregationists' apologists but in the formal advent of a single people unique and richly dimensioned."

None of us was immune. We seemed to need that myth—needed it to shape, if we could, a new sense of national possibilities—and so, in an odd way, the South replaced the West as the mythic American frontier. After being closed for more than a century, this was the territory that was opening up—not in the literal pioneer sense, not in the sense of homesteads and free land, but certainly in the sense of development and growth, and, more significantly, in seeming to offer the resources and experience for an age which no longer took for granted the old American immortality, which recognized that the belief in some national immunity to error, limitations and tragedy was an illusion. At the same time the contemporary South was closer to its own history, closer to the frontier, more visible still as a distinctive American place. The connections between past and present come easily:

one did not have to travel far from the new plants and suburbs to be swallowed by the region itself—by the climate, the trees, and red soil—or to be engulfed by that Gothic sense of doom which still lingered in the small towns, in the shacks of the croppers, and in the mists that rose from the streams and swamps during the night. It was the last American region, and anyone concerned about the country's future had eventually to return (or go for the first time), to see what had changed, to test his own versions, to see how it felt *down there* looking up. And yet, the very need betrayed more than a hint of disillusionment, a growing doubt about what the country had achieved, where it was going, and what progress meant.

Clearly there was something new, and what was new extended beyond the obvious artifacts of "progress"—the new shopping centers, the factories, the rising levels of regional income, and the declining level of racial invective—beyond the endless announcements that the South was becoming less Southern and more like the rest of America. Jackson, Mississippi, in 1972 was not the same town it had been in 1960 or even in 1969. Could one imagine, right here, integrated groups of blacks and whites eating in the restaurants of Capitol Street? Could one imagine a black candidate for governor of Mississippi speaking unmolested from the steps of nearly every little county courthouse in the state? Could one imagine that the citizens of Sunflower County would try the white killers of a black girl before a jury of nine blacks and three whites? Could one imagine witnessing a scene in which the black sheriff of Greene County, Alabama, in a mod Italian suit, was inspecting the watermelon crop on a thriving four-thousand-acre farm owned by Muslims? Could one imagine the governor of Georgia announcing that "the time for racial discrimination is over," or Senator John C. Stennis of Mississippi urging his fellow politicians in that state to start paying attention to the demands and power of the newly enfranchised black voters? Most of all, the South *felt* different, and every outsider who returned after an absence of a year or two perceived it:

one could generally assume, lacking evidence to the contrary, that the men with the shotguns in the pickup truck following you on the rural roads of Alabama or Mississippi were in fact hunters, not Kluxers, that a talented high-school halfback would be cheered by the local citizens regardless of his (or their) color, and that a white waitress would rather serve a black customer than trade places with the underpaid all-black crew that cleared the tables and scraped the dishes.

And yet the differences did not answer questions—they only changed them. Ever since 1968 the media had represented every new Southern politician as a moderate: Carter in Georgia, West in South Carolina, even Waller in Mississippi. If a man didn't talk like Lester Maddox or John Bell Williams, if he didn't shout "nigger" during his campaign or sport buttons saying "Never," he must be a progressive. The editorial writers in New York and the national politicians of the Democratic Party appreciated manners; Maddox and Wallace were too dirty and scruffy for their taste, too obvious, too demagogic. But when a man talked about reason, economic growth and industrial development, when he said something about black and white working together, he was appreciated as a realist and a gentleman. And so we suffered from a sort of split vision, a vision on the one hand of the South catching up with America, a vision on the other of the South as a source of political and cultural renewal. At the close of the sixties, wrote Paul Gaston in *The New South Creed*,

the myth of the New South appeared to be losing its *raison d'être*. Southerners accepted new racial patterns that gave to the black more dignity and greater opportunity than he had ever known before—only to see sharply highlighted the inadequacies of integration and the immensity of the problems caused by a heritage of oppression. The region's continuing economic progress, more substantial than ever before, was beset by the same kind of critiques that confounded national advances. Its growing identity with the national viewpoint, made possible initially by the nationalization of the race problem, was unrewarded by a sense of relief and achievement because the nation itself appeared to have lost a sense of destiny. Thus deprived of the larger frame of reference which had always conditioned its character and given it its special appeal, the myth paradoxically pictured a regional way of life in harmony with a mirage.

The consequence of such perceptions, however, was not despair or resignation but a kind of instant replay. In the South the exhausted liberalism of the thirties still seemed to make some sense; it had not yet been fully tried and had therefore not yet had a chance to fail. At the same time (for a minority of others), the South still seemed to offer possibilities for a renewed radicalism, for a resurgent populism uniting blacks and poor whites against the power of banks, utilities and large corporations. The South bemused us all, bemused us with its tension between civility and violence, with its pervasive sense of politics—politics as second nature, politics as every man's preoccupation, politics and courtesy as two sides of the same coin—and with a sense (our sense, perhaps our projection) of opportunities not yet closed, racial opportunities, opportunities for the good life, opportunities for a new sort of politics. Maybe the South was, after all, better than America itself, perhaps the South, as a relatively underdeveloped region, as a place where "the races have always known and understood each other," as the one region which had known defeat and tragedy, was now better prepared for the future than any other region in America, maybe out of it some restorative hope would enter the mainstream of American life. "Hell," said young Hodding Carter to Willie Morris, "it might just work here someday. Wouldn't *that* surprise 'em?"

II

Greene County, Alabama, is located at the edge of the Black Belt forty miles southwest of Tuscaloosa, where the university is located, an irregular cone-shaped area formed by the Tombigbee River on the west and the Black Warrior on the east. Its population, estimated at eleven thousand people, was eighty percent black, predominantly rural, and one of the poorest in America. What made it unique in its region, where many people were poor and black, was that in two elections in 1970—one a special election ordered by a federal court in the summer, the other in November—the poor, black people of Greene County elected a black sheriff, a black probate judge, a black school board, and black county commissioners. Of the major political leaders in the area, only the judge of the circuit court, Emmett Hildreth, who represented three counties, was white. Greene County's government was therefore as black as or blacker than any in America.

There are three of us in the car, Tom Gilmore, the black sheriff, Bill Field, a white student from the University of Alabama, and myself. A makeshift blue light has been mounted on the dashboard, but the car is otherwise unmarked. Gilmore, in his gray pinstriped suit, looks more like a lawyer or writer from New York than a thirty-year-old country boy who was raised on a farm no more than twenty miles from this spot, going south on U.S. 11, where we are now driving. For a time he had been away, two years at a Bible college in Selma, two years in Los Angeles, but most of his life he has been here, preaching, organizing for SNCC, talking up the potential of political power, and reassuring the fearful that "we'll always be here" to protect them if the gun-toting sheetheads should come around in the middle of the night. And since Gilmore is also a part-time student at the university, he further confounds the image with the paperback books on the front seat: Camus, Rollo May, B. F. Skinner. Is this really the county sheriff? "I'm just like my prisoners in the county jail," he would say later. "I'm in a cage, too. It's just that the bars aren't iron and the walls aren't concrete."

Gilmore is taking us on a tour of the county, a tour of places and of time. To come even this far was an incredible achievement —the casualties were all around, evicted sharecroppers, people hounded for the repayment of debts they never knew they owed —and still it was only the beginning. Political power alone was something, but without economic power it would not be worth much. *"Why the hell do you think the elections were so close?"* *someone had asked me. "With eighty percent of the population, they should have run away with it, but they didn't. Think of all those chattel mortgages held by whites, mortgages on land and cattle and cars, going back thirty years. All those chances to remind people to stay in line. That's where the power was."* "Their jobs weren't jeopardized," Gilmore says as we drive, "because most of them worked outside the county; they work in Demopolis or in Tuscaloosa. But their homes are here; all through the registration drive and the campaign we had to find places for evicted people to live. See that place over there? All the newer houses were built for people who were run off by white landholders after they went to register."

He knows all the names, the stories, the landmarks, knows, it seems, the history of every acre—who owned it and who was dispossessed. Close to 40 percent of the population was out of work, the median per-capita income was about $600, and more than 80 percent lived in substandard housing. In Eutaw, the county seat, a number of new alphabet organizations were trying to create local community-controlled corporations, seeking employers and jobs and money to train workers to fill them, organizing a land-buying association, planning low-income housing, trying to sustain the hopes of people who, on the one hand, expected too much from political victory or, on the other, expected nothing at all. But even these considerations might be secondary to the staggering pattern of personal debt—debts owed by blacks to individual whites. In Tuscaloosa a white lawyer who helped litigate a string of Greene County cases through the federal courts—cases of intimidation and election fraud which ultimately led to a criminal-contempt sentence against the white former probate judge—estimated that it would take $5 million just to free the county's blacks from their creditors. Until that freedom is bought, he says, political power means nothing.

Gilmore and his fellow black officials were understandably

reluctant to speak too much of what might yet be. The problems were too staggering, the possibilities too uncertain. Even before the 1970 election several hundred whites, anticipating the inevitable, had begun to move away; a third of the stores in Eutaw were closed, and there was no telling who was friend and who was just waiting until disaster struck. Across the street from Gilmore's office, Ralph Banks, a white lawyer and landholder who had served as county attorney under the old regime and who helped lead the resistance against the black candidates, had offered his cooperation and was apparently giving it. "Sure I thought it was going to be pretty damn bad," he had told me, looking across at the courthouse. "But I changed my mind." Tom Gilmore had done that: "He wants to do the right thing." Other whites—a few, at any rate—were accepting the change, and a handful who had moved away were coming back, disappointed by "those sorry white folks" in the white-majority communities where they sought refuge. It was their county, too, and they meant to make the best of it. Still, there was neither enthusiasm nor warmth. That would take time. Judge Hildreth might later speak about how blacks and whites had always gotten along in Greene County, how they understood one another, how they had always eschewed violence and in fact there had been little violence, but he could not speak persuasively of any great passion to cooperate. Gilmore still had one white deputy—"to keep an eye out for the white folks on what the blacks were doing," someone said—and Banks was helping with the legal work, but for the most part the whites were simply sitting it out.

"I want people to reach the level where they can be fully human," Gilmore had said, "and we're not there yet." We were driving past fields of corn and cotton, flat, rich ground rising gradually into rolling hills where the crops yielded to pasture. Occasionally Gilmore would stop to point out a landmark: the home of William McKinley Branch, the Reverend Branch, now county probate judge; the Ebenezer Baptist Church near Forkland where "the movement began"; the dirt roads where Gilmore and his friends had once walked as children, going to school or to the store; the homes of dispossessed people who had been relocated on an acre or two donated by black farmers, new clusters of houses, little communities rising out of the dislocation of people whose first trip to the ballot box had produced this change, creating an entirely new history, an intrinsic history joining land and people in bonds they could not have imagined before. The other South belonged to someone else, to another time. Maybe, Gilmore suggested, "the Black Belt was really named for us, and not for the black soil. A lot of us are buried here; we're the ones who bled for it." Still, this time the link might have a different meaning, might produce a different vision. Branch, who once taught school, was fired for his activities in voter registration; Gilmore had been beaten up; there had been boycotts in Eutaw, and some stores had been forced to close; Rap Brown had been there, and SNCC and SCLC and SEDFRE; and there had been that succession of court cases which culminated in the special election of 1970. The former county judge had refused to put the names of the black candidates on the regular election ballot, even after he had been ordered to do so by a federal court, and so he was held in contempt, and fined, and a special election ordered: That was the new history, a history in which blacks were protagonists and not just victims.

Already there was a different mood. Black people, as someone said, could stand "a little taller," could congregate around the courthouse, *their* courthouse, and see their people getting the county jobs. Black people were wearing uniforms and badges and giving black (and white) folks the big hello on the courthouse steps, could talk politics with some expectation of meaning and success, could even engage in all the intrigues and maneuvers that political power made possible. There would be evening meetings in the upstairs courtroom to discuss other campaigns—the coming city election in Eutaw, for example—and to talk of road repairs and housing. There would be talk of new plants, foundation grants and federal assistance. And there would no longer be the possibility "for them to send out the sheriff and have him mess with people."

There were some things about the sheriff's business, Gilmore said, that he didn't want to learn. His own political career had begun in an encounter with a state trooper. His car had spattered mud on the trooper's car. "The trooper stopped me, cussed me out, and pulled his pistol; he told me if he ever saw me again he'd blow my brains out." Two years later, he said, he was beaten up by the sheriff, a former All-American tackle at the University of Alabama whose family had controlled the sheriff's office for forty years. "When he beat me up," Gilmore said, "I decided I'd beat *him*." But he also decided that he would become a different sort of cop, and so, shortly after the election, he had started going through the records of the local court to see which former residents of Greene County now incarcerated in state prisons could be returned home in the custody of the sheriff; he wanted to try some serious work in prisoner rehabilitation, had already sent a couple of county prisoners back to school, and had found a job for another. Each week, moreover, he conducted meetings with his prisoners, served them coffee, and discussed their problems; perhaps he could get federal money for prison reform; perhaps this might be a model; perhaps . . . Still he was reluctant to talk. "If I say too much I'll telegraph my plans, and the opposition can set up a good defense. The system, you could say, was almost made to make men destroy each other. Maybe if I knew as much as Skinner I'd try to do things his way. The whites in the South conditioned the blacks—and each other. Maybe I could do a different kind of conditioning."

Even this much was hard to comprehend. They were all trying to live together at the same moment, the whites and the blacks, the old fundamentalist preachers, the economic planners, the kids, yet each person's clock seemed to be set to a different time and to run at its own pace. Within a few hours and the space of a few miles you could hear them all: Gilmore's chief deputy, a large black man named James Flanigan, talking about his son Arthur, a student at Swarthmore, who was spending his junior year at the Sorbonne; Ralph Banks in his law office recounting how, generations ago, his family had come to Alabama to escape a slave revolt in Haiti, how they had run once and were not about to move again; the young activists down the block discussing tax policy, small-business loans and the habits of New York foundations; and, ten miles down Route 43, in a little country church, an old preacher telling how he always used to remind his flock that when you beat up someone who broke the boycott you were doing the Lord's work: "When you hit that man, He *knew* you had love in your heart."

There were other things, too: the eighty little churches—seventy-nine too many, Gilmore would say—with their endless round of revivals, their hymns, their nickel-and-dime collections, and their holy-card-Jesus-picture fans advertising Gandy's Funeral Home ("One Call Does It All"), perched uneasily between this world and the next; the precarious houses, lacking foundations, sitting on cinder-block posts, with their broken furniture and the ubiquitous magazine pictures of the black man's trinity, Jesus, Kennedy and King; the school system, about ninety-nine percent black, desperately trying to institute new programs that would really teach kids to read, trying to get federal money, sometimes over the veto of George Wallace and the state bureaucrats; and, most of all, the people standing at the crossroads, or riding in the rusty cars with the sagging springs, or walking along the side of the road much as they had for a hundred years, not quite certain what time it really was. It was all precarious and ambivalent, life at the margin, at the intersection of ages and states of mind, but the most ambivalent element of all was religion itself, religion as energy, religion as inertia. "I know," Gilmore had said, "that it was the white man's religion, and that the churches were used to keep us apart. I know that. But now we're going to use the churches against them." Perhaps the Word itself could be redefined.

There was no longer a single vision, if indeed one had ever

existed; the nineteenth century had not yet ended, and the twenty-first had already begun. And so new visions had to be created, and new techniques invented. There was no money, and while a few new employers were expected to come in—and some already had—the possibilities for industrial development were limited: all Greene County could offer was the promise of enlightened government and cheap unskilled labor. Possibly, just possibly, there might be something in the land itself, in the historic ability to endure, and in the puritanical toughness of the people themselves. For Greene County, after a year of black government, the model enterprise was not a factory or a state agricultural project, not the schools or the hospital, but the Muslim farm. The farm, for obvious reasons, was unmarked; east of Birmingham, in St. Clare County, Muslim cattle had been poisoned, and at other Muslim farms shots were fired. Even here there was still fear and suspicion: There had been some threats from passing motorists, and twice U.S. Army helicopters had landed on the farm—ostensibly through mechanical failure—because some idiot in a uniform suspected that the Muslims were using the place to train guerrillas. In fact there was not even a Muslim on the farm—it was run by a hired professional named Ollie Hall, the Muslims just owned it—yet there were still local blacks (not to mention whites) who believed that any contact with the place was tempting the Devil.

But they were making a go of it, farming nearly four thousand acres of their own, leasing another 2,600, growing corn and cattle, soybeans and watermelons. (On the day of my visit Hall was proudly showing off the watermelons; it was the second crop of the season, and if the frost held off another ten days he would have done something that had never been accomplished in that region before.) Hall employed eight men full time, and more during the peak seasons, paying wages double the going rate for agricultural work: tractor operators who had been getting $30 a week were earning $65; the two assistant managers were earning $100. "It's hard to find good people," Hall said.

"They've been kept down so long; the white man destroyed initiative, and now we've got to recreate it." We were walking through the fields together: Gilmore, the black sheriff in the Italian suit; Hall, the farm entrepreneur; Bill Fields, the white student from the small town in south Alabama; and myself, the writer from New York, who could hardly tell a soybean from a tomato. We too represented four separate worlds, four versions of time, but each of us knew that we all wanted this to succeed. Next year, Hall said, there would be more cotton; if he could grow a thousand acres it would pay him to build and operate his own gin, and to do some ginning for others; they were still clearing land, would use every foot of the place, would try other crops, take on more people, might indeed build an entire food-processing plant. Already they had harvested enough watermelons to market forty-nine semiloads of 55,000 pounds each, with another harvest yet to come, had three hundred acres in cotton, four hundred head of cattle and six hundred acres in corn. But what was most important was to restore that initiative, to regain the use of the land, to rebuild, to renew. "We've got to have that initiative back," Hall said, "or we'll all die," appealing now to the oldest form of Americanism of them all: hard work, thrift, enterprise. If Nixon really believed all that stuff about work, I thought, stepping over Hall's watermelons, maybe this is where he should have his picture taken.

It wasn't enough, of course, didn't even make sense in most of the rural areas whence it came and where it once seemed so apt. A few rich men, almost all of them white, owned the land, the money, the equipment, and this, finally, was just a corporate farm that happened to be owned by an organization of blacks. Gilmore and Branch had no answers, except to speak about the political changes that had already occurred, nor was there any assurance that a black government, on issues other than race, would be any more saintly or successful than one run by whites. Even Gilmore had been thrown back on the old Southern mystique. "This," he had said, "is the best place in the country for blacks: Alabama and Mississippi. If we're going to make it, we'll have to make it here. Here the relationship is closer—we're all kinfolks—and the races aren't strangers to each other." And yet perhaps this was all there was. All through the South there were people who couldn't leave, couldn't, in a sense, even find the road into town or, if they did, couldn't survive when they got there. The cities were full of the casualties. If the future was doubtful here, it was even more uncertain somewhere else. There was no place left to go. "We can get it together," Gilmore had said, "can do it with people in the community. People who got involved in the movement will never want to be white again. Damn that skin color, it keeps everybody from being human. But we'll do it, one thing at a time—we can't take on the whole system at once. First we'll deal with race, and then with the money thing, and then maybe with the guns."

III

They all spoke of possibilities now—the striking woodcutters of southern Alabama and Mississippi, the young academics, the kids, the liberal lawyers, the organizers, the black politicians (and the white), the bankers and editors—as if possibility itself had become the new creed. People who had conducted lonely fights through impossible years—the people who got the burning crosses and the midnight phone calls—and people who had never dared speak at all had become part of organizations, were surrounded by movements, and began to talk. The civil-rights movement and the federal laws it produced emancipated a piece of everyone, and even the white politicians, excepting only a few, were willing to admit it. Yet even those changes resolved nothing, and people now were just as ready to fight about the meaning of the new faith as they once were prepared to fight for (or against) its coming.

The most fashionable of the new sects was Lamarism—the L. Q. C. Lamar Society—and in the long run it might well become the strongest. Its natural habitat was the academic study, the boardroom, the hotel convention and the country club, and its most concise objective, according to its own literature, was "practical solutions to the South's major problems and constructive change." Although anyone could join for an annual fee of twenty-five dollars, the Lamar Society was, in fact, on the way toward becoming the voice of the New South establishment, an organization of "moderate" businessmen, lawyers, newspaper publishers, politicians, university presidents and professors. It was integrated—its directors included John Lewis, director of the Voter Education Project; Vivian Henderson, president of Clark College; and Maynard Jackson, the vice-mayor of Atlanta, all of them Negroes—and seemed to share some spiritual kinship with John Gardner's Common Cause. Against the stridency of a Wallace or a Maddox it was liberal, but in the more subdued context, the *politesse*, of Jimmy Carter's Georgia or John West's South Carolina it was very much middle-of-the-road. "From now on," said one of its members, "the decisions of the South are going to be made by a center coalition," and that, one could safely assume, was something like Lamar.

Organized in 1969, the Society "brought together persons who believed that the South's progress had been too long delayed by preoccupation with racial integration and disregard of other pressing regional problems." It was to be conscientiously nonpolitical, looking, according to its own literature, for "Southerners who are long on imagination, innovation and professional competence, short on political dogma." That, of course, was in itself a form of dogma. "If you take anybody and accept everybody," a black activist had said at an organizational meeting, "then it's like having an organization with nobody." But in fact, as one of the officers reminded him, they weren't about to get everybody, nor were the decisions going to be made by just anybody. The organization's primary objective, at least on the surface, was to sponsor studies, encourage regional planning, and "present the people who make decisions with realistic alternatives." They were not, according to H. Brandt Ayres, the Society's president, "going to be ideological cheerleaders." Yet clearly they would like nothing better than to be regarded as the embodiment of the reasonable New South.

The abiding principle was caution. Lucius Quintus Cincinnatus Lamar, for whom the Society was named, was a nineteenth-century Mississippian who served in the U. S. Senate during Reconstruction and later became the only man from his state ever to sit on the Supreme Court. "The Society believes," according to its brochure, "that the type of behavior exemplified by his struggle for reconciliation between the races and regions of this country in the divisive 1870s is worthy of emulation by his fellow Southerners in the 1970s." The brochure said nothing about Lamar's role in arranging the Compromise of 1877 by which the Southern Negro lost the protection of the federal government, nor did it say just what black people had done to whites and why, therefore, "reconciliation" was the proper word. It was not surprising that a leading Lamarist could therefore propose that the way to resolve the regional controversy about the playing of "Dixie" by high-school and university bands was to pair it with something like "We Shall Overcome"—as if the two were, in fact, symbols of similar movements, attitudes and experience: first they'll play their fight song, then we'll play ours.

Given its style and structure, and considering its membership, Lamar was more likely to be a nonmovement than a cause, more apt to represent a mood than to push a program. It would not *do* very much as an organization other than sponsor research, meetings and publications (e.g., "The Urban South: Northern Mistakes in a Southern Setting?"), but no establishment organ ever did. Ayres, who was also editor and publisher of the Anniston, Alabama, *Star* and who, as much as anyone, was Lamar's chief organizer, suggested that someday the Society might become a sort of "distant early warning apparatus" with an executive committee that could deal with crisis situations. That day had not yet come ("We can't even deal with crisis situations in our own communities"), yet Lamar's influence, even as an informal communications device, could be substantial: As in most establishment situations—at the country club, the informal lunch, or the Council on Foreign Relations—the more private the decisions, the more effective they were likely to be.

The impact, despite all the disclaimers, would obviously be political: compromise over contention, gradualism over militancy, "progressivism" over populism. Lamar would not create that impact but give it focus, respectability and support. Privately Ayres believed that Lamar itself was "an expression of a new progressive movement in America. Populism is limited by its mode of attack, although it has some real substance. The progressives in America are taking over the agenda and starting to implement it." In concrete terms, that meant tax reform, ecology, regional planning, legislative reorganization, and expansion of higher education, all of them accomplished through moderation, reason and compromise. For clearly there were things worth preserving—courtesy, civility, due process; no point in "destroying each other in contentiousness." Civilization was too precious and precarious for that. What a stupid thing it was to bus schoolchildren just to achieve an abstract mathematical formula. "We've got to learn to live in communities, as friends and neighbors, and not just as contending factions."

In more general terms it meant other things; meant, for example, that the moderating level of racial conflict must not be replaced by class conflict—that the blessings of this economic order, properly adjusted to accommodate certain environmental considerations, would (hopefully) be extended to increasing numbers of people without restructuring the order itself. Thus the populism of Wallace—his attacks on banks and utilities—became as much of a threat as his racism, and the redneck, cleansed of his backwardness and his nigger-baiting, became a recruit for the great ascent through Upward Mobility. There might be a lot of nostalgia about those colorful old politicians, a lot of talk about populist grandfathers, about Huey Long and Tom Watson and Pitchfork Ben Tillman, but those days were past. You took it gradually, calmly. There was no point in raising the wages of textile workers if the higher scales meant destroying the industry, no future, as a university president said, in "two yards and a cloud of dust." One had to "extend privilege, not shift it from one group to another."

The great hope lay in education and research, planning and intelligence, all of them items that, in the South, had special meaning. For one thing (like liberalism itself), they had rarely been tried; for another, and more important, they looked especially attractive against the lingering fear of strife and violence. For no matter how joyful the professions of a new Southern mood, new attitudes about race, integration and all the rest, every Southerner knew that there were a lot of guys out there with guns, and that while Northern radicalism might be a parlor avocation, an element that blended into the background of New York or Cambridge like long hair and pot, it—and most other forms of political immoderation—constituted fighting words at home. Populism could go to the right or to the left, could turn moralistic and reactionary, could be racist or egalitarian, or even both in the same moment, could turn on Jews or capitalists or intellectuals with equal fervor. They also knew that for a century the region had been dominated by the economic power of the North, by paper companies, steel mills, utilities and banks whose directors and senior management sat in New York and Pittsburgh, not in Atlanta or Birmingham. "Until the late 1920s," said a Lamar flier, "largely non-Southern interests exploited the region's resources—its land, timber, minerals and human resources—for short-term gain, without regard to the long-range implications of their actions." In fact, of course, that era extended beyond the twenties, and even beyond World War II, and it was difficult to imagine what that situation produced in a patriciate with illusions of grandeur; in their hearts most of them must have known that they were lackeys. With hindsight we may eventually conclude that those days came to an end at the close of the sixties, that the psychology of outside domination and the penchant for direct violent action faded together, but so far there was no way to be sure. The special political skills of the South were themselves products of that historic threat of violence: It was always hard to tell which part of a man was simple charm and grace and which was political calculation, because they were inseparable; people learned their gentility and their politics together, partly in self-defense against the economic and political power of the North, partly against those at home whose honor and convictions were offended too quickly. Out of the sheer necessity to survive, the Southern Negro learned to con the white man; for related reasons the Southern white learned to con his rich cousins up North and his poor kinfolks at home. Often they did it the same way.

Beyond the fear of violence there was simple self-interest: to protect and enlarge possessions and control. Nigger talk had historically been sufficient to put down any class movement, to keep the unions on the defensive, and to keep white upstarts in their place. If a man refused to work for $1.75 a day, someone had said, "the boss would hire a nigger who'd work for a dollar"; and when the unions did come, they were conned with nigger talk, too. Now for the first time there was a problem. The old form of discipline was becoming increasingly less effective: Wallace had failed on race, Maddox had failed, Faubus had failed. In Mississippi alone, six thousand people were sending their kids to White Citizens Council schools, and no one was sure how many thousands more were supporting private academies, but they were going broke doing it and were therefore beginning to suspect that when it came to money and public services they were no better off than the blacks. "Now," said George Dean, an American Civil Liberties Union lawyer, "some of them are going to start thinking. Race was the last solid support, and once that's gone they'll know they're getting fucked; they won't take much more: it's time to roll up your sleeves and go after those banks and those corporations." Here and there, where schools were *de facto* integrated poor whites were already joining with blacks to get better textbooks (or to get free textbooks at all), to demand more money, to get a response from the bureaucrats, and in the backwoods of Alabama and Mississippi eight thousand woodcutters—60 percent black, 40 percent white —had organized to strike mills and lumberyards. So far such people had no real voice—"God has to send us *someone*," Dean had said—but it was possible that something could happen, that in this, the poorest of all American regions, the diminishing satisfaction of being white was no longer enough. "At the dawn of the 1970s," said Virginia's Governor Linwood Holton in his inaugural address, "it is clear that problem-solving, and not philosophical principles, has become the focal point of politics . . . old clichés have now blurred and old dogmas have died." One had to take those echoes of John Kennedy and Daniel Bell as an attempt, once and for all, to put the fire-eaters in their place. But as quoted in the literature of the Lamar Society, they could also be interpreted as a way of resisting any radical resurgence, of trying to assert economic home rule, and, simultaneously, of showing the rest of the nation what reasonable people Southerners had become.

The Southern moderate was not the first to discover that reason itself could be a political device to keep the class structure intact, the wages low, and the tax system regressive. The credo of Lamarism dwelt a great deal on the potential of a uniquely Southern course of development, progress without Northern mistakes, but no one at Lamar had any clear idea of what that meant. There was talk of new cities, new highways, of governmental reform, and of the danger that the region's cities would become just as stratified, ugly and polluted as New York and Chicago, but no specifics—other than "research" and reason— about solutions. In North Carolina, Terry Sanford, former governor and now president of Duke University, was speaking

THE NEW SOUTH SHALL RISE AGAIN

about the construction of superhighways and the development of new towns along their routes, and in Arkansas Dale Bumpers, the young governor, had managed to ram a law through the legislature permitting cities to annex adjacent suburbs in order to permit metropolitan planning without the drain of resources to the periphery. At the same time, there was still little talk about the regressive tax structures; despite all the claims about how heavily the South must tax itself to maintain state and local services, no one said much about the fact that a major share of the burden came in the form of sales taxes—even on food and medicine—which fell most heavily on the poor, or about the expense and drain of an industrial base attracted through special write-offs, tax immunities and other subsidies. Welfare payments and support for public health, state mental hospitals and other public services remained scandalously low, and while there was considerable concern about raising expenditures for public education at all levels, the focus tended to be on benefits for a rising middle class rather than on the provision of minimum support and security for the poor. "We know," said a college president who supported Lamar, "what some of the pitfalls are. We don't know the precise direction, but we know it's around here somewhere."

Beneath it all there remained the more ominous possibility that, in the great orgy of Southern moderation, another Compromise of 1877 would be reenacted. John Mitchell and Richard Nixon had been quite willing, even eager, to dilute the Voting Rights Act of 1965 when it came up for extension, thereby throwing blacks back into the hands of Southern election boards, registrars and legislatures. The act had been extended by a close congressional vote in 1970, but enforcement by the Justice Department of school integration orders and civil-rights laws had, at best, been unenthusiastic. The federal government sent "observers" to Mississippi for the 1971 gubernatorial election between Charles Evers and Bill Waller, and subsequently filed suit charging intimidation in one county, but failed to prevent the countless instances of voter intimidation and harassment reported by the Northern lawyers and students who served as Evers' poll watchers. And while Nixon was ostensibly searching for a Southern judge to sit on the Supreme Court—nominating Haynesworth, Carswell, and finally Powell—he consistently overlooked Frank Johnson, the most respected federal judge in the Deep South, a Republican and a conservative, who had rigorously enforced civil-rights laws and decisions. The Southern strategy failed for the Republicans in the 1970 elections—the old Wallace vote went overwhelmingly to the Democrats—but the consequences for the South itself were not so plain. (Nixon, of course, carried the South in 1972, but the Republican Party fared little better than it had before; since that left most of the South a one-party region, the black vote, lacking anyone to bargain with, was likely to remain marginal. Senator Eastland of Mississippi was Nixon's candidate.) Obviously the changes of a decade in race relations could not all be undone, but with the disarray of the civil-rights movement, the nationalizing of the race problem (as manifested, for example, in the issue of busing), and the general eagerness to regard nearly every Southern governor as a moderate, the pace and direction of further change were doubtful. There is no point in debating again whether Southern racism and discrimination were worse than they were elsewhere, because conditions and points of departure were so different. But it was clear that there were still vast regions of the South where blacks were systematically intimidated, exploited and, on occasion, murdered; that there were places where the entire public bureaucracy—the welfare system, the dispensers of food stamps and commodities, the schools, the politicians, the agricultural agents, the public health and medical services —discriminated against all the poor, and against the black poor in particular. In ninety-five percent of the counties of the Deep South the sheriff was still the black man's enemy, could still be sent around "to mess with people," and the courthouse was still white man's turf. Greene County and Macon County and Fayette, Mississippi, and the handful of other places where the newly enfranchised blacks had some political control were models of possibility, but they didn't yet reflect a pattern. Blacks had been purged from the voter rolls before, and no moderate had been able (or willing) to stop it.

Once again there was a chance that history might repeat itself, a chance for implicit arrangements between the leadership of the South and the economic and political power of the North, a chance for "reconciliation" accomplished under the cover of benign neglect. National power, however hesitantly, had been on the side of the Negro since 1932. Now things might again be different. In a small Alabama town near Montgomery, where so much of this movement had begun in the fifties, an aging Southern liberal reflected on his own struggles by observing that however lonely his own position had been in the South, that loneliness was always mitigated by the general direction of national power and opinion. "Roosevelt," he said, "gave his blessings to the struggle for the right to vote. Now Nixon is packing the Supreme Court with people who don't give a damn for the Negro, and there's no assurance that the federal government won't withdraw its protection of the right to vote. No assurance at all."

IV

James Simmons of Forest Home, Alabama, called himself a redneck. In 1968 he voted for George Wallace for President. In 1971 he endorsed Charles Evers, a black man, for the governorship of Mississippi. He was a slow talker, perhaps even a slow learner, and spoke of himself as a man of little education, the last of the all-American blue-eyed, bull-necked backwoodsmen. "Four years ago," he explained, laconic as ever, "if anybody had told me that I'd ever appear at an Evers rally, I would have told him he was crazy." But in four years a great many things had happened, and James Simmons, president and chief organizer of the Gulfcoast Pulpwood Association, changed his mind and his politics.

The central event in that conversion was The Strike: A few thousand woodhaulers, men who cut and trucked pulpwood from the forests of Alabama and Mississippi to lumberyards and hardboard plants and paper mills, took on some of the most powerful people in the South, defied the local press (which either ignored them or called them Communists), and began to unload the burden of a century of acquiescence and self-denial. There was no idealism in the strike, nothing theoretical or highfalutin; from the start it was a straight matter of survival. The precipitating incident had been a decision by the companies to enlarge the measurements for each unit of wood they bought, thereby lowering the price.

> On September 1 [said an Association flier], Masonite installed scales at its Laurel woodyard. They charged 7,100 pounds of wood per unit. This was the last straw for hundreds of Mississippi woodcutters. The unit is not standardized by state or federal law and can be anything the companies want it to be. We know of one place where a company is charging 8,100 pounds per unit. The use of the "unit" means that paper companies have the sole power of determining how much a woodcutter makes for his work. The woodcutter becomes a slave to his dealer and the paper companies.
>
> We are determined to have a standard and fair procedure for selling our wood to dealers and paper companies.
>
> We have never known anything but poverty and exploitation; we've been cheated and lied to and this strike is *our* effort to help ourselves.

People like Simmons were not given to rhetoric, and men who averaged $2,000 a year for hard physical work were not likely to walk off the job on impulse. Most of them were already in debt, often to the companies for whom they hauled and cut wood; the cutters "owned" their trucks and equipment, but the loans were secured or extended directly by the dealers ("Who the hell is going to give credit to people like us?" one of the cutters asked), and so the mill was not only the buyer of wood but also the bank, the credit bureau and, in some instances, the company store. "It's the same system as sharecrop cotton," Simmons said. "They handle the money and we do the work. The woodcutters have been going broke for years." There were times when a man and his sons would work a week cutting timber, deliver the wood to the yard, and discover that after debts were deducted the settlement sheet came out to zero. There were times when a man who had been paying installments on his truck for years would demand to see his account and be told that it was all taken care of—that he'd just made his final payment. There were times when there was only one place to borrow—for equipment or gas or medical bills—and no way to survive without it, and so the debts were endless.

The boycotts began in 1968—sporadic strikes punctuated by threats or token increases in compensation—but they did not escalate into a regional movement until late summer of 1971, when the Masonite plant in Laurel, one of the largest hardboard manufacturers in the world, changed the weight factor. In the meantime Simmons had been driving hundreds of miles each week, talking to woodcutters, organizing, trying to talk up the cause. There were, he estimated, seventy-five thousand cutters in the Southeast who depended on the yards and the mills—seventy percent of the paper manufactured in America was produced in the Southeast—and so a membership of eight thousand was only a small percentage of the potential. But what had been done, given the resources and the manpower and the region's history, was nonetheless phenomenal. There was no strong tradition of union activity, no sense of political potential, only a belief that to be a white man, an independent white man, no matter how poor, was better than being a nigger. To associate with blacks in a movement was unthinkable. They had broken all that, had developed an integrated organization even though, as they all conceded, there were places where you couldn't get any blacks and other places where you couldn't get any whites.

Even now they didn't want much, were asking only for a uniform standard of measurement and what they regarded as a fair price, but that proved hard to get. In Washington County, Alabama, police and sheriff's deputies bristling with guns had surrounded a woodcutters' meeting in an effort "to prevent violence"; in Laurel, Mississippi, someone tried to run down a couple of men standing on a picket line; and in Jackson, *The Daily News*, reflecting the common sentiment of the Mississippi press, published a cartoon of a woodpile labeled "Laurel Pulpwood Agitation" which partially covered a flag with the hammer and sickle. (One of the woodcutters later said that he went to the dictionary to discover the meaning of "Communist" and learned that, among other things, it had something to do with equal rights to property: "I guess that was us all right.") Inevitably, however, the harassment led to bigger confrontations, to general threats of violence, to anonymous phone calls about bombs, and finally to unexpected action from the local welfare agents, who cut off the strikers' food stamps. Suddenly they were no longer eligible, were making too much money, didn't qualify because they were on strike, didn't understand the rules, had falsified their applications. And so Simmons turned to the politicians: to Senator James O. Eastland of Mississippi, whose assistants patronized him and suggested he stop associating with agitators, to John Sparkman of Alabama, to the candidates for governor of Mississippi, to anyone who might help. Only Evers came through; within a few days he had Simmons and a handful of others on a plane to Washington to see George McGovern and Teddy Kennedy, and within a few days after that the food stamps were restored. Subsequently there was other help: the NAACP provided emergency funds for food; a couple of New York foundations made small grants; and when John V. Lindsay came to Laurel to campaign for Evers, Simmons and his colleagues, who were on the platform, got the attention of the national press. Here was the genuine article, a good ol' boy from the sticks of southwest Alabama who wasn't going to take any more shit.

Still, it was only the beginning, small and painful and uncertain. The Association was an integrated organization—there were perhaps three thousand whites and five thousand blacks—and its leaders had begun to understand what it meant to buck the system. They had been thrown out of a house in Laurel which they used for an office, because blacks came and went freely through the front door, had discovered that the influence of the yards and the mills ran right through the political system, the newspapers and the television stations ("They're like a bunch of drunks," Simmons had said, "all sitting around the same table and swigging from the same bottle"), had even begun to suspect that on a good many political questions they had been wrong all their lives. Simmons still thought that Wallace was a good man, but he conceded that his old resentment of Bobby Kennedy might have been unjustified. "I thought he just came to Alabama to mess around, to tell folks what to do. Now I think I might have been wrong."

They had learned other things as well, had discovered, for example, that they were officially regarded as "independent contractors" and were therefore not covered by the collective-bargaining provisions of the National Labor Relations Act; discovered that the unions themselves were reluctant to provide support, that a man who cut and hauled wood, who lived in a little shack on the side of a red dirt road, was not covered or protected by anything and, in an official sense, was not supposed to exist at all. At the same time they had begun to learn something about their own power—about the ability, through collective action, to make yourself visible. When the yards and the mills began paying strikebreakers double compensation for hauling wood they knew that the companies were beginning to hurt, and when Masonite tendered invitations to negotiate they understood that for the first time they had won.

But what they won was not clear, and would not be clear for years, if ever. The test would not come in the first round of negotiations, or perhaps even in the second or third, but in the pattern of demands that the cutters pursued and in compromises they were willing to accept. And those decisions might well have to be made after the woodcutters had faded from the headlines and from the list of worthy causes that national philanthropy was willing to support. What were they willing to settle for if they found themselves alone? How much had their politics really changed? It was always tempting to envelop people like Simmons in the reflected glow of our own ideology, to see in the beginning of any organization, any strike, any conversion, the seeds of a regional or national movement, a new populism, a new political force. Here were men who, as one of them said, "found themselves faced with a thing we thought only happened to somebody else." In a sense they knew now who the enemy was. And yet it was still too easy to exaggerate the possibilities, too easy to unload our visions of radical reform on their cause. Simmons and his colleagues were not ideologues: their strength was precisely in their limited objectives, in the relentless test that always asked, "What's in it for us?" (Simmons once explained that he didn't support the civil-rights movement of the sixties because "there didn't seem to be anything in it for me.") At the same time there would always exist the overwhelming financial pressure to settle, to take a little and go back to work. They had always settled for a few dollars before, and the negotiations now in progress might produce no more than conditions just barely above the intolerable. All they were asking was a fair standard of measurement and a fair price. Perhaps Simmons and some of his colleagues had begun to explore a new kind of politics, but out there on the back roads lived 75,000 poor men whose only chance of survival was to cut and haul wood.

V

The more one pursued the changes, the more one found the residue—situations, people and attitudes that had hardly changed at all. Some were obvious—the poverty, the racism, the continuing sense that nothing could be done. At the same time there was something more subtle, perhaps more important: In the newer suburbs of the cities, in the football stadiums and country clubs, in the motels and bars, in the vast region of the pin curl, the tease and Miss Teen Age America, the great battle was still the struggle against time itself. It was not simply that they were trying to stop history, for the Old South had become a sideshow, a sort of legitimizing background for a rootless (and, in that sense, new) existence. It was rather that they were trying to forget that they were growing old, that here especially the pinnacle of life was still the sorority dance, the engagement ring, the moonlit night, and the game, and that everything thereafter was a bitter retreat. In some ways, of course, all of that was universal, was certainly American, but in the South, which was now supposed to have a lot to be young about, was supposed to be free of its old chains and inhibitions, the battle against age became particularly grotesque.

The residue was not 1840 or 1870 or 1910, but 1945. No riverboats here, honey, no plantation houses, no happy darkies. They were embalming something else. It was the Pride of Mississippi Orchestra at the big political bash for the state's regular Democrats playing "Moonlight Serenade" and "String of Pearls" —vintage Glenn Miller from World War II; it was the crowd flowing from Legion Field and Denny Stadium and a dozen others, weekend after weekend, through Holiday Inns and Ho-Jo Motels, the women in their bouffant hairdos, the men with their pinky rings, clinking glasses, how-ya-doin' across parking lots and lobbies, desperately laughing through a thousand pregame parties, shouting To Hell With Mississippi, To Hell With Tennessee, knowing that those boys down on the field are "fighting all our battles for us"—Archie and Steve and Bobby Jo, new faces every other year, but the bodies always lithe and beautiful and young; it was the Texas Rangerettes from Kilgore Junior College learning to smile, smile, smile, no matter what hurts, smiling so long that it often seemed like an effort to get your face together again.

At the heart of it was football. Not football as the national Sunday madness, the solitary television-filtered escape, but the special version of *Southern* football that knows levels of meaning, intensity and violence entirely foreign to other regions. In Alabama and Arkansas and Mississippi, they used to say, football means more because "they don't have much else to be proud of, in everything else they were always last," but that was only the beginning of an explanation, for football was also a surrogate for the promise of youth, for the closed frontier, and, finally, the forum of the battle against time itself. It was the realm of undivided loyalty, uninhibited expression and unrestrained confrontation, a relief from the imperatives of civility. Football gave life a focus; football stopped the clock: Each week they moved from place to place, from Athens to Tuscaloosa, from Knoxville to Jackson, converting vacations into a succession of catatonic Saturdays and laryngitic Sundays, hiring special trains, meeting the old crowd, talking real estate in Tupelo and weddings in Biloxi, but returning always to that game, reliving without end the glorious moments of another day. They were facing not the future but the past of their own lost youth.

It was a complex and arduous ritual, a fantasy of the race, where the time is always 1945 or 1950, a time between times, the Old South with the promise of Northern prosperity, the New South without integration or social ambivalence, the time when the war had ended, the South had at last rejoined the Union, and the Brown decision in the school cases would never come. It was a fantasy of a time when, despite the Claghorn jokes and the endless taunts about Southern nigger-baiting, being a Southerner had been rapidly losing its liabilities and being an American had still been the most unqualified of all assets. One of the things that had always made the South so difficult to understand was that the man who behaved like a corporate executive on the job often imagined himself to be Colonel Beauregard at home. They would have their modern gadgets, their factories, their suburbs and their highways, would be free of their Gothic legacies, would trade their Baptism for something more tolerant, their bourbon for Scotch, but would also be free to keep their mammies, their cheap labor and their patronage.

Two elements were essential, the Negro and the Woman. Because each could be cast at will (alternately and exchangeably) into the role of adult or child, tower of strength or reed of frailty, each helped sustain the white male's adolescence. The woman as mother or daughter, the Southern woman who, on the one hand, as Virginia Durr had said, "bears all, suffers all, endures all" and was rewarded with a pedestal to her own purity, and, on the other, could be the perpetual coquette, the cute little girl; the black as boy or as mammy, irresponsible child or faithful retainer. The ritual was threatened now by the Negro's refusal to play his part, for if he insisted on being a man then the white boy must become a man as well. The Negro was time's intruder: Each time he carried the ball or knocked down a white with a block or demanded political parity another crack opened in the adolescent cocoon. Put a party of blacks into a motel dining room and the decibels of pre-football revelry begin to sink and the level of decorum begins to rise. Take the black servants out of the sorority houses or have them refuse to address little girls from Mobile as "Miss Susan" or "Miss Mary Jo" and the girls begin to wonder. If they were not Southern belles, what were they? While they were taking care of the white boys who would take care of them?

Because of their impact on the struggle against time, the integration and emancipation of blacks from social subservience was likely to have effects far beyond the semblance of "equality." In 1971, for the first time, Coach Paul "Bear" Bryant played blacks on the University of Alabama varsity football team; in 1971, for the first time, a Southeastern Conference team, the University of Tennessee's, had a black co-captain. What would happen when there was a black quarterback at Alabama or Ole Miss? What would happen when black cheerleaders had to throw white girls into the air, or when the black beauty queen had to be kissed by the white president of the Student Council (or vice versa)? So far those problems had been averted by careful selection, by eliminating portions of the ritual, by letting blacks run with the ball, or block, or tackle, without letting them dominate the game. But each time you amputated a piece of the ritual, each time you canceled a traditional dance or a ceremony of custom, each time one of *them* participated in something that used to be exclusively your own, resistance became more difficult.

And yet the ritual continued. The growing resistance among blacks was hardly universal and might, in the long run, channel itself into the enlargement of parallel black bourgeois structures, encapsulating white fantasies without destroying them; where black power and identity were recognized they were generally seen in political rather than social terms—you negotiated with Julian Bond or Charles Evers or John Lewis, but dealt with the maid, the cook and the gardener in the same old way. More important, the white woman had barely begun to resist, and her collaboration alone might be sufficient. She had been emancipated into the realm of booze, tobacco and profanity, but had not yet been removed from her crumbling pedestal. It was not simply that she was, as W. J. Cash wrote, "the perpetuator of white superiority in legitimate line . . . a creature absolutely inaccessible to the males of the inferior group," but that she had also become, as a consequence, a person whose very identity required isolation from worldly taint, and whose self-esteem depended absolutely on the protection that a man could provide. It was possible that exhaustion of the political possibilities of nigger talk would eliminate a major barrier to a common class consciousness, and clearly, as in the case of the woodcutters' strike, there was some evidence that it had, but there were also contra-indications that no major movement could ever be organized as long as women, white women of all classes, continued to serve their double function: dirty workers on the one hand, perpetuators of the mythic bloodline on the other. "The women tend to be receptive," said a community organizer in a poor-white neighborhood of Jackson called Battlefield Park. "They are interested in day care, abortion counseling and all the rest. But the men are afraid they'll lose power over their wives. They want to keep them down, keep them at home. And the important thing is for every woman to have a man. You don't count for a whole lot if you don't."

Rather than just dreaming, they practiced their fantasies. What the future closed off could be reinvested in one's children, not *for* them primarily, but for oneself, not for their future, but for the perpetuation of adult adolescence. Of course they wanted the kids to succeed, to make it, but such things were secondary to the exploitation of the kids themselves. In no other region were there as many teen-age beauty contests, as many drum and bugle corps and marching societies, as many bands and carnivals, or as much vicarious intimacy with college and high-school football stars. In no other region had people been as infuriated by the politicization and militancy of the young, and by the incipient schoolhouse revolt against adult authority and the rituals adults support. That revolt had not only offended the South's political conservatism but, more significantly, threatened the whole system of youth ritual and adolescent fantasy. An assertive kid was like an uppity nigger; because he was essential to the maintenance of a social mythology, his refusal to cooperate and his attempts to be an adult become invitations to violence. In America generally, the counterculture was primarily an offense to manners; in the South it was also an assault on illusion. "Don't use my name," said a white student who was working for Evers in the 1971 campaign, "but my father just called to say he'd made an appointment for me with a psychiatrist. He thinks I've flipped out."

For a time in the late sixties it appeared as if the national militancy of the young would spread through the South. A demonstration at the University of Alabama against the invasion of

Cambodia in the spring of 1970 turned into a major confrontation with the Tuscaloosa police; some two hundred students were arrested, and when the cops charged into a fraternity house looking for demonstrators, the resident whites began to reach for their hunting rifles and their target pistols in defense of their turf; that house, someone said later, "was like an armory." Earlier that year Alabama students had heckled George Wallace (a university alumnus) so effectively that he was unable to complete a scheduled address; Wallace vowed to return to "finish that speech" but never did. In the meantime underground papers had been started in Tuscaloosa, in Birmingham, in New Orleans, in Atlanta and in a dozen other locations; William Kunstler and Abbie Hoffman spoke on (or near) Southern university campuses, usually to capacity crowds; draft resistance spread and, despite the South's particularly strong tradition of military service, became respectable on college campuses. What was most significant was that a growing number of Southern university graduates, lawyers, teachers, social workers, resolved to stay in the region to launch legal-services projects, community action programs, and other reform organizations: in Laurel, kids out of Mobile were working with the woodcutters; in Tuscaloosa Jack Drake and Ralph Knowles, both graduates of the University of Alabama Law School, were specializing in civil-liberties cases; and in Jackson a young woman named Donna Berry had joined with a half-dozen others, all of them white Southerners, to operate an organization called the Rankin Street Center which served poor whites. The Southern activists seemed to have a particular sense of place; they were angry about the inequities and the stupidity, but they loved their land, were, as someone said, "always coming back." Their commitments had more to do with the region's tradition of radical populism than with the more familiar brands of liberal-middle-class alienation that had been so visible in the late sixties. Patriots, not expatriates. "People like us are interested in something more than discussion societies," said a young graduate of Tulane who campaigned with Evers. "A lot of kids have begun to understand about the hypocrisy of Southern politics. What the hell have Stennis and Eastland ever done? What can the old liberals do now? We've been through the era of doom; this is the time to build, to build here."

There was a chance that all of that would survive and grow, even without a serious national youth movement in politics, that there would be more activist lawyers, more organizers, more kids who would not be patronized, would not play the game, would not be hostages to time, but that chance was still small while the pressure to acquiesce remained immense. (George Wallace had not been their man; his style antedated 1945, contained too much cottonseed and piney woods. Wallace, someone said, scratched his crotch too often. But Dale Bumpers of Arkansas, Jimmy Carter of Georgia and John West of South Carolina were something else. They had about them the scent of Northern approval, the sweet smell of reason, the aroma of Lamar.) For most of the kids now in college the most visible future lay, therefore, in the conventional American route: into business, into the suburbs, into the proper civic organizations, the hospital boards, the YMCA, the School Committee. They would conduct themselves honorably, trying to trade their adolescence for paternalism, updating their music, modernizing their racial rhetoric, talking about development and growth, yet knowing also that to confront the old fantasies head on, to break the ritual, to grow up too fast, was to risk forms of chaos and violence that the region might not survive. (Among lower-middle-class whites Wallace had his youth movement, too; his support did not come primarily from the old rednecks who were dying out, but from the young underclass which was not. Wallace was also a class symbol.) In the South, wrote James Clotfelter, *"no majority can be created that does not include some whites who are hostile to integration."*

Nothing, therefore, was certain. To have known the dark, tragic side of life—to have lost a war and a cause—did sometimes lead to a more mature confrontation with the limits of existence, to a suspicion of extremes, and to an appreciation of the importance of civility. It could produce a Faulkner or a Flannery O'Connor or a Martin Luther King. It could produce the blues. But it had also produced that compulsive escape into fantasies of youth, violence and direct action: When Willie Morris returned to Mississippi in 1970 and wrote of a premonition "that I would meet there, on my home ground, a violent death" nobody laughed. Most significantly it could create—and had created—a moment that seemed to be severed from time itself, when neither the regional past nor the national future represented any strong attraction. The conventional route might lead nowhere, might not provide either the growth or the satisfaction that would, in another day, have made it worthwhile: "a regional way of life," as Gaston said, "in harmony with a mirage." And so the temptation to suspend time increased; there would be more football, more contests, more indulgence. In some ways we were all doing that, but few of us were making claims that a new era was at hand.

VI

To say that the South was catching up with the nation was, at best, no more revealing than to say the nation was catching up with the South. There was evidence for both, but neither meant much unless there was some agreement about direction. Per-capita income in the South rose sharply through the sixties; the landscape was covered with new developments, new factories and highways; the major cities, with some exceptions, operated with the same public assets and liabilities as the cities of the North and the West; and the public-opinion polls suggested that on most issues—busing, the economy, Vietnam, drugs, crime and all the rest—the South did not differ very sharply from the rest of America. At the same time, the problems of Northern cities, as we had all heard time and again, were, in some important respects, the converted problems of the South brought North, rural unemployment and deprivation turned into "ghettoes," "welfare" and "crime"; the statistics (on income and attitude) were therefore evening out not only because many Southerners were better off, but because a million others, most of them poor, were now counted as part of New York, Chicago and Cleveland, and not with Georgia, South Carolina or Mississippi.

Until the mid-fifties we had been able to berate the South for its insularity, its racism and its backwardness because we still took for granted the legitimacy and permanence of national progress and rectitude, still had unlimited confidence in ourselves as a nation. Now, having lost that confidence, we had become more tolerant of the South and, at the same time, had begun to look to it for those possibilities we could no longer find in ourselves. Shortly before the 1971 election I asked Charles Evers whether it would be easier for a black man to become governor of Mississippi or to become Vice-President of the United States. "Governor of Mississippi," Evers answered. "I expect to become governor." In fact, of course, he was not elected and didn't expect to be, although he clearly believed he would do better than he finally did. (He received approximately twenty-two percent of the 700,000 votes cast.) And yet there were people in Mississippi and elsewhere, reasonable people in most things, who not only believed that it would be easier for a black man to become governor of Mississippi—an indication, surely, of how we now thought of our national racism—but also believed that Evers, once a Chicago pimp and hustler and now the mayor of Fayette, really had a chance of being elected. What would have been a joke ten years ago—a Flip Wilson routine, perhaps—had become an article of hope in 1971.

The Evers campaign was more than a curiosity; it was, as much as anything can ever be, a landmark of how far, and which way, the South had come, a measure of possibilities and rhetoric and resources, and an indication of what others had come to expect. It also indicated how difficult it would be to separate the South from its mythology and from the burdens that outsiders were trying to impose on it. Occasionally Evers himself would treat the campaign like a joke, the best hustle of his life. One morning a few days before the election he showed up at the Governor's Mansion in Jackson for an "inspection." The mansion had been closed as unsafe; it required structural repairs, Governor John Bell Williams was living elsewhere, and the expense of restoration had turned into a political football. The reporters and cameramen were at the gate, but were not allowed in. Still Evers made the best of it. "This is dirty," he said, running his hand over one of the columns. "Now, if John Bell would get a little soap and water and do a little cleaning twice a year this place would look a lot better. They talk about black folks not taking care of their places. . . ." Then he went inside, quickly made the rounds, and delivered another statement, the black operator talking about the white governor as nigger. "It's not in such bad shape, a little plaster falling in one of the bedrooms, but mostly it needs cleaning. It needs a coat of paint. It's just another place they're trying to keep closed; I'm going to move right in after the election and then it's all going to be open, all the state facilities, because they belong to the people, the black, the poor, everybody. We're going to have barbecues here, fish fries, picnics—open it to the people."

It had been the Great Entertainment—the reporters, the bodyguards, the rallies, the statements, a black man standing on the courthouse steps in dozens of small towns, packing the meeting rooms at the Black Elks, jamming the churches, passing through the whole geography of Southern racial violence, West Point, Philadelphia, Clarksdale, McComb, Grenada, Indianola, the landmarks of death, telling how he was going to be governor, was going to fire the chief of the highway patrol, was going to get more federal money for schools and health, would build more roads, would permit liquor sales in every county and legalize gambling in the state. He was going to end the hypocrisy of the whole Mississippi system, would get the sheriffs out of the boot-legging business—they were the profiteers of local prohibition—would appoint blacks to the highway patrol, and would chase every man who deserted his wife, bring him back, and make him support her. The great entertainment—part hustle, part revival, the Biblical cadences strung out against an organ continuo and punctuated with hallelujahs and amens: "We're going to turn that State Capitol inside out; we carry no racism, no hate, we'll just carry our sorrows. . . . Precious Lord, take our hand. Precious Lord, lead me on. . . . We're going to take it into the Capitol, and we're not going to do it no different." Then it would turn worldly: He had gotten federal and foundation funds for development and health programs in Fayette, and he knew where to get them for the state. "They keep talking about how they never ask for anything; I've never seen people with so much pride in nothing." The money would bring a lot of other things, including respect, and he could talk about getting it as if he were discussing a connection with a client on a Chicago street. If you knew how to operate you could get anything. Running Mississippi was another hustle. "I've already won," he had said to me a week before the election, had already demonstrated that it could be done. "I'm having the time of my life. They're so confused, they don't know what we're doing."

In the end, the hustler had been outhustled. "You're learning your first political lesson," Ed Cole, Evers' campaign manager, had said to a white worker as the returns were coming in. "*Blacks never win.*" But it was not just the losing, or the harassment by local election officials, or the instances of outright fraud that had constituted the essence of defeat. What did hurt was the miserable showing in the counties: they had expected that the Evers campaign would help elect at least twice as many local black candidates as it did, would create more of an impact, would represent the beginning of a genuine political force. They thought they knew what they were doing, but in the end it turned out that while they had estimated, had counted on, some

300,000 or 350,000 registered black voters, there seemed to be only 200,000. And even on that they could not be sure, could not be certain how many corpses had voted, how many blacks were registered, or how many votes were stolen. They knew, in fact, almost nothing. But the thing that hurt most was simply this: that in the end it had not been Evers who proved it could be done, but his opponents. They got the credit for moderation, for conducting a decent campaign, for the fact that Evers himself had not been physically attacked. Evers got used in the name of the New South. "One can only wonder," wrote one of Evers' white press people after the election, "if the 'acceptance' of Mayor Evers's candidacy was not part of some grand design to insure that the wrath of the national media would not subject Mississippi to the shame it has been so accustomed to since the beginning of the Civil Rights Movement. . . . Many a reporter came, visited, and spent a day on the campaign trail before returning to New York, Washington or Atlanta to write his story about the changing South. Mississippi ostensibly setting an example of tolerance. . . ."

They had all used him: the Northern liberals who came to work, the Southern moderates, the press. He would demonstrate the South's new racial tolerance, its changing political climate, and its mythic capacity for an honest confrontation of those historic inequities and limitations that the rest of the nation still managed to ignore. He was to be the link between the Old and the New, the bridge across the adolescence of the fifties. It had been possible for his liberal adherents to be romantic about his Old Black South style, his revivalism, his hymns and his Bible talk, and, in the same moment, to see in him the embodiment of a contemporary political movement uniting the young, the black and the poor against the establishment. Charles Evers would lead the kids and the rednecks against the barons of Capitol Street; if we couldn't beat them in Manhattan we would take them on in Jackson and Tupelo. What they never understood was that they weren't merely fighting racists, were certainly not just fighting the "establishment," but were up against a collection of dirty little political machines which had been running the counties of the Deep South for a century, stealing, intimidating, killing when necessary, machines which were not about to tolerate challenges from anyone, white, black or brown, and certainly were not about to be beaten by a collection of upstarts. In Greene County, Alabama, where the population was eighty percent black, it took five years, two federal court orders, three foundations and nearly every civil-rights organization in America to dislodge the machine. This was where the Old South was. The liberals from the North were hooked on honeysuckle and magnolia, were mucking around with Old South fantasies and dreams of a populist revolt, but they were fighting an enemy they didn't understand and, until election day, couldn't even find. Charles Evers, they thought, might be the black Huey Long of Mississippi, but he had nothing to offer the local pols except black replacements, and that, needless to say, was not enough.

Nearly three hundred black candidates ran for local office in Mississippi in 1971; all but thirty-two lost. It was the New South that permitted them to run; it was the Old South that beat them. Both the Old and the New could therefore be regarded as winners. They had always had their implicit understandings, their arrangements of convenience—tax breaks and utility rates for the boys downtown, road contracts and a little patronage for the county politicians—and those understandings, though perhaps subject to alteration, would continue. The attorney general of Mississippi, despite affidavits of complaint and intimidation from the Evers poll watchers, quickly declared that he had no authority to investigate voting irregularities unless complaints were brought by the local election boards themselves; that was the system. It was also the system to select officeholders in the primaries, to fight things out within the machines, within the party, and not in the general election. This election was therefore unprecedented, a triumph for the New South abroad, a reaffirmation of established practice at home. The Republicans hadn't managed to break the system very much in 1970, and Evers' Independents could do no better in 1971.

There *was* a New South, a region creeping hesitantly past the year 1954 into acceptance of school integration, black politics and an appreciation of the subtleties of public relations. There was even a possibility that the Evers campaign and the hundreds of thousands of new black voters in the region would, in the future, add a major element to the calculations of every politician, that unless they could be purged or intimidated, they would have to be reckoned with. Racism was bad for the image, violence was out as official policy, and public nigger-baiting was probably over. In Jackson people could speak with some pride of the fact that they were doing appreciably better with busing and school integration than Pontiac, Michigan, or Boston or Chicago. Bill Winter, the lieutenant governor of Mississippi and one of the most liberal politicians in the Deep South, was sending his daughter on a bus five miles across town, to a school that was slightly over fifty percent black—not many politicians up North could make the same claim—and even Bill Waller, who beat Evers so badly and who was endorsed by Stennis and Eastland and John Bell Williams, could remind the skeptics that he was the district attorney who had prosecuted the accused killer of Medgar Evers, Charles's brother, had worked hard to convict him, and had done so in 1964, a time when prosecuting white assailants of blacks, especially of civil-rights workers, had not been regarded as the most auspicious beginning of a career in Mississippi politics.

There were other things as well, some subtle, some obvious. "We've seen the results of unbridled, unplanned industrial development," Winter said. "We were getting industry on whatever terms it wanted to come; we were so poor we had a hard time worrying about the conditions—we took it any way we could get it. But I think there's going to be a change in public attitudes and some tightening up on taxes and pollution." (Almost at the moment we were talking, Reubin Askew, the new governor of

Florida, was carrying his state with a popular referendum imposing corporate taxes for the first time in Florida's history and thereby helping to establish himself as a possible vice-presidential candidate for 1972. In Alabama, meanwhile, an ambitious young attorney general named Bill Baxley had taken on some of the state's largest corporations in pollution cases.) There was a new generation of people in the South, said Winter, who were not conditioned to automatic acceptance of a system that imposed "external limits," where "the black man was automatically expected to live in a menial role" and where a "warm paternalism" was the highest civic virtue. The blatancy of racism was over, and although the subtleties would be there for a long time, even they might be mitigated by small-town familiarity, by politeness, and by the fact that social relations in the South did not have to be a "faceless thing." The most promising thing, and one could hear it all across the Old South, was that the region was a more attractive place to live in: if they could get more professional people to come in, or to stay, if people "don't have to feel they're living in a colonial or a provincial area," then Jackson or Charlotte or Montgomery would have so much more appeal than Pittsburgh, Chicago or New York.

For a New Yorker, the comparison was obviously embarrassing. For a century the country had tempered its Jeffersonian suspicion of large cities with an ambivalence about the excitement and opportunities of the Big Town; now they were all defining themselves as non-New York, non-Chicago, non-urban, even if that meant, as it usually did, ignoring the parallel problems of the small city. (Jackson and Charlotte and Montgomery, God knows, have their slums, too, and generally they are more neglected than the slums of New York.) It was not merely that it had become difficult to be ecstatic about the prospects of life in the large cities, but that the very ethic had changed, that some of us, at least, were flirting with a new social mythology and a new sort of geopolitics that demoted the process of making it—the big money, the big challenges, the big jobs—and elevated the ideals of the good life. One night, riding from Laurel to Jackson, the Atlanta correspondent for a California news syndicate expounded to his fellow passengers on the limitations of the South. The climate was too warm, he said, the region too insular; there were no white ethnic minority groups, no foreign interests, and not enough creative energy and frigid weather to produce the activity that characterized the development of the North. What Southern climate had ever produced anything without slaves? One person in the car began to debate the accuracy of the observation—hookworm, after all, had been eradicated, air conditioning was universal, and black people offered enough cultural energy to satisfy anyone—but the question no longer seemed quite as important. The new Sun Belt of the Southwest might appear plastic and vulgar because it was full of petty-affluent insecure people who had come without history, tradition or a commitment to place, but the idea of sunshine and all it represented was still attractive, more attractive now than ever before. Somehow there was in the larger national atmosphere a sense that the era of rampant development had come to an end, that the necessity of work might still exist but that the romance had faded, that there were values other than making it, and that we had better learn to cultivate them. The South, however corrupt and unjust, seemed to know more about that than New York City.

We were all hooked on magnolias and honeysuckle, had all moved a few degrees South. But the South was not yet in a position to save anyone. The pressure of an organized underclass, black and white (should it ever come), combined with the new official tolerance of the establishment, might mitigate the vast inequities of status and income that had always characterized the region. Under the right conditions, with luck, with great skill in organizing, with the proper leadership, the South might even enjoy a resurgence of moderate populism. Running for governor of Virginia in 1969, Henry Howell had made a surprisingly strong showing with a populist campaign that included exemption of food and patent medicines from the sales tax, control of utility rates, and reduction of auto insurance premiums; in 1971, with a similar appeal, he was elected lieutenant governor. His support came from urban blacks and whites, the unions, the young and the old liberals; he was relatively weak in the rural areas. In the same period, however, two traditional populists, Albert Gore and Ralph Yarborough, were defeated, Wallace won again, though by a narrow margin, and Evers was crushed, suggesting again that the elements of reform and populism were elusive, and that the populist impulse itself had its dark side, its racism, its narrowness and its reaction. The activist kids and the Northern reformers might be quite right in regarding people like Evers and Simmons and Ed Cole as the real hopes of the New South—and as the only individuals who also offered something for the social inequities of the rest of the nation. "When everything's ironed out," Medgar Evers' widow had said one night, "Mississippi is going to be the best place; what happens here will ripple out, and all America will benefit. . . ." But that still remained a dream; there was no way to be certain, even of the people who were supposed to be on your side.

All of it remained fragile. The wisest political management could find itself overwhelmed by the poverty or suspicion of its own constituents and by the power of the absentee-owned corporations which always dominated the region's economy. It was hard to romanticize poverty as "the good life." The South's civility, moreover, that courtesy and understanding of which it spoke so much, had not yet been tested without the props of class structure and racial separation. In its confrontation with the civil-rights movement it failed miserably, ran before demagoguery, hysteria and violence. Civility with paternalism was easy; without paternalism it required the kind of maturity that the region badly lacked. Most important, the South still had no clear vision of its future, no persuasive dream about its own version of the good society. There were pieces of it, but no coherent whole, and many of the people who should have been most concerned with its formulation were too immersed in the preservation of an adolescent fantasy to be involved. What the South did know was that things in the past decade had gotten a great deal better; but from the outside, where things had become more doubtful, if not actually worse, the prospects of the South appeared even more hopeful than they really were.

The choice was not the old against the new, but what portion of each and how combined. In the long run, the advertised version of the New South might, by itself, become nothing more than the old class system buttressed by smooth talk, public relations, and the veneer of industrial progress, might be nothing more hopeful than Mississippi catching up with Ohio; in the long run, the Old South might offer only black suffering, subtle violence, exploitation and sentimentality. If the great thaw had really come, then there was a chance that the New South might borrow some of the populism and egalitarianism of its Jacksonian ancestry, and that the Old might absorb a little of the tolerance and skills of the New. If they did not, they would continue to coexist with their arrangements of convenience, their tensions and their petty exploitation: two versions of time, each with its own pace, each with its own dead end.

SIX:

THE DEMISE OF THE
MAD SCIENTIST

I

Our last great romance, and perhaps the most significant, was our brief, torrid affair with Brains. Partly as a consequence of World War II and of Sputnik and of the infatuation with the Blessings of Technology, and partly in response to the closing of other "frontiers," Americans after World War II transformed the future from an article of the common faith into a semiprivate preserve for technicians and intellectuals. The future had always been the ultimate colony of the West, the last territory of empire, but henceforth the pioneers would be Specialists, while the rest of us—waiting for new gadgets and new blessings —were at least partly persuaded that we could no longer manage for ourselves what we once regarded as our most precious possession. We were, needless to say, not the only nation which made futurism into a sort of academic discipline, nor, again, was literary or scientific speculation about the future particularly novel with our generation. The Greeks, said Robert Heilbroner, "consulted the oracles; the Middle Ages the clergy; the Enlightenment the philosophers and historians." But we, the Americans, once regarded ourselves unique in the belief that the future was the possession of the common man, that destiny, to put it crudely, might be individualistic and democratic, and that possibilities were unlimited. A half century ago Frederick Jackson Turner, the historian of the American frontier, suggested that the brain, through education and science, might someday replace the physical frontier as the source of new possibilities and therefore as a means of maintaining an open society and a national spirit of optimism. But the suggestion assumed that all men might be participants and not merely subjects or passive beneficiaries; Turner, moreover, did not—could not—fully anticipate the brevity of the honeymoon between the brain, lately called the knowledge industry, and the frontier, nor could he imagine the rapidity with which yesterday's dreams might become tomorrow's nightmares.

The latest version of the dream had lasted barely a decade. Beginning in the late fifties with the suddenly growing national commitment to education and science, it reached its apotheosis in the first moon landing in 1969. In the interim the federal commitment for research and development grew from an annual budget of some $2.7 billion to a figure exceeding $16.5 billion; at the same time national expenditures for education grew at a rate nearly double the annual growth of GNP, and the expectation developed that the commitment, though it might overemphasize the military or the scientific, would properly grow forever. Like all dreams, this one had its faddish pop-cult qualities: everything that science fiction once imagined was coming true, and nothing, if we really set the best brains to the task, was beyond achievement. The crises of the sixties seemed always to derive from ever-rising brain-demand curves: where would we get the engineers, the scientists, the college teachers, the trained manpower to fill the need? Was there a way to produce a quicky Ph.D.? Could we use paraprofessionals to expand the efficiency of the physician, the scientist and the teacher? Every day the papers were full of ads for research directors, project engineers and systems analysts, and every week some corporate official announced that his company's research effort was limited only by the shortage of scientists to carry it on. Normal schools became colleges, and colleges universities, and every academic with an ounce of enterprise created new divisions, departments and schools. To John F. Kennedy, the Apollo program must have been a perfect symbol for the adventure deriving from scientific development, for the energy and thrust that the mind could generate. Here was the new frontier, and most Americans seemed to accept it in the spirit it was offered. It did not occur to most practitioners (or to anyone else) to ask whether the thing they called the explosion of knowledge was rooted in useful considerations or in demonstrable epistemology, or whether it was merely the product of a lot of people writing a lot of learned papers—whether, in short, it was produced by overemployment in research.

In the interim, however, something else had happened. Research must, by its very nature, justify itself by appealing to the future; if we spend the money now, we will have better cars next year, better television sets, better medicine. Better living through chemistry. But even when the research and the educational expansion of the sixties were promoted in terms of specific programs or products or services—and that was not always the case—the cumulative effect was so general as to encompass the future itself. Here was paranoia in reverse: *they*—the planners, the scientists, the technicians—were taking care of things. It was inconceivable that there might be a serious problem that they couldn't solve (or that there might be personal problems that could not be converted into social problems and thus made manageable by social or behavioral experts). *They* were conspiring to make us happy. At the same time there was the millennial appeal of the year 2000 itself, which, when viewed from the ebullient perspective of the mid-sixties, appeared manageable, thinkable, and, in some versions, as imminent as tomorrow morning. With the prospect of constantly growing everything—research money included—research would be future-oriented not merely by implication or inference but by subject. We would study the future itself. In a period of a few years, therefore, futurism had become a profession surrounded by an industry. Dozens of corporations hired social scientists, philosophers and planners to think twenty-five or thirty years ahead; management institutes and seminars were organized to ponder the world of the year 2000; the American Academy of Arts and Sciences created the Commission on the Year 2000; a group of veterans of the Rand Corporation established the Institute for the Future; the World Future Society was organized; and in almost every think tank between Santa Monica and Cambridge (and in several overseas) teams of "experts" established projects to study "alternate futures."

The techniques employed were often identical to those used by intellectuals to study military strategy. Here was a world devoted to cross-impact matrices, scenarios, the Delphi exercise, morphological analysis and relevance trees. Game theory, conflict resolution and systems analysis were appropriated for the great battle ahead (which included, among other things, the problem of assuring the survival of the Hudson Institute and the Rand Corporation in the unlikely event that peace broke out and military research funds dried up). The possibilities of new drugs and new learning techniques were assessed in precisely the same way as the possibilities of new missile systems; the behavior of black activists, union leaders and corporate managers was "gamed" much in the manner of Russian generals and Chinese premiers. The intellectualized warfare of force and counterforce, zero-sum games, second-strike capabilities and deterrence (which had itself borrowed ideas from mathematical game theory) was escalated to include everything from university students to Brazilian peasants. Alvin Toffler, whose pretentious book *Future Shock* had to be taken seriously (if only because it became a best-seller among those who liked their clichés hardbound), described the possibilities of these ventures in a tone bordering on ecstasy. What we needed, he wrote, was a system of "future sensors" (I imagine no pun was intended), "imagineers," "utopia factories" and a "world futures data bank." Man already knew more about the future than he had ever tried to formulate or integrate, Toffler said. "Attempts to bring this knowledge together would constitute one of the crowning intellectual efforts in history—and one of the most worthwhile."

Here was futurism at its most promiscuous—the intellectualizing of everything. Although Toffler wanted to democratize futurism —everybody must somehow get into the game—the existing enterprises were passionately elitist. Inevitably they divided the universe between "us" and "them," planners and subjects; there was after all, no other way to do it, no language which did not assume that some people would do the thinking for others. "It is possible," wrote Daniel Bell, chairman of the Commission on the Year 2000, "to direct some of this change consciously, and because a normative commitment underlies any humanistic approach to social policy, we can try to widen the area of choice. Looking ahead, we realize that the rebuilding of American cities, for example, entails a thirty-five-year cycle, and one can rebuild cities only by making long-range commitments." Clearly there was an assumption here that some individuals would "widen the area of choice" for others, that some would plan and some would be served by the planners, and that the future, if things were to be properly directed, could be entrusted only to professional management, thereby creating the most dangerous of class divisions, that between those who possessed what Ivan Illich called "knowledge capital" and those who did not. Some members of the Commission understood the problem—"How," asked the psychiatrist Leonard Duhl, "do you live with the anxiety of not really comprehending the thinking people around you?"—but it was generally ignored in the general euphoria of colonizers surveying virgin land. Bell, now a professor of sociology at Harvard, later said that his colleagues were never as optimistic about their powers—or the possibilities for the future—as the general press suggested, but the publications and the recorded conversations of the mid-sixties made the assertion questionable. "The heightened prestige of science and the crucial role of research," wrote Bell in 1965, "have brought with them a new, optimistic temper about the future. Science, by its nature, is open, self-corrective, and often cumulative." Moreover, said Bell, "within less than a decade, more than a dozen men have orbited the earth, space shots have reached the moon and have probed Mars, and a communications satellite that provides instant television and telephone linkage among almost all parts of the world has become a fixture in the skies. Thus man's technological powers have been given a new dimension and a new dramatic demonstration. The jump-off into space is also a jump-off into future time." Optimistic? "There now exists the sense that social change, inevitably linked in its effects, must be guided in some conscious direction. Though this may not create the changes themselves, it will at least anticipate their direction and effects, and [one can] plan accordingly. In other words, we have become oriented toward the future." Bell did not say who that "we" might be, but the context was clear. "We" were the intellectuals, and the ebullience among them could hardly be contained. When, early in 1971, the British economist E. J. Mishan surveyed the rhetoric of the futurists, he concluded that, in their view, "man's powers . . . are growing all the time and doubtless he will meet the challenge when he has to. A decorous concern was admissible, but there was no cause for alarm."

What I want to emphasize here is not simply the optimism of the scientists and the planners (however qualified that optimism may have been) but, more significantly, the general identification of the future with the knowledge industry and its certificated professionals. Once such a belief was transformed from a private and general faith into the possession of a priesthood, only a revolution could succeed in winning it back. Inevitably, given the resources and the attached prestige, the professional thinkers could be expected to arrogate to themselves the study of "alternative futures." What greater empire could anyone desire? What was surprising was that Americans, with their history of anti-intellectualism, would allow them to get away with it. For nearly a decade university presidents promoted their institutions with pictures of cyclotrons and lists of Nobel laureates; for nearly a decade no academic enterprise and no program of research was too abstract or expensive to find support. The text of the fund raiser was a study by a University of Chicago economist named Theodore Schultz, who argued that social investment in education had more payoff in gross national product than equal investments in land or capital; similar studies were undertaken—inconclusively, as it turned out—for investment in research. We had no way of measuring the productivity of brain work, but the few rough indications that existed suggested that cerebration, unlike factory work, was no more productive in 1965 than it had been fifty years before. Nonetheless the faith (especially when it was implemented with tax money) persisted. We were going to send half the population to college and, at the same time, use organized brain work to solve all the problems of hunger, poverty and disease at virtually no cost to anyone.

The whole decade had a Faustian quality about it: we were offered a future of robot maids, commercial space travel, effective weight and appetite control, human hibernation, weather control, genetic manipulation, direct electronic communication with the brain, and all the rest. "We must pursue the idea," said Glenn T. Seaborg, chairman of the Atomic Energy Commission, "that it is more science, better science, more wisely applied that is going to free us from [our] predicaments. What I am speaking of . . . is the application of science and scientific thinking both to alleviate immediate ills and to set the underlying philosophy for a rationale for the future handling of our technological and social development." I have no idea how many Americans bought such ideas, but they tended, more often than not, to behave as if they did. Common sense lost its nerve and Main Street its self-confidence; the magic and the power now rested not in the dynamo of Henry Adams' era, but in the laboratories of Cambridge and Berkeley. And where the magic was, there also was the future.

The bust was probably inevitable. The late sixties were, as we all learned, disastrous for the brain business: aerospace engineers selling hot dogs; people with shiny Ph.D.s from the Ivy League teaching freshmen in junior colleges (if they could find jobs at all); men of prestige scratching for funds to support their laboratories and their shrinking teams of assistants. The American Institute of Aeronautics and Astronautics (AIAA), the professional association of the onetime glamour boys, estimated early in 1971 that between fifty thousand and a hundred thousand professionals were out of work in that field alone; figures from the Bureau of Labor Statistics, moreover, suggested that unemployment in professional and technical occupations, which had been negligible in 1968, tripled in the next three years and had begun to approach the average for other occupations. What the figures could not estimate was the level of underemployment or the extent of the psychological depression among people whose self-esteem depended not only on a job, but on a job with prestige. Beginning in 1969, AIAA ran hundreds of workshops for its unemployed members to teach them how to write resumés, compose letters of application and conduct themselves in interviews, but the sessions almost inevitably turned into group therapy for men trying to find their bearings in a world where, for the first time, they had to look for work.

At the Glastonbury, Connecticut, high school, a group of 120 engineers and technicians meet for the first of three evening workshops. They have been laid off by Hamilton Standard, United Aircraft and other aerospace contractors in the Hartford area: radar project engineer, combustion engineer, process engineer. (You remember the titles from those pages of glamour five years ago that appeared in The New York Times *and* The Wall Street Journal: *$20,000 a year with liberal benefits; $22,000 in Santa Monica; $25,000 in Fort Worth.) Some of them are young men only a year or two out of college, but many are well over forty and a few are close to sixty. After a general meeting in the auditorium they are divided into groups of six or eight, each of them with a "counselor" to discuss their common problem. In Room 106, where one of the small groups is meeting, the regular daytime teacher has posted old* Time *and* Newsweek *covers depicting the Apollo moonshot, the astronauts and* *assorted spiny space vehicles. (During the day the kids are being motivated by this vision of the future; in the evening the men who helped design it are learning how to fill out resumés.)*

"No jobs in pollution," says one of them. "No jobs."

"Dallas is very bad right now," says another man. They talk about the B-1, the F-14, the F-15, and the space shuttle—"What if they go down the pipe?"—and about the fact that companies are simply not hiring older men, even if they have openings. "They'd rather have the young guys; they're cheaper." Not a bright side anywhere, says the counselor, a personnel manager for a local company; go to your friendly banker and tell him you have trouble and he'll probably try to work things out for you—what the hell would the banks in Seattle do with twenty-nine thousand empty houses? We're telling people to get out of aerospace; it's not going to come back, it'll never come back like it was.

The manifestations of this "recession" were more visible on the faces of people than they were in "For Sale" signs on the lawns of the new developments that surrounded the boom regions of the sixties: Cape Kennedy, Route 128, Sunnyvale, Seattle. A man could live off unemployment insurance, he could drive a cab or he could do odd jobs for local industry, but there was no point in moving: things were as tight elsewhere as they were at home. Those most visibly affected were people who lived off the fat of the fat—restaurant and nightclub operators, car dealers, real-estate promoters—but the most profound impact was more subtle. One could read it in the statistics and hear it in the anxiety in people's voices. The wow was gone. Four years before, that ever-rising federal commitment to research and development had leveled off and, in terms of constant dollars, had actually begun to decline. (No talk then about an overheated economy or about curbing inflation—that was to come later.) And what happened first with federal dollars for aerospace and military hardware also began to happen in education, in medicine, in local school budgets, in television and advertising and publishing, and in almost every other sector of the knowledge industry. And so we entered the era of overruns, cutbacks and layoffs, and the talk began about conversion budgets, about reordering priorities, and about the pressing needs of the domestic economy in housing, transportation, pollution control and health. But still the depression seemed to run deeper, ran to the very fount of faith in science and brainwork. The vote against the SST might have been a vote for reason, as Daniel Bell claimed, but it was also a vote of no confidence in the planners and the engineers. "People simply didn't believe what the engineers told them," said a public relations man for one of the ailing aircraft companies. More important, the onetime stars of R and D were now often regarded as pariahs by other industry. "Those guys keep getting told that they're not cost-conscious, that they've been living so long on cost-plus contracts and unlimited government money that they simply can't operate in a competitive market. That's not true, of course—many of them are doing well in other industries—but that's what they keep hearing when they apply for jobs. There isn't much blue sky left."

If the vote on the SST had indeed been a vote of reason, then how did one explain the growing revolt against school bond issues, university budgets and medical research? The conventional answer was "the general recession in the economy," and the common solution (as proposed by most politicians) was to shift military money into brain work for peace. If the Democrats were elected in 1972, Bell had said in 1971, things would turn around; a temporary problem, said Olaf Helmer, the president of the Institute for the Future and one of the high prophets of futurism, there was no reason for pessimism: "After this depression the ebullience will return." Late in 1970 the Nixon Administration appropriated funds to convert unemployed aerospace engineers and scientists into ecologists, urbanologists and experts in surface transportation, but at AIAA in New York, where the models of new planes and rockets adorned the office shelves like so many relics of antiquity, men with long faces were calling the program a "forty-two-million-dollar boondoggle" to train engineers to fill nonexistent jobs. Not surprisingly, therefore, every Democratic challenger for the presidency made an issue of the "reordering of priorities," turning the conversion of technical manpower from military research to such problems as housing and ecology into a staple of the political arsenal. What could be easier than to put all that talent to work on the *real* needs of the nation and the world? "There is no permanent decline in our sense of possibilities," said Helmer. "We have a repressed potential in this country. We behave as though we're poor, but we are not poor. It would be easy to transfer the talent we have. The basic methods are not too different."

Despite such optimism there were unmistakable indications that the problem was more complex, that there was (at the very least) a possibility that the nation now had a knowledge establishment considerably greater than it could use, that the belief in the possibilities of research and education had measurably declined, and that conditions in the next two decades, rather than getting better, would actually get worse. Allan M. Cartter, now the chancellor of New York University and long a critic of the ebullient expansion of the intellectual community, told the American Association for the Advancement of Science late in 1970:

We should not attribute today's problems just to a temporary cutback in federal funds for education, research and development. Even without the topping out of federal support, we would have begun to have an abundance of doctoral scientists in most fields of specialization in the early 1970s. . . . We have created a graduate education and research establishment in American universities that is about thirty to fifty percent larger than we shall effectively use in the 1970s and early 1980s, and the growth process continues in many sectors. The readjustment to the real demands of the next fifteen years is bound to be painful.

Cartter's argument was that even with optimistic projections of growth in all scientific sectors there were already too many specialists in the academic pipeline. "Doctorate holders will tend to 'bump' those with lesser credentials in many types of positions. However, an increasing proportion of these specialists will not be employed in jobs for which they were trained, or to which they aspired. . . . The price of a surplus of Ph.D.s is not unemployment but rising underemployment." Coupled with this problem was the danger of an increasingly aging academic faculty. In most universities there were large (and growing) numbers of tenured professors who would (under current policies) not reach retirement age until after the year 2000. If the need for new faculty declined sharply in the late 1970s and early 1980s (when, Cartter predicted, college enrollment will actually decline in absolute numbers), the universities would be victims of an aging professoriate unrelieved by transfusions of younger blood.

The meeting of the American Association for the Advancement of Science at which Cartter spoke was a depressing gathering of already depressed people. On the day after Cartter's speech, the assembled scientists were subjected to an even more sobering appraisal from Bentley Glass, the retiring president of AAAS. What Cartter had said about academic manpower Glass applied to the scientific enterprise itself. There was at least a possibility, said Glass, that "we are like the explorers of a great continent who have penetrated to its margins in most points of the compass and have mapped the major mountain chains and rivers. There are still innumerable details to fill in, but the endless horizons no longer exist." Although Glass left open the possibility that new developments would create unexpected horizons—"What remains to be learned may indeed dwarf imagination," he said—"no rate of scientific development equal to the past half century can be long maintained." Exponential growth, however measured, could not continue forever. Glass listed some of the factors which tended to limit such growth: population density, the exhaustion of sources of energy, pollution, and, most significantly, the mounting expense of each new development. Historically there had been a compulsion to pursue whatever development was considered possible, regardless of the benefits or the cost: we climbed the mountain simply because it was there. The reaction against the SST may have indicated that an ethic of curiosity based on individual scientific or intellectual initiative (a Pasteur, a Galileo, or an Eve Curie working essentially alone) would not be applicable to huge collectives of researchers—corporate science—supported by millions of dollars from the public treasury. (Many of these issues, incidentally, were raised by René Dubos in 1968 when the general euphoria was still going strong, but "the public's disenchantment at the realization that science cannot solve all human problems" and the doubts of the professionals about "the wisdom and safety of extending much further some of the applications of knowledge" had appeared—at the time—to be more rhetorical than passionate. Dubos was serious, but I'm not certain that anyone else was.)

What was most significant in the remarks of people like Cartter and Glass lay in their fundamental lack of optimism about the scientific future. Clearly some of this sobriety—or, at any rate, the willingness of professionals to listen—came from the depression in the knowledge industry; nobody laughed or hooted when Glass spoke (even though some of his listeners were well aware that similar prophecies had been made by scientists as long as seventy-five years ago). But the erosion of confidence seemed to go beyond the immediate shortage of jobs or grants, to the desirability of the enterprise itself.

The prime difficulty [said Glass] is that so many persons, not only in the highly industrialized countries but even more among the peoples of the underdeveloped countries, now see their hopes for the future bound up with the continuation and extension to all mankind of the progress hitherto limited to a few fortunate lands and people. The momentum of these processes is furthermore such that measures to apply the brakes to population growth or to reclaim and preserve our environment, even if the measures are firm and effective, will take at least one generation—say until the year 2000—to reach full effect. . . . In future histories of the world the decade of the 1960s may be known not significantly for the miserable Vietnam war but as the time when man, with unbridled lust for power over nature and for a so-called high standard of living measured by the consumption of the products of an industrial civilization, set in motion the final speedy, inexorable rush toward the end of progress.

This was not simply the standard argument for ecology and population control or the conventional cry of *mea culpa* of a "responsible" scientist, but a more fundamental question about the association of "science" with the future. Clearly Glass was an advocate of planning, but planning for a future that was limited rather than infinite, a future in which neither science nor knowledge was of itself to be regarded as an unqualified benefit to be supported without reservation. What it suggested, although Glass never said it, was that "reason" without limits—unplanned and uncoordinated—could create its own jungles and wastelands. There was little here with which futurists like Bell or Herman Kahn or Olaf Helmer would have disagreed, except perhaps the bearishness of the tone, but it begged a string of questions that had rarely been discussed, either by the futurists or by anyone else. Having ceded management of the "frontier" to professionals, how would the man who was promised unlimited blessings in return respond to the caveats of finitude? How would he react when he discovered that the magic that promised robot maids, superdrugs and supergadgets turned instead into a bitter choice between *their* version of control (of population, growth and, therefore, of life itself) and environmental destruction? What sort of social reaction could one expect when the life and activities which represented the ultimate frontier were themselves restricted to a minority of privileged people, and when the rest of society was regarded as surplus? What Glass and Cartter seemed to be saying was that this frontier was also closing.

"The scientist or academic, though his work subjects him to the most grueling pace," wrote Mishan in *Encounter*,

believes he has some compensations—recognition of published work, intellectual communication with others in his field, occasional mention by the press. I believe that he, too, is under illusions that he will not weather the future. But we shall let that pass, and turn instead to the greater part of humanity. *For it is the ordinary men and women that are destined to become the victims of the future.* [Italics mine] Social workers may teach [the ordinary man] to play games for his health, and suggest recreations to soothe his thwarted instincts. But as an ordinary human being he will have nothing really to offer society. He may be regaled with goods and privileges. But nobody needs him. He will live by the grace of the Scientific Establishment, earmarked as a drone, protected for a while longer by social institutions and the remnants of a moral tradition, yet transparently expendable.

Mishan, a member of the faculty at the London School of Economics, had been a critic of growthmanship long before such questions became fashionable (and thus, of course, a crackpot), but his blast at the scientific establishment, the "high priests of the new ecumenical faith," now took the sobriety of the Cartters and the Glasses a step further. Mishan wrote the script before anyone seriously expected that it might correspond to reality; now the reality was, at the very least, a possibility: "If present trends in mass education continue, there is every likelihood of millions of dissatisfied ex-students milling about American cities, their frail expertise unwanted (how many sociologists can the nation employ?), unable or unwilling to fit into the uninspiring niches provided by industry and government, and inevitably forming a sort of intellectual *lumpenproletariat* that will go far to aggravate the general unrest, dissent and desperation."

The sum of all this arithmetic suggested that there was only one thing more dangerous than a brain elite based on a faith in the future, and that was a brain elite based on no such faith. Having acceded to power on the basis of promises that were economically and ecologically beyond fulfillment, the new priests of science and technology were likely to try to hold on with the argument that they were the only people who could hold off a technological apocalypse, and that the rest of us had better come along if we didn't want to face total destruction. Given the context and the tone in which it was made, the call for a "reordering of priorities" sounded more like a way of keeping intellectuals occupied than an expression of confidence in resolving genuine social problems. No one had yet confronted the question of whether the conversion of engineers, scientists and technicians from the design of military hardware to the construction of housing or the solution of other social problems would, in effect, become the pacification of America by the same people (and the same attitudes) who tried to pacify Vietnam. What evidence did we have that the Department of Health, Education and Welfare, the Department of Housing and Urban Development, and the Department of Transportation would be any more benign than the Pentagon? What models provided assurance? The Bureau of Indian Affairs? The federal highway authorities? The Atomic Energy Commission? "An all-powerful scientific establishment," Mishan wrote, "clearly has no need of some thousand millions of now useless mortals moving about the globe and cluttering up the limited space of the planet-laboratory. The prospect of diverting resources to provide them indefinitely with goodies and to ply them with entertainment and medicines will not be attractive. The temptation to be rid of them will grow stronger. . . ."

The conventional defense of "research" rested in the argument that new developments would alleviate the plight of the poor, heal the sick and improve the "quality of life," but there was ample evidence that all "development" created corresponding underdevelopment—that kidney machines, supersonic transportation, and the other elegant products of advanced research were available only to a small minority, and that higher education itself (even in the United States) favored the affluent at the expense of the poor. Economic studies of public universities had produced considerable evidence that while the children of the affluent received a disproportionate share of the benefits, the poor (through regressive sales taxes) paid a disproportionate share of the cost. For at least a generation, "development" had enlarged economic and technological gaps; the specialists in designing the gadgets of the future created products to be used, operated and maintained by other specialists: the expense of operating one kidney machine would feed ten starving people or provide minimal medical service for a hundred. Research and education thus became corollaries to capitalism, knowledge was treated like property, and the future became the possession of those who were presumed to know most and who had the most to spend.

The new frontier served the same political function as the old. A century ago, the open spaces of the West—that Virgin Land —had been regarded as the nation's social-safety valve, an escape from the inevitability of Marxist class conflicts; only a minority benefited, but the promise was sufficient. And when the frontier closed, it had been replaced in American mythology by the schools, the colleges and, most recently, research itself. These things had come to represent the future, were arguments against revolution, soporifics to an underclass which demanded more equity in the distribution of economic benefits. When the NASA budget for space exploration was cut in 1970, a collection of true believers headed by a self-styled "space philosopher," who called themselves the Committee for the Future, proposed a "Citizens' Mission to the Moon" ("New Worlds for All the World") which, they suggested, would solve most of the problems of mankind. Welfare recipients, they said, would be offered new opportunities—"New Worlds can provide a new Homestead Act"—and college graduates would be offered an "unlimited frontier . . . a future based on positive values." We would farm Mars, mine the moon, colonize Pluto. Thus the argument came full circle: there was no need for a class struggle in America, no need to reexamine values, because the frontier (or the schools, or science, or the moon itself) created opportunities and benefits for all men; what was not available today research and education would make possible tomorrow—a precise duplicate of the classic argument for capitalism. (In their last foray, the moon missionaries were trying to raise $100 million for an expedition.) For deliverance, Mishan had said, men "turn from Mammon to Science. And, when the time comes, Science, in its turn, will consign them to oblivion."

II

There were growing indications that the romance was, indeed, coming to an end, not only among a number of scientists and intellectuals, but among the public at large. The political revolt, local and national, against mounting budgets for research, education and development obviously reflected the tightened belts of the Nixon recession, but it also pointed to a more general disenchantment with that version of the future which had been so widely promoted a decade before. (The efforts of congressional Democrats to restore cuts in the federal appropriations for education were motivated at least as much by a primitive urge for revenue sharing—to bail out the local taxpayer—as they were by enthusiasm for the enterprise.) Ronald Reagan's attack on the budget of the University of California (which, as much as any institution, had stimulated the academic bull market in the late fifties) had been prophetic rather than pigheaded. What Reagan said about the university in 1967 and 1968 had, after all, been not so different from what Mario Savio and the Free Speech Movement had been saying about it three years before: Here was a monster that seemed to operate independently of any popular controls (by students or taxpayers) and that appeared more concerned with technical and professorial prestige than with democratic service. The Nobel laureates and the cyclotrons were still there, but, just as they had once been symbols of the promised golden age, they now were becoming tokens of elitism and irresponsible complicity with corporate and military research—were, in effect, the tools of the Devil. (However one may have felt about student protests against university administrations, they did suggest that *something* was wrong.) Educational budgets continued to go up, but the problems, instead of being solved, only seemed to get worse, and so the disenchantment of the students slowly began to spread to their parents and to the taxpayers.

The arguments had become all too familiar—too much rat race, too much trivia, too little personal attention, too little student participation—but one thing remained: going to college had become more a matter of survival than the initial step into an exciting tomorrow. One had to go (because there was no other choice, because of the draft, because college was the only mode of education or training that was so lavishly subsidized), but one defended oneself with increasing skepticism about the official version of rationality practiced by the apostles of higher learning. The choice, all too frequently, had been between, on the one hand, the *reason* of the builder of economic models, the theoretician of conflict resolution and the mathematical social scientist and, on the other, the unreason—if that's what it was —of intuition, personal experience, mysticism and vibes. (The kids did not, however, reject the complicated, involuted reasoning of people like R. Buckminster Fuller, whose "science" confirmed personal experience and seemed to provide mathematical and engineering support for a world view that rejected older views of national sovereignty, exploitation and conflict. At the same time, it may have been the quality of mysticism itself and not Fuller's reason that made him a hero to the kids.) At any rate, it was absolutely inconceivable that there would have been a counterculture without the technocratic elitism of the late fifties and sixties: this had been the response to the futurists and to the future they offered. If that's what lay ahead, the hell with it. One would live in the present, or in the past.

The sense of time was crucial. For the kids the magic had tarnished quickly; their parents were perpetually trying to catch up. (Not one of the members of Daniel Bell's Commission on the Year 2000, incidentally, would be less than seventy in the year 2000, and a couple of them, if they lived that long, would be more than one hundred.) It had been said that no one who reached adolescence after Hiroshima ever believed in a future anyway; perhaps, in any case, the futurists tended to be too Strangelovely to allow anyone to forget the Bomb. Yet for those who had gone to college in the sixties there had been a double dose: the academy was presumably the place that offered the best, the most positive and the most sophisticated of everything. If anyone could cope with the pressing social issues, could offer hope and the techniques to go with it, he would be somewhere on campus. But he wasn't. All one could find, excepting only a very few, were people who understood the skills required for accommodation into the system that already existed; the academic version of the future, if you really looked at it, was only an extension of the uglier aspects of the present.

What the kids had really discovered on campus were Allan Cartter's statistics and E. J. Mishan's pessimism. The familiar argument that the young felt guilty about their privileges and therefore wished to "serve mankind" to soothe their consciences was far less revealing than the fact that going to college after 1960 no longer qualified a person for membership in any elite. Until 1968 or 1969 there had been a choice of good jobs and a miscellany of other perquisites, but people who might have expected to become "leaders" by virtue of the degree, or who did expect the academic system to impose a slightly higher order of honesty, social concern and honor, discovered instead that institutional emoluments—grades, credits, degrees—were accessible to any hustler who played the game no matter how calculating or inhumane he really was. The crowd on campus was too big; even if there were jobs it was inconceivable that there would ever be honor or status. The revolt on campus was, at least in part, a status revolt. It must be hard to tell your father, after he had worked all his life to send you to college, that there were millions just like yourself, that most of them were average, and that going to college was no big deal. It was just another mob.

Not surprisingly, the professional futurists didn't have much use for a collection of unreasonable kids. In one article in *Commentary*, Bell characterized the counterculture as "the democratization of Dionysius," meaning, I suppose, that a large portion of an entire generation was composed of self-indulgent hedonists who responded only to their own gut and rejected serious cerebration. Shortly after the Columbia University demonstrations in 1968, Zbigniew Brzezinski, also a member of the Commission on the Year 2000 (and, like Bell at that time, a member of the Columbia faculty), put down the entire youth movement as reactionary, a last Luddite stand against the blessings of technocratic planning. (Brzezinski had always regarded "public pressure" in policy-making as somewhat annoying and inefficient; France under de Gaulle was more to his liking.) The recurring admonition directed to the young was that they didn't know anything, didn't understand the social and technological complexities of their time, and weren't interested in finding out. Institutional and technological reform (they were told, *ad infinitum*) was a sensitive and difficult business. This was an admonition that always sounded like a substitute for the schoolmaster's stick—a demand that people get into line and apprentice themselves to the journeymen of technocracy (Sit down and shut up or technology will get you)—but it also stood as a monumental refutation of the argument that technology would make life more leisurely, manageable and pleasant: The road to the happy future seemed to lead through an everlasting series of intolerable presents. Even for someone of imperfect logic it must have been difficult to understand the connection.

But alienated students—the intellectuals of the year 2000—were no longer alone, were not the only people who had serious doubts that there would be a future. There were still regions and sectors of optimism in America, still places and groups where people felt that they could control the future—and that there was a future to manage—but it had become increasingly difficult to find them. By the end of the sixties most Americans had become schooled; they had been persuaded that only expertise could confront the major problems of technology and society, but they had also learned that the brilliant future that expertise was supposed to bring had not materialized. It may well be that popular belief in the possibilities of science and education was exorbitant ten years ago and that it was (therefore) unduly depressed now. But it was not the familiar seesaw between utopia and apocalypse, Great Society and sick society, that was now most apparent; it was rather a coming to terms with an indefinite present, with a sense that tomorrow will not inevitably be better than today, that the more things seemed to change, the more they stayed the same.

There was no end of evidence: people who once were willing to believe whatever the school superintendent told them and who responded with extravagant support for every educational innovation voting against budgets and bond issues without even a tinge of regret; first-generation students in junior and community colleges (who were supposed to represent the "blueing of America" by an upwardly mobile class of new technicians and engineers) dropping out because the effort didn't seem worthwhile; gleeful legislative votes against university superchairs (established a decade before for the prestige of the academic stars they would attract) because "the people of New York shouldn't be paying $100,000 a year so Arthur Schlesinger, Jr., can write his memoirs." In a period of four years the entire foundation of public policy changed orientation: in 1965 we were making the future; in 1969 we were talking survival. "Our national apparatus for the conduct of research and scholarship is not yet dismantled," said Philip Handler, the president of the National Academy of Sciences, "but it is falling into shambles." The most passionate rhetoric that the Administration could muster was something about "the lift of a driving dream," a phrase that suggested moon dust without moon magic. (When Mr. Nixon tried to sound idealistic he seemed to be compulsively attracted to the echoes of John F. Kennedy.) Even the reordering of priorities could not capture the public imagination; the trumpet sounded but nobody marched, because the whole thing had the ring of a street and sewer project and lacked coherent vision. We were suffering not future shock but future deprivation.

The short of the argument was simple: Americans entrusted the future to experts, lost faith in their investment, and were now, hesitantly, uncertainly, trying to put the experts in their place. (The Mayday Tribe, the Redstockings, Nader's Raiders, the Yippies and Wallace's voters were all descendants of a great amateur self-help tradition.) Perhaps we would never have made the investment in the first place had we trusted our own individual capacities to manage the world; perhaps the experts, had they really applied expertise, might have accomplished something during the optimistic years of the New Frontier and the Great Society. Daniel Patrick Moynihan always attributed the failures of the poverty program to a "latter-day obscurantism" among social scientists whose programs raised "the level of perceived and validated discontent among poor persons with the social system about them, without actually improving the conditions of life of the poor in anything like a comparable degree." The social scientists, said John Gagnon, a sociologist at the State University of New York at Stony Brook, "knew plenty" about alleviating poverty and other specific problems, "but everybody converted their private anxieties into social necessities."

Robert Heilbroner leveled a similar criticism at the futurists themselves. The Commission on the Year 2000, he said, "for all its scientific air," had "not really performed its task in a scientific way" and was never clear whether it stood above the system, "seeking to analyze and report its trends with all the aloofness of the astronomer plotting the movements of the planets," or whether its members stood within the system, "working *for* social change." If the task of the Commission was to imagine a better world, he added, "it will need the radical and bold outlook of those outside the Establishment quite as much as the measured banalities of the professordom." Daniel Bell subsequently acknowledged that the Commission was insufficiently sensitive to cultural issues—"we were too preoccupied with social policy" —which one might take as an admission that the society was still too diverse, too messy, for the sort of social forecasting and planning that educated men of absolute reason sometimes dreamed about. But there also seemed to be some doubt—if not in Bell's mind, then certainly in the minds of others—that the year 2000, metaphorical or real, was something that could realistically be defined, managed or even studied. Somehow the next thirty years seemed longer now than the next thirty-five appeared in the mid-sixties. Perhaps we had learned something about the political and social consequences of "accidents," assassinations and collective unreason. (The Vietnam War had been the most "scientific" and intellectualized encounter in military history, but it was also the most inconclusive, the most frustrating and, ultimately, the most stupid.) Perhaps the absolute lesson of a decade of intellectual futurism was the heightened importance of the principle of uncertainty. Every "advance" and each new development made systems more vulnerable to sabotage and guerrilla attack, and increasingly the onetime symbols of the golden future—the schools, the universities, the computers, the planes and the laboratories—required protection from armed guards. Perhaps this would also be seen by future historians as a temporary outburst of Luddite revolt, perhaps we would (through the pressure of economic recession, through police action or through simple exhaustion) bring the rebels into line. Perhaps. But the consequences, as Mishan noted, were not likely to be pleasant.

When the Commission on the Year 2000 had its first meetings, Fred Charles Iklé, perhaps the most sober member of the group, presented a paper in which he argued the case for uncertainty. "I wonder," he had written, "if we are not seeing the world from a rather narrow perspective, somewhat like the medieval scribes who saw their past, present and future only in terms of religious and ecclesiastical events. While we find it well-nigh impossible to visualize our future without further technological developments, we can nonetheless visualize that the march of science might not turn out to be the cumulative enterprise we had thought." Iklé raised the possibility that most of the predictions of the futurists were only projections of their own personal goals. (The agenda of the Commission, he pointed out, was almost identical with the agenda of President Johnson's Great Society program of the previous year.) It was possible that by the year 2000 "economic growth will be smaller than we now project on the basis of the trade-off between more goods and more leisure. By the same token people [may] *care* less about economic growth . . ." When it comes to predicting our goals, he had concluded, "we are perpetual 'revisionists,' for we know that we can only follow the light at the prow of the ship."

No one made much of Iklé's argument in the mid-sixties (although it was clear that some of the futurists recognized it). Now its implications were becoming crucial. The business of futurology had been unequivocally based on assumptions of prosperity (despite its occasional warnings of international famine, nuclear war and other holocausts) because futurology itself was created by affluence, by an economic surplus that permitted societies of scholars and corporations the luxury of pondering not merely the problems of the next year or of the next product, but also of the next century. By 1970 it appeared that even without the recession, the optimistic forecasts of economic growth (perhaps even the desire for unchecked economic growth) would have to be qualified, that what ecology and shrinking natural resources did not do Japanese competition might, and that a certain humility therefore became urgently necessary.

The tempering of optimism in the possibility of brains had, and has, two related intellectual consequences. Both tended to be utopian (and, in that sense, totalitarian), but while one pretended to use intelligence to throw man into a new harmony with nature, the other, espoused by Harvard psychologist B. F.

Skinner, escalated applied intelligence into a behavioristic super-science that transcended all the paltry attempts of the past to manage the society and the universe. The first, represented by Fuller and the recycling-ecology-whole-earth freaks, assumed that with a proper understanding of "synergy" and "ephemeralization" the world could provide all the energy and resources to feed, house and transport its population handsomely. Fuller believed that existing resources had been used for goods that were (because of improper design) too heavy and too costly in energy and materials to be tolerable. Ephemeralization was the process of creating something that was "greater" than the sum of its constituent parts. (Tungsten steel, for example, has a tensile strength greater than the total strength of its constituent metals; the geodesic structure, which Fuller designed, was simultaneously lighter and stronger—and less costly in material —than conventional buildings.) In response to the various zero-sum games, which always assumed competition and struggle, Fuller designed a "world game" founded on ephemeralization and on the principles of what he called synergy (the idea that everything affected everything else—that the universe and all its parts must be regarded as a total system). The world game presumed that, contrary to all Malthusian and Darwinian ideas, survival and development were possible only in a setting founded on collaboration and on the principle that proper design could create technologies and social institutions that transcended the limitations which conventional attitudes impose upon them. The intellectual crime of convention was overspecialization, the inability to understand the total (synergetic) attributes of a problem, and the corresponding commitment to such unnatural principles as national sovereignty, competition and class. The remedy for such ideas, Fuller maintained—and the only hope for survival—was an understanding of the ephemeral possibilities of creative (and collaborative) endeavor. "Only mind can discover how to do so much with so little as forever to be able to sustain and physically satisfy all humanity." All value was created by mental activity, and increments in the quality of life did not, therefore, deplete the world of its resources or its possibilities. Yet even Fuller appeared more concerned with the totality of planetary planning (the title of a lecture he delivered in 1969) and world survival than with the aspirations and activities of individual men. The involuted complexity of his prose, the quasi-mystical rendering of ideas (e.g., "the NOVENT continuum permeates the finitely populated withinness and comprises the finite NOVENT WITHOUTNESS"), and the tendency to substitute metaphors for ideas ("Operating Manual for Spaceship Earth") made Fullerism fair game for cultists, for curbstone intellectuals and for new generations of elitist planners ready to impose collaboration and ephemeralization by coercion or persuasion. The world game would turn the data banks and the computers over to a crowd of people too tender to contemplate international struggle, arms races and resource depletion, but eager nonetheless to become members of the intellectual management of other people's futures. Perhaps that judgment would turn out too harsh, but there was always reason to suspect a man who wrote, "It is clearly to be UTOPIA or OBLIVION—and no half measures."

The second response to the declining confidence in brains, the Skinnerism of *Walden II* and *Beyond Freedom and Dignity*, ran in a slightly different direction and appealed to a different sort of person. It asserted that intelligence really hadn't been tried and argued that the whole thing must be escalated to a higher level. In other words, it turned quite mad. The argument was basically simple: Since all behavior and all attitudes were the consequence of conditioning, it became imperative to condition man to insure "the survival of the culture," and since science had revealed that concepts like freedom and dignity were illusions anyway, "what we need is more control, not less, and this is in itself an engineering problem of the first importance." The society should therefore create an environment that reinforced positive behavior—not to induce people to be good but to induce them to behave well—because "a culture that for any reason induces its members to work for its survival is more likely to survive." We already had a technology "of behavior . . . which would more successfully reduce the aversive consequences of behavior, proximate or deferred, and maximize the achievements of which the human organism is capable." It was only the "defenders of freedom" (that illusive quality) who resisted its implementation, thus exacerbating social dislocation and suffering. We could, in other words, condition men, and must condition them, to insure the survival of culture just as effectively as Skinner himself had conditioned pigeons to play ping-pong. The point was to rid ourselves of outmoded unscientific ideas—of assumptions about the innate attributes of man which, like prescientific notions of gravity or combustion, wouldn't stand the test of empirical examination.

It was easy to quarrel with Skinner; the argument was full of inconsistencies: If all was environmental conditioning and reinforcement, why try to persuade people with a book? Whose science and whose version of the culture would form the basis of the new conditioning? And was the technology, in fact, already available? If it was, why hadn't we had more success (or why hadn't the Russians or the Chinese) in predicting and conditioning behavior? "If there were some science capable of treating such matters," wrote Noam Chomsky in a review of Skinner's book,

it might well be concerned precisely with freedom and dignity and might suggest possibilities for enhancing them. Perhaps, as the classical literature of freedom and dignity sometimes suggests, there is an intrinsic human inclination toward free creative inquiry and productive work, and humans are not merely dull mechanisms formed by a history of reinforcement and behaving predictably with no intrinsic needs apart from the need for physiological satiation. Then humans are not fit subjects for manipulation, and we will seek to design a social order accordingly. But we cannot, at present, turn to science for insight into these matters. To claim otherwise is pure fraud. . . . It would be not absurd but grotesque to argue that since circumstances can be arranged in which behavior is quite predictable—as in a prison, for example, or the concentration camp society . . . therefore there need be no concern for the freedom and dignity of "autonomous man." When such conclusions are taken to be the result of a "scientific analysis," one can only be amazed at human gullibility.

What was significant about Skinnerism, however, was not the novelty or the degree of persuasiveness of the argument, nor the resulting questions about freedom and fascism, but the impact and the response: the cover of *Time*, the major excerpt in *Psychology Today*, the conclusion by a *New York Times* reviewer in 1971 that it was the most important book of the year, and a sale that put it on every best-seller list in the nation. Part of the explanation lay in a review by Richard Sennett (also in the *Times*) some months after the book was published. Under the skin, Sennett said, Skinner was an old-fashioned, small-town moralist. His beliefs "should sound familiar. They are the articles of faith of Nixonian America, of the small-town businessman who feels life has degenerated, has gotten beyond his control, and who thinks things will get better when other people learn to behave. . . . As a moralist who believes in a way of life that is rapidly dying, Skinner has contrived the best possible defense for his value judgments: science—modern, up-to-date, hard science—stands ready to support him." He offered his reader the old verities—decency, civility, "culture"—and, at the same time, permitted him to regard himself as thoroughly modern, technological and scientific.

But there was something else as well, and that was the appeal to the Faustian legacy of applied intelligence. Skinner seemed to restore the new frontier intact: he cranked up the juice, wired everybody to the apparatus of social conditioning, and promised the good society. What the nineteenth-century American attempted with preaching and moral persuasion, what the liberal of the twentieth tried with social programing, New Deal projects, public housing, wars on poverty, and economic planning, and what the post–World War II brain business claimed through "research" and education, Skinner would now achieve through conditioning and positive reinforcement. What no one fully pointed out, however (other than to charge Skinner with the desire to operate a concentration camp, a charge that gave him too little credit for good intentions), was that Skinnerism, that last outgrowth of the last frontier, slammed the door on all frontiers, that in wishing to enlist intelligence for the ultimate of social-engineering projects, it discarded all individual intelligence into the same heap with freedom and dignity. For the point of all futures, all frontiers, all optimism, was their common quality of unpredictability, their scruffiness, their elements of high risk. Skinner believed in hermetic man, and his appeal, finally, was to those who could not tolerate the chances that attend freedom or frontiers or intelligence. What he appealed to was the desire to be safe, the sort of safety that admits of no real future.

What the futurists shared with Skinner was an intellectual imperiousness, a desire, Vietnam style, to regard the failures of the past as evidence that what was required was more of the same at ever higher levels. And yet half measures might be all that reasonable men could expect. The message of the counterculture of the late sixties, when it was not viewed in its most extreme moments, had always included the premise that the future was made in the present, not by planners talking about the year 2000 but by the way people would live tomorrow morning. Inherent in that assumption had been the crippling belief that by tomorrow morning everything would have to be different; its arrogance was the arrogance of time rather than scope. Nonetheless its attitude toward the future had been more humble and tentative, its forms of extremism respectful of nature and resources. To go crazy recycling paper and tin cans or eating organic food was considerably saner than the opposite madness of napalm, strip mining and protective-reaction strikes. The quarrel of the counterculture was directed precisely at Bell's observation (or at Skinner's assumption) that "what has become decisive for society is the new centrality of *theoretical* knowledge, the primacy of theory over empiricism, and the codification of knowledge into abstract systems of symbols that can be translated into many different and varied circumstances. Every society now lives by innovation and growth; and it is theoretical knowledge that has become the matrix of innovation." If theoretical knowledge was central, then clearly people who sat in studies were more important than those who planted seeds, ran sewer plants or organized new schools. But what if growth was limited—in the brain business and in the economy generally—and if the problem was not the training of more skilled people (or the creation of utopia factories and other such nonsense) but the misapplication and misdistribution of the talent the country already possessed? Obviously there was an uneven distribution of resources between research for war and research for health, housing and transportation, but, even more significantly, there were inequities between theoretical and applied brain work. For generations, but particularly in the previous twenty-five years, the nation's talent had become increasingly segregated: in nearly every profession status went not to service but to nonservice. In teaching, in medicine, in law, the emoluments were inversely proportional to the number of clients; the highest rewards went to those who worked only with their peers and who remained isolated from the general market of men. At the same time entire regions and populations lacked adequate medical and dental services, intelligent local news programs and papers, competent teachers, mental-health programs and (frequently) even the mechanical skills to repair the unnecessarily complicated machines that "theoretical knowledge" designed for immediate obsolescence. Middle America, so called, was a huge region from which talented people had fled while the marginally competent remained.

The recession in the brain business, if it lasted long enough, might drive some of that talent back to Main Street, to the inner cities, and to the other regions and activities which required it. (Again the kids of the counterculture seemed to have anticipated something that the futurists neglected.) If knowledge was the new property—as Charles Reich, among others, described it—then perhaps the principles (if not the law) of antitrust applied to concentrations of talent just as appropriately as they did to concentrations of capital. Yet even if they did not, there remained fatal limitations in a future where the horizon could be enlarged only at exorbitant expense in resources and personal alienation. The only alternative to that future was an ongoing popular revolution against the claims and elitism of the professors of "theoretical knowledge"—the high priests of futurism themselves. The objectives of such a revolution would be to recapture and reinvent the skills and confidence of one's own possibilities and to convert theoretical knowledge into those tools and technology that would not only serve men but allow ordinary men to operate them. The problem was not how Man would control the planet but how men could manage their lives, how to save the future from collectivization.

A century ago John Stuart Mill had suggested that a "stationary state" of capital and population was more desirable than indefinite growth. Such a state, he wrote,

implies no stationary state of human improvement. There would be as much scope as ever for all kinds of mental culture, and moral and social progress; as much room for improving the Art of Living, and much more likelihood of its being improved, when minds ceased to be engrossed by the art of getting on. Even the industrial arts might be as earnestly and as successfully cultivated, with this sole difference, that instead of serving no purpose but the increase of wealth, industrial improvements would produce their legitimate effect, that of abridging labor. Hitherto it is questionable if all the mechanical inventions yet made have lightened the day's toil of any human being. They have enabled a greater population to live the same life of drudgery and imprisonment, and an increased number of manufacturers and others to make large fortunes. They have increased the comforts of the middle classes. But they have not yet begun to effect those great changes in human destiny, which it is in their nature and in their futurity to accomplish. . . .

Many people in America had become doubtful about the future because they were beginning to feel in their bones what Mill discussed; the future they had been offered for more than a decade promised nothing but more of the same. Under those premises, planning for the year 2000, or even thinking about it, had no charm whatever.

SEVEN:

THE EUROPEANIZATION

OF AMERICA

I

If the sixties taught the country anything, it was the importance of a certain modesty. The representative demons of the Right and the Left seemed to spring from the same liberal soil—"permissiveness" and social perfectionism on the one hand, Vietnam on the other; Jerry Rubin, Abbie Hoffman, Walt Rostow and McGeorge Bundy were more than contemporaries of coincidence. The counterculture and the war escalated at the same time; Altamont and Tet were part of the same debacle. Providence was indifferent after all, perhaps even hostile, progress was not necessarily indefinite, and the American empire might not last a thousand years, perhaps not even a hundred. "The United States," wrote Andrew Hacker in 1970, "no longer has the will to be a great international power, just as it is no longer an ascending nation at home. We have arrived at a plateau in our history: the years of middle age and incipient decline." America's history as a nation, he concluded, "has reached its end . . . Americans will learn to live with danger and discomfort, for this condition is the inevitable accompaniment of democracy in its declining years."

It was a familiar refrain, and it obviously found its corollaries and reinforcement in national behavior: in the conservation and ecology movement and the corresponding disenchantment with growth, in the Metternichean, Central European conduct of foreign affairs under Nixon and Kissinger, in the growing sense of embattlement, alienation and frustration among large segments of the population, and in the new fashion of intellectual resignation and benign neglect of unresolved social problems. Most of these things, of course, were not new to the West—not, at least, in spirit, and frequently not even in substance—but America, despite its exposure to the intellectual pessimism of Europe, was singularly unprepared for the change. Europeans, with their feudal heritage, had always lived with assumptions of class difference; they had had their personal experience with war, destruction and tragedy, had never believed they were exempt from mortality, had long understood about limited possibilities, and had developed the intellectual equipment and institutions to deal with them. Not that those institutions were necessarily just or efficient; unlike American institutions, however, which were usually designed on assumptions of growth and human perfectibility—peculiar adaptations from the Enlightenment and the Romantic Era—the institutions of Europe were designed to cope with limits and to deal with the effects of inequity and accepted class difference. Socialism never made it on this side of the Atlantic—we had no Labor Party—and while Catholicism did, it was always trying to be more puritanical, entrepreneurial and nationalistic, more worldly and American, than to be pietistic or "universal." The great American Catholic edifice was not Chartres or Notre Dame of Paris but Notre Dame of South Bend: it was the Fighting Irish. European charity was designed for the maintenance and relief of the poor and afflicted; American philanthropy was organized to enable the needy to rise above their condition, to transform them.

The most significant difference between the worlds, however, was in the conception of time itself. The idea of history as progress, of course, was European as well as American, but while it represented a temporary intellectual current in the Old World, a kind of overlay that lasted roughly from the Renaissance to World War I, it was the very basis of life in America. Gibbon, among others, had spoken about "the pleasing conclusion that every age of the world has increased, and still increases, the real wealth, the happiness, the knowledge, and perhaps the virtue, of the human race," and Acton, in 1896, referred to history as "a progressive science" in which "we are bound to assume, as the scientific hypothesis on which history is to be written, a progress in human affairs." By the end of the nineteenth century, however, and certainly by the end of the First World War, much of that faith was gone, swallowed in the horrors of war, fascism and mass murder. Only America seemed exempt; this was still a New World and had, as we always knew, the benefit of special Providential blessings. What had been a period in the intellectual history of Europe was the birthright of life in America; every day things would get better, the curves were rising indefinitely, and perfection was the fundamental law of (American) history. America was created by European optimists and institutionalized European optimism.

The end has been a long time coming. Thoreau thought he saw it in the advent of the railroad, the machine defiling the garden; the historians of the twentieth century saw it in the closing of the frontier or, later, in the Depression or technology or the possibilities of nuclear war. Yet, as I suggested earlier, American pessimism, like European optimism, was, for most of our history, a kind of overlay, a special attitude only remotely connected to the realities of everyday expectations and almost totally unrelated to political decisions and the mainstream of national life. "Only recently," wrote R. W. B. Lewis, "has the old conviction of the new historical beginning seemed to vanish altogether, and with it the enlivening sense of possibility, of intellectual and artistic elbow-room, of new creations and fresh initiatives." Lewis was writing in the early fifties and dealing with American literature; yet even then the social possibilities had not been exhausted: there still existed the frontiers of science and social science and education; the universities were full of people and ideas ready to be used for a new assault on the heights of development and perfection. If Eisenhower would stop playing golf with his businessman-cronies and begin listening to the intellectuals—and if he were only willing to use the powers of government—a great many problems could be solved overnight and the national future could be rescued from the suburban plasticity in which it had temporarily become stuck. Science, education and government were the ultimate weapons. While John Foster Dulles was talking about massive retaliation should the Russians begin war over Berlin or the Middle East, the intellectuals were dreaming, on the one hand, about massive assaults on poverty and other domestic problems, and, on the other, about the intellectual weapons—conflict resolution, bargaining theory and strategy games—for the successful management of the Cold War.

Everyone knows what happened: the secret weapon didn't work. It produced the New Frontier and the Great Society and Vietnam, and while the measures associated with those efforts are still being judged by different people as partially successful or as too little, too late (not enough money for poverty, insufficient determination to "win" in Southeast Asia, treason in high places), none of them produced the victories that had been advertised and expected. What they generated instead was a new cynicism not only (as in American tradition) about politicians and professors, but a more fundamental disenchantment with the political system and the possibilities of social action. In partisan political terms, it was the Democratic Party which suffered most, because it had always been, willy-nilly, the party of reform and social change. But, more basically, the victims were hope and reason—replaced now by pessimism and mysticism—and, along with them, the American conception of time itself. If progress and social betterment, even with the assistance of what David Halberstam would call the best and the brightest, were not manageable (or, perhaps, even possible), then the whole meaning of America was up for grabs.

The moment of political disenchantment coincided with rising doubts about growth, the nature of affluence and the good life.

Wealth in America had not been regarded as static or as mere possession of goods; it was dynamic, expanding, and included the expectation of future wealth; the country was what Daniel Boorstin once called "a consumption community." The question of redistribution was mitigated by the assumption of growth—hence no socialist party—and the necessity for what might be called a "post-achievement ethic" was perpetually postponed in the euphoria of continuous advancement and progress. Yet the more "advancement" the country enjoyed, the more evident the disproduct. While the issue of pollution was first raised a generation ago in the context of the atomic bomb, it soon managed to give content to a broader set of frustrations and disaffections, creating a sort of global consciousness about a whole catalogue of pollutants. Although atmospheric testing of nuclear weapons was stopped by the major powers (though not by France and China), we discovered that we could still poison the atmosphere and the earth with a nearly unlimited set of industrial effluents from DDT to mercury dioxide, that, in fact, "progress" itself was already causing such destruction, and that the ghost of Malthus was still haunting the earth. The corresponding decline of marginal satisfaction with new goods among the affluent—the accumulation of consumer products without the sense that the good life had been achieved—exacerbated that consciousness. We were supposed to be rich but often felt poor, and so we began to see the dirty streams, the dying lakes, the stripped hillsides, the oily beaches, to smell the dirty air, and to count the dying species (seeing in each an omen of human death), and to measure resource depletion, the exploding population, and the years we had left before the apocalypse. In the context of the environment—the earth itself—it wasn't simply that time was no longer on the side of man, that the curves had stopped rising; time was now an enemy, and the symbols of progress—the automobile, the smoking factory chimney, the growing population—became symbols of danger and degeneration. The open society was not only running out of space but running out of time.

America was rejoining the West, but it did so with an ambivalence born of peculiar historical conditions. There was no Conservative Party to take over, no vestigial class structure for comfort, no socialism, no appropriate political language, and no fully applicable tradition. The so-called conservatism of the Nixon Administration (which, characteristically, had no ideological label, not even a name on the package) was largely a way of buying time and maintaining some semblance of social order, no matter how imperfect, until the country could come to terms with its new limitations. A great deal of it was European: wage and price controls and what was essentially a managed economy, the Kissinger foreign policy, the proposals for a Family Assistance Program, and, most of all, the calls for an end to "permissiveness" and the restoration of "self-discipline," which in the European context would be labeled austerity. Nixon thought we were too rich and too spoiled. But it lacked the European tradition which took certain limits for granted (and which had never expected as much of the future) and which therefore accepted a certain minimum in social services: national health programs, adequate public transit systems, state subsidies for the arts, and a general responsibility for the maintenance and support—not the transformation—of the poor and the lower middle class. While Nixon was speaking about corporate tax reductions to induce growth, the Japanese, with far smaller income disparities than the Americans, were enjoying the highest growth rate in the world, and while the nation accepted the idea that further tax increases would be intolerable, nearly every country in Western Europe functioned with substantially higher tax rates than the United States. Family assistance had been invented in Europe (and borrowed from Canada by Daniel Patrick Moynihan), but it was sold—unsuccessfully so far—as a way of getting people off welfare and reducing the maintenance budget. The refrain about getting people off the welfare rolls and onto the tax rolls seemed to assume that no one required any permanent public support, with the possible exception of blind paraplegics, and that every support program was, at best, temporary. Self-discipline did not mean higher taxes for the rich to improve social welfare and the incomes of the poor, but a return to the jungles of scarcity.

The conventional analyses of the sixties described Nixon's policies as a reaction to the programs of the Great Society and to a general attack on inflated expectations, but beyond that it was a political expression of the declining faith in liberalism itself—liberalism as free enterprise, liberalism as social reform, and liberalism as an assumption of national growth. Since it was un-American to talk about distinctions of class, the Administration had to justify the existing inequities of income and life style—which it often tried to enlarge—in traditional terms (e.g., "the work ethic") without offering the traditional remedies for the future (e.g., more education, training or other "new" frontiers). At the end of Nixon's first term, many of the old indices of "growth" had started rising again, at least temporarily, but even the official unemployment figures, which did not include the millions who were subemployed or had simply given up looking for work, or had retired early, remained almost as high as they had been in the trough of the recession. The prime beneficiaries of the new policies were corporations and individuals in the higher tax brackets; their incomes were rising even as the Administration went about the business (often with limited success) of trying to cut transfer payments to the poor and pruning back the Great Society. Beyond the sheer economics of class, however, the ethos of class was itself being encouraged through what seemed like a public commitment to permanent distinctions. The liberal view that the poor were a middle class in the making was slowly being replaced by the reimposition of a permanent taint which regarded poverty either as an indication of intrinsic character flaws (laziness, for example) or, among intellectuals, as the consequence of unfortunate genetic limitations beyond the power of government to change. Under the surface there floated a new and respectable science of race—"proof," for example, that even in so-called culture-free tests of intelligence blacks did worse than whites—which could be used to justify the inequities of the nation and to assuage the consciences of the advocates of status-quo politics. The uprisings and minirevolts of the sixties (and especially those of the black and poor) were powerful reminders to the middle class of what it was not (often by inches), what it had escaped, and the rediscovery of the blue-collar class did a great deal to assuage the guilt of affluence. We were all victims, all sufferers, and we could tell ourselves (with a little cheering on from Nixon and Agnew) that whatever we had we had earned. The "permissiveness" of the sixties would be brought to an end through an invocation of specters and spooks, a resurrection, wherever possible, of the mind-set of the fifties which included, among other things, the haunting memories of the Depression. By lumping the whole middle class together, the affluent could disguise themselves as struggling workers, and the lower middle class—even if they couldn't manage to see themselves as affluent—could take pride in the status they shared with their economic superiors. At least they weren't on welfare.

II

Richard Nixon was buying time not only with particular programs and policies (or with opposition to programs) but also by trying to cheerlead a mainstream revival. White House prayer breakfasts, Sunday football, and a synthetic Protestant ethic (the carrot) were combined with a concerted assault on political and cultural dissent—the intimidation of radicals, police harassment, selective enforcement of civil-rights laws, and prosecution of the activists of the Left (the stick). The bloody shirt was labeled crime, drugs and busing (with minor references to abortion, pornography and general smut), but beyond those labels was the larger problem of national identity and the failure of traditional myths, symbols and heroes to command allegiance. If the age had a characteristic figure, it was not a great entrepreneur, a poet or a military leader, it was Lieutenant Calley, the soldier as killer and as victim, a symbol of brutality to the doves and the characteristic victim of a no-win futility to the hawks, and if it created any heroes, they were the heroes of separate cultures and groups, Castro, Cleaver, Angela Davis, the Berrigans, Marcuse, Jerry Rubin, Joe Namath, John Lennon.

The new particularism in American culture worked largely to Nixon's political advantage, since most of the separate groups were far more likely to be the natural allies (or former adherents) of the old Democratic coalition than to regard themselves as fallen-away Republicans: it was their defections from Humphrey in 1968 that had made Nixon President in the first place. And yet the cheerleading had little effect in creating any new sense of national identity, in part, of course, because the war remained a painful and divisive embarrassment—and might remain an embarrassment even after it was all over—but more significantly because the country had no history and no future apart from liberalism, abundance and growth, no royal family, no aristocracy, no church, no transcendent institutional mystiques which had meaning simply because they had endured. American civilization and civility offered little reassurance because they had never been tested in genuine adversity, because our generosity and openness had always enjoyed the reinforcement of abundance and future possibilities. "For a nation to exist," Ortega once said, "it is enough that it have a purpose for the future, even if that purpose remain unfulfilled." The problem was to reinvent a future.

There was obviously a great deal to do, not only in the realm of what might loosely be called social justice, but in regenerating the possibilities of meaning. Even in the late sixties it was still easy for Americans traveling overseas to learn how different they were from Europeans; people were forever returning with a renewed sense of their Americanness—the smart set from London, the radicals from Cuba and China, the deserters from Stockholm, the tourists from Paris. Despite Vietnam, it seemed, we were not Germans, and while the casual sense of superiority (moral, political and economic) was no longer possible, the styles and modes of thought generated by two thousand years of coming to terms and accepting limited possibilities were almost as foreign as they had ever been. While we were looking, sometimes with envy, at Swedish socialism and British health programs and Japanese industry, or, more lately, at the Chinese sweeping the snow off the streets of Peking, we also managed to see bureaucratic regimentation, social stratification and, often, a dreariness of outlook that made American possibilities seem brilliant by comparison. Had any nation ever tried its own "war criminals" or been more tolerant of political and cultural dissent? Did any country in Europe treat its ethnic minorities better than we had—the West Indians in London, the Algerians in Paris, the Jews in Moscow, the Palestinians in Israel? Americans came home not only because this was where they were comfortable—because it was home—but because, however reduced the possibilities, more remained here than anywhere else. Next to Europe, this was still a country of great expectations and unrestrained individualism. The problem with borrowing was to make any foreign comparison favorably persuasive; models were scarce.

The question was not how or when we would go Swedish or British or German, but whether the country would use the time Nixon was buying to reinvest the wreckage of the liberal future with new cultural and political options. George McGovern had failed dismally as a candidate of reform in 1972, and while that failure was generally interpreted as a rejection of an excessively "radical" program, there was every chance that the issues would survive. Nixon had not built a new majority, certainly not a new party; he had merely built an election on a platform of apathy and deferral. America would inevitably become more

European (even while we were selling Pepsi-Cola to the Russians)—would continue to have a managed economy, a growing bureaucratic apparatus, public and private, a foreign policy committed to a balance among military and economic powers, and an increasingly modest attitude toward time and the traditional future. We had already discovered how "peace" could raise the price of bread in the supermarket (for hadn't the Russian wheat deal constituted the *quid pro quo* for Soviet accommodation to the Vietnam settlement, including the mining of the harbors and the bombing of the north?) and how American influence was tied precariously to everything from jobs in the textile industry to the safety of airline passengers—how every American, in other words, was a hostage to accommodation. Nixon, moreover, had suggested that the sensitivity of international negotiations and the precariousness of the domestic order demanded concentrations of executive control which would once have been regarded as intolerable by a majority of Americans. Attempts to impose prior censorship on *The Washington Post* and *The New York Times* in the Pentagon Papers case, and the subsequent effort to prosecute Daniel Ellsberg and Anthony Russo for violations of the Espionage Act and conversion of government documents, represented the first formal measures in American history to impose what would in effect be an official-secrets act (without the prosecutorial self-restraint of the British) and to develop a theory of information which invested the government rather than the public with preemptive rights to official documents. That theory was reinforced by Nixon's assertion that he would hold press conferences only when they were "in the public interest" (as determined by him), the Administration's concomitant efforts to intimidate newspapers and networks, and the rise of an unofficial ministry of information extending from the Pentagon propaganda apparatus to the White House "director of communications," to the Corporation for Public Broadcasting, which was coming under increasing White House pressure to broadcast only programs politically acceptable to the Administration. What was happening, in effect, was that the Administration was slowly developing a political theory of "national security" which, while it was unjustified by foreign attack or any serious threat of domestic revolt (or any Congressional or constitutional sanctions), nonetheless attempted to institutionalize a synthetic sense of "wartime" crisis into a permanent element of domestic life. Combine that with the vastly expanded machinery of domestic surveillance made possible by computers and the installation of data gatherers in the police business, and the development of accompanying theories of justification (fighting organized crime, subversives and drug dealers in the interest of "national security"), and you had the outlines of a still more grand theory of the state as an inviolable entity above the considerations of civil liberties and individual freedom, the first shades of a religion of the state. When Nixon spoke about decentralizing domestic programs and power he said little about the bureaucracies of war, information and repression; they would presumably remain intact, more European than ever now that an entirely professional volunteer Army would replace the last of the citizen soldiers and march the country several steps back toward a certain view of the Old World. It was not merely Metternich who was influencing White House policy, but Clausewitz.

And yet the possibilities for resistance remained substantial, even with a Nixon Supreme Court and a Nixon Attorney General and a Spiro Agnew to cheer on the police. America, wrote Hannah Arendt in her study of totalitarianism, "knows less of the modern psychology of masses than perhaps any other country in the world." If the old Democratic coalition had proved fragile, the synthetic Middle American ethos which elected Nixon (or, at any rate, defeated McGovern) was even more precarious as a political entity; this constituency had not yet become what Arendt called "the fragments of a highly atomized society whose competitive structure and concomitant loneliness of the individual had been held in check only through membership in a class." There was no pervasive "isolation and lack of normal social relationships." The hypothetical American middle was and had always been a collection of coalitions—people belonging to distinct and identifiable groups which, while they might now be increasingly uncertain of their relationship to the "mainstream" or the national structure, nevertheless remained intact. Alienation in this country was not, for the most part, atomization, the loneliness of the individual produced by the dissolution of class or national feeling, but, more often, a change of uniform (from middle class to counterculture, from factory worker to taxpayer, from housewife to liberated woman, from WASP to ethnic and back again), just as, in Madison's view, faction supposedly checked faction and majorities were forever fluid. Nixon had managed to make many of them feel more threatened than exploited, and to see the threat as coming from below rather than above; there remained, moreover, the possibility that the dissolution would continue and the sense of political futility would grow. Hoggart, at the conclusion of *The Uses of Literacy*, his study of the transformation of the English working class after World War II, had conjectured that "even if substantial inner freedom were lost, the great new classless class would be unlikely to know it: its members would still regard themselves as free and be told that they were free." Clearly the American majority has been willing to accept things they would not have tolerated before (and would not have needed to tolerate before—a standing army, a centralized police establishment, inconclusive wars and general depersonalization by the various bureaucracies), and they might, given the proper conditions, learn to tolerate more. And yet it was striking how little impact the politics of repression had had in particular cases—how resistant, for example, courts and juries had been in the celebrated "political" trials of the age of Nixon: the Chicago Seven conspiracy case, the Angela Davis case, the Panther cases, the Harrisburg conspiracy case. Apparently people who were willing to tolerate a general disregard for constitutional liberties by the Administration and the police were still scrupulous when it came to individual defendants and to the defense of individualism, no matter how unrespectable some of the accused might be in the view of individual judges and jurors. There were signs, moreover, that impositions that might be tolerable in the abstract were likely to generate rebellion in the particular: commuters taking over trains on the New Haven railroad in protest against poor service, federal bureaucrats in the Immigration and Naturalization Service filing complaints against their superiors charging cozy relationships with fat-cat smugglers, military personnel resisting racism and arbitrary treatment by senior officers. Where the American ethic of the small town was confused by the escalated immorality of Vietnam or the atmosphere of general intimidation produced by wiretapping and police harassment, it often managed to reassert itself in specific (i.e., "small-town") settings involving particular actions against particular people. It was the intervening bureaucracies—the dirty workers—which made brutality and repression possible.

But if there were conditions which might increase political alienation and cynicism and thus abet repression, there were also situations likely to generate an expansion of the welfare system not only as an *ad hoc* solution to "short-run" problems but as an ideologically accepted element of the permanent social order. The continuing intractability of domestic problems (including welfare) and the growing recognition, at least in the particular, that social services were in poor shape were almost certain to increase the demand for "European" programs in health, welfare, transportation and taxation (meaning income redistribution) and to drive the disparate subculture minorities into new coalitions. If the sixties had produced anything permanent, something not totally vulnerable to reduced budgets and unilateral action by the administration, it was a network of counterinstitutions living in uneasy coexistence with the organizations of the welfare state: neighborhood legal services, free clinics, Head Start parent groups, alternative schools, community corporations, tenant unions, consumer lobbies and welfare-rights organizations—vested interests in political or cultural resistance. Since most of them sprang from the old liberal reformist impulses, many of them remained uncertain and divided about how they connected with the official system: were they in the business of reform or should they be trying to create a wholly new structure? Were they temporary remedies to short-term problems or were they the permanent skeleton of a growing institutional network designed to serve the equally permanent underclass of an increasingly static society? Through the sixties the number of jobs provided by the state and local governments had grown substantially faster than employment in private industry; without these jobs the social services would be in even worse shape (presumably) and unemployment politically intolerable. Most of those jobs, of course, were in the old-style bureaucracies—school systems, welfare offices, state and municipal government—yet even they represented a potential constituency in support of expanded social services, income redistribution and a European view of growth, time and social mobility. Although its members often behaved like the white-collar class that C. Wright Mills described twenty years ago ("political eunuchs . . . without potency and without enthusiasm for the urgent political clash"), they were also showing surprising powers of self-protection and political action. The more pressure for reduced budgets, the more often school systems faced the chance of having to close down entirely for lack of funds, the more certainly the public-service bureaucracies were becoming established lobbies (in self-interest if nothing else) to create public acceptance of a permanent system of social maintenance and expanding social services. "The overriding lesson of the 1960s," wrote Bennett Harrison, an economist at the University of Maryland,

is that short-run, "reform-minded" manpower policies that concentrate on "supply-side" variables such as education and training are doomed to failure, given the chronic shortage of jobs at decent pay in the economy. Public Service Employment, however, unlike any other single policy on record, suggests short-term (labor demand–stimulating) and long-term (social system–transforming) implications that are mutually consistent. This means that alliances are possible on this issue, especially among radical organizers, non-radical wage and salary workers, and decidedly non-radical political liberals.

It had been a familiar dream, especially in the late sixties, yet it may well have been overoptimistic, even from a "radical" point of view. Liberal institutions in America—the schools, the foundations, the welfare organizations—had generally been more concerned with the processes of mobility and transformation than with the protection of individual rights and personal freedom of choice, more devoted to social management (planning and "reason") than to the irrational and possibly anarchic elements of life. The assumption of nearly a century of liberal policy was that all Americans, other things being equal, would choose to join the mainstream; it was therefore the function of social institutions to make things equal and thus facilitate the process for those who had been left out. Under conditions limiting growth and mobility (which would be labeled "technological complexity" and invoked to enforce discipline), that devotion was likely to increase the temptation to trade civil liberties for the blessings of central planning and to regard the residual minorities outside the mainstream with enduring contempt. The advocates of benign neglect and genetic determinism tended increasingly to view those minorities, and especially the poor and the black, in a quasi-institutional context and to treat them as candidates for custodial care. Beginning in the late sixties, for example, the burden of discussion about the schools of the major cities shifted from the possibilities of transformation—compensatory education, Head Start and all the rest—to the problems of management and security: guards, closed-circuit-television monitoring systems, and the use of drugs to keep restless or uncooperative children quiet. The schools themselves, not the junkies on the street, became the nation's biggest pushers of amphetamines. And while some states were attempting to reduce the population of their mental hospitals—to go from custodial care to halfway houses and local clinics, again with a heavy use of drugs —the growing pressure to establish a national system of day-care centers for very young children was on the verge of generating a vast expansion of institutional situations and a concomitant enlargement of the custodial mentality. The American adaptation of the European solution tended toward the imposition of social ghettoes instead of social classes, institutions to replace communities. The meritocracy would segregate according to what people could "contribute" to the technological apparatus and how they could accommodate to it—the technology was given, human beings were the dependent variables. And as fewer people were required to maintain given levels of productivity, more would be regarded as marginal—too old, too young, too dumb, too difficult —and relegated to "service" occupations or welfare institutions, the "growth" sectors of the economy. The ability over the past generation of oligopolistic corporations to fix prices and overcharge more or less at will made it possible for them to maintain thousands of employees who contributed little to production or efficiency and thus to run a sort of private welfare system. Accommodation to the system was obviously more important than skill or work accomplished. But that form of welfare was clearly limited, and the chances of growth in other areas were almost certain. The question therefore was how the system would treat people in those sectors, whether they would be regarded as the leavings of the technological economy—wards of the state, jailers and inmates caught in the same prisons—or whether their potential and individuality were recognized and honored. The service sectors in transportation, education, health, housing and welfare could obviously become among the most creative and useful areas of American life, yet the specific institutions charged with them had developed reputations as the most mismanaged and abusive enterprises to be found anywhere. Did anyone really want to entrust the restructuring of society to organizations of schoolteachers, social workers and cops? More

303

important, could economic planning be compatible with cultural pluralism or would the expanding service institutions assault all diversity as antagonistic to orderly management? What was the price of economic rights?

III

The impositions of bureaucratic institutions were certain to grow, either in the name of order or in the name of welfare, and the expectations of an American future were likely to diminish, no matter how bullish Merrill Lynch was on America. But there was still no certainty about how the country would adjust to the changed meaning of time—whether, for example, reduced expectations themselves would create a new sense of liberation, some freedom from the pressure to make it, or whether they would simply continue to exacerbate personal anxiety and social tension. "Many of the tendencies of world history," Heilbroner had written in the late fifties, "are likely to manifest themselves in a worsening of the outlook. We may well be tempted to interpret this growing intractability of the environment as the metamorphosis of progress into retrogression." What he was suggesting was identification not with the conventional "Western" idea of progress but with "the sweep of history," meaning, finally, an abstract idea of humanity beyond the ordinary social calculus. Here again the residual American minorities, and especially the blacks, seemed to offer some cultural leadership; they had never been able to expect as much from progress and had thus always been forced (or permitted) the luxury of an aristocratic conception of time and leisure. They had endured as Americans and had, despite everything, preserved their humanity. It was clear, moreover, that much of the counterculture of the sixties (which often took its style from blacks) had been searching for elements not dependent on conventional ideas of success, growth and satisfaction, a groping for those "inner" frontiers which were founded on assumptions of a transcendent, universal humanity. That it often failed was not necessarily a repudiation of the idea but only an indication of the difficulty of execution and of the veto power of older assumptions and practices. The idea was too radical and its practitioners were not radical enough. It was difficult to transform middle-class college dropouts into holy men, or to keep the Hell's Angels out of the Garden of Eden.

The Watergate disclosures, which raised the most serious possibility of impeachment in a century and which implicated the highest officials of government, including the President, seemed, if anything, to underline the return of American political institutions to worldly imperfection. The country's capacity to function and the President's capacity to govern were undoubtedly impaired, but the limitations on those capacities did not spring full blown from the revelations; in part one could almost as accurately say the reverse: it was because consensus had broken down (in the matter of leaks of official information, for example) and because problems had seemingly outgrown and outrun principles, that the White House turned to burglary, espionage and sabotage. Long before the disclosures it was fairly apparent that Nixon, Haldeman, Ehrlichman, Mitchell and other members of the administration had never regarded themselves above such tactics, if they thought they were warranted. Similar tactics had been used by Nixon people in his campaign for governor of California in 1962 and in his campaigns for Congress as far back as the late 'forties. What Watergate did do was to take some of the awe and mystery out of the American presence overseas; it pierced the shell of what was supposed to be (at least at the highest levels) an immaculate government at home; and it punctured the mystery of transformation which was supposed to attend the elevation of a politician into a President. Watergate was somehow symbolic of the end of the pretense of higher American principles. In one way it might, as some hoped, radicalize American politics—people might never trust the White House in the same way again—but in another it might also confirm the feeling that politics in Washington was, finally, no different from politics anywhere else. Watergate was, at least for a moment, a touch of the neo-gothic, a Byzantine revival on Pennsylvania Avenue.

Among the ironies of the reign of Nixon was its ability to revive some of the assumptions of a common political ethic and, beyond that, of a transcendent worldliness. It seemed to prove that the alternative to utopia was not necessarily apocalypse and that the end of presumptions of moral perfection and unending growth did not immediately bring on unmitigated barbarism and decay. Although Nixon had been around for four years, the country was still here, time had not come to an end, and the sun was still rising in the east. "The presumption of an end of history," wrote Edward Hallett Carr in *What Is History?*, "has an eschatological ring more appropriate to the theologian than to the historian, and reverts to the fallacy of a goal outside history." The very fact that McGovern's supporters could indulge themselves in the pursuit of their separate salvations—women's liberation, abortion, amnesty and all the rest —suggested that more fundamental political freedom could still be taken for granted (at least among the movement people at Miami Beach) and that the end was not yet at hand; they themselves were living denials of the prophetic voice. Nixon's commitment to the cooling of America did not create any new future, certainly not an American future, but it did suggest, in a way that John Kennedy's magnificent liberal globalism never did, that the United States was now part of the imperfect world, that we had at long last rejoined the West. The country would never be as wonderful again, never as grand in its expectations or its innocence—and was, therefore, less of a country—but neither was it likely to be so demanding and pretentious. Nixon was the last of the old liberals but also the first of the Europeans. As the country approached its bicentennial in 1976 it was, in a way, like starting all over.

INDEX

Abel, I. W., 68
Abzug, Bella, 64
accommodation, vs. growth and
    freedom, 37, 153, 166, 303
Adams, Henry, 38, 259
Adams, John Quincy, 48
Advertising Age, 41–42
affluence: myth of, 86, 94–95, 129–
    130; national compulsion toward,
    142; partial, 110–11
AFL-CIO, 64, 68
Agnew, Spiro T., 59, 93–94, 97,
    118–19, 294, 298
Alabama: New South and, 211–14;
    University of, 212, 237, 239–40
Alexander, Shana, 83
Alioto, Joseph, 203
All in the Family, TV serial, 124
Alsop, Joseph, 84
American Academy of the Arts
    and Sciences, 256
American Association for the Ad-
    vancement of Science, 263–64
"American Century," fantasy of,
    92
American Civil Liberties Union,
    225
American dream, 15, 145, 175
American entropic consciousness,
    40
American future, *see* future
American idealism, 62

American Institute of Aeronautics
    and Astronautics, 260, 262
Americanism: ethnicity and, 116;
    national identity and, 15–16;
    "traditional," 52–53
American liberalism, decline of,
    58–59
"American malaise," 38
Amercan Melodrama, An (Chester
    et al.), 53
"American Pie" (McLean), 37–38
American politics, crisis in, 12–13
"American resignation," 38, 54
American Telephone & Telegraph
    Co., 167
American West, "loss" of, 169–205;
    see also West
American worker: apathy of, 138–
    139; democratic style of, 159; dis-
    sonance and, 163; future of, 154;
    permissiveness and, 162; prob-
    lems of, 123–30, 166–67; "pros-
    perity" and, 143; urgent con-
    cerns of, 160; voting registration
    for, 159, 162; *see also* blue-collar
    worker; white-collar worker
Amiotte, Cindy, 162
Anderson, Tena, 48
Apollo space program, 254–55, 260
"Appalachia East," unemployment
    and, 135–36
Arendt, Hannah, 298

McCarthy, Eugene, 54, 65
McCarthy, Joseph R., 85
McCloskey, Pete, 45
McDonnell-Douglas Corp., 191
McLean, Don, 37
McGovern, George, 16, 63, 296,
298, 305; betrayed by background, 74–75; blue-collar workers and, 66; California voters and,
195; campaign speeches of, 23–
25; charisma of, 65; clichés of,
49–50; at Democratic National
Convention, 47; Democratic
Party establishment and, 77;
"disorganized" state of campaign, 45; on healing and reconciliation, 29; insecurity of, 72;
vs. "interests," 70–71; labor and,
67–68; liberal elitism of, 68;
Middle America and, 75; mili-
tary-budget proposal of, 49;
moral fervor of, 80; in New
South, 232; Nixon voters and,
78–80; as 100-to-1 shot, 63–64; as
populist, 67; poverty and, 72;
reform of Democratic Party and,
32; small-town ethic of, 107; as
"wrong man," 75
McPherson, Aimee Semple, 176
Meany, George, 68
Melville, Herman, 38–39
Metternich, Prince Klemens von,
298
Mexican War, 193
Miami, Fla., Republican National
Convention at (1972), 44, 53
Middle America, myth of, 26, 74,
84, 101–02, 106–07, 115–19, 283,
299
middle class, 84–87; amusements of,
150–51; busing problem and, 157;

college education and, 145, 150–
151; establishment press and, 93;
factory owners as, 118, freedom
and, 153; labor problem and, 167;
Nixon and, 127; "opportunity"
ethic and, 121; pop cult of, 115;
reformers from, 168; scarcity
and class distinction in, 118–19;
white lower middle class and,
123
Mill, John Stuart, 284
Miller, Glenn, 235
Miller, Robert, 192
Miller, S. M., 43
Mills, C. Wright, 84, 86–87, 91, 144,
301
Mineral King development, 184
mine workers, doubt and apathy
of, 140
Mishan, E. J., 109, 258, 266–67, 272
Mitchell, John N., 17, 29, 61, 227,
305
mobile homes, 199–200
mobility, government jobs and,
301–02
Model Cities Program, 132
Modern Times, 128–29
moonlighting, 124
moral code, inversion of, 62
Morris, Willie, 208, 211, 242
Moynihan, Daniel P., 43, 60, 275,
292
Music Man, The (Willson), 102
Muskie, Edmund S., 65, 69, 168
My Lai massacre, 51, 85, 91, 150

Nader, Ralph, 63, 109, 152
Namath, Joe, 295
NASA (National Aeronautics and
Space Administration), 191, 195,
269

nostalgia, for 1950s, 62, 83

O'Connor, Flannery, 242
Odets, Clifford, 91
oil fields, Texas, 192–93
Old South: populist revolt in, 247; as "sideshow," 235; *see also* New South; South
Old West, mythology of, 188, 204; *see also* California
optimism: end of, 289; vs. entropic consciousness, 40; as flaw in American thought, 38
Orange Co., Calif., population and life style in, 192–95
Organization Man, The (Whyte), 90
Orr, John B., 96
Ortega y Gasset, José, 295
Orwell, George, 62, 151

Page, Bruce, 53
Paine, Tom, 60
Pasteur, Louis, 265
Peace Corps, 31
Peale, Norman Vincent, 84, 97
Pentagon Papers, 107, 297
Percy, Charles H., 45
permissiveness, American worker and, 162
pessimism, cultural predisposition to, 166
Ph.D.s, demand and supply of, 254, 264
Playboy, 101, 113, 143, 176
Podhoretz, Norman, 59–60, 68
Poirier, Richard, 60–61
pollution problems, 56, 109, 291
population growth, prosperity and, 41, 291

Populism, rise of, 28, 74, 166, 223, 250–52
Populist Manifesto, A (Newfield and Greenfield), 159
Portola Institute, 199
Potter, David M., 33, 122
Presley, Elvis, 84
problems, as "aberrations," 33
product cycle, goods production and, 165
productivity, GNP and, 40–41
progress, idea of, 288–89
Proposition 19, 184
Protestant Ethic, 88
psychosurgery, on prisoners, 205
Public Interest, The, 94
pulpwood strike, 230, 238

racism, South and, 157–58, 208, 248–49
Radical Suburb, The (Orr and Nicholson), 96
Rand Corp., 256
Ratner, Ronnie Steinberg, 43
Reagan, Ronald, 45, 77, 189–90, 270
recession: "Nixon's," 59; unemployment and, 134
Reconstruction Era, 222
redwood forests, cutting of, 184
Reeves, Richard, 74
Reich, Charles, 59, 97, 284
"reordering of priorities," 268
Republican National Convention, Miami (1972), 44, 48, 53
Republican Party, 79, 228
research and development, federal expenditures on, 254
Reston, James, 83
retirement, unemployment and, 135
Reuther, Victor, 159

316